Falling Apart in One Piece

*One Optimist's Journey
Through the Hell of Divorce*

Stacy Morrison

Simon & Schuster Paperbacks
New York   London   Toronto   Sydney

Simon & Schuster Paperbacks
A Division of Simon & Schuster, Inc.
1230 Avenue of the Americas
New York, NY 10020

First Simon & Schuster trade paperback edition March 2011

SIMON & SCHUSTER PAPERBACKS and colophon are registered
trademarks of Simon & Schuster, Inc.

From *Letters to a Young Poet* by Rainer Maria Rilke, translated by
Stephen Mitchell copyright © 1984 by Stephen Mitchell. Used with
permission of Random House, Inc.

For information about special discounts for bulk purchases, please contact Simon &
Schuster Special Sales at 1-866-506-1949 or business@simonandschuster.com.

The Simon & Schuster Speakers Bureau can bring authors to your live event. For
more information or to book an event contact the Simon & Schuster Speakers
Bureau at 1-866-248-3049 or visit our website at www.simonspeakers.com.

Designed by Jill Putorti

Manufactured in the United States of America

10 9 8 7 6 5 4 3 2 1

The Library of Congress has cataloged the hardcover edition as follows:

Morrison, Stacy.
    Falling apart in one piece : one optimist's journey through the hell of divorce.
        p. cm.
    1. Divorce. I. Title.
    HQ814.M64 2010
    306.89092—dc22
        [B]   2009029759

ISBN 978-1-4165-9556-4
ISBN 978-1-4165-9557-1 (pbk)
ISBN 978-1-4391-9985-5 (ebook)

For Zack,
My bright little lion

And for Chris,
Because without you there would be no book,
in more ways than one

The point is to live everything.

Rainer Maria Rilke

Contents

Falling Apart
in One Piece

We Begin at the End

I suppose I should start where it all started. Or, more specifically, started ending. The night Chris told me he was done with our marriage.

I can recall exactly what I was doing on the June evening this one-way conversation started: I was standing at the sink in the kitchen area of our one-room first floor, washing a bunch of arugula, my favorite salad green, pushing my hands through the cold water in the salad spinner to shake the dirt loose. I was looking out the window over the sink, marveling at the beautiful backyard of our Brooklyn home: an actual lawn, its bright green grass thick as a carpet; a wood deck; and a pergola with grapevines climbing over it in curlicue abandon. The yard was my favorite thing about our house, a house that we'd bought and moved into just five months before on a freezing-cold January day, when our son, Zack, was just five months old. Stationed in his bouncy seat on the floor in the empty living room, he'd watched with wide eyes as everything we owned was marched through the front door in big cardboard boxes.

I felt lucky to live in this house every single day, especially now that the backyard had come to verdant life. Every evening after I took the subway home to Brooklyn from my job in Manhattan, I'd pick up Zack as I walked in the door and nuzzle his soft, sweet skin, say my goodbyes to his nanny, and head out the back door and lie down in the grass while Zack crawled around. I'd stare up at the soft blue sky, drink in the smell of the green all around me, and think, I can't believe how lucky we are. I cherished that skyward view: a simple pleasure that made me feel small in the best way, as if I were being cupped in the hands of the universe. Simple and small were antidotes to the way I had been living my life for so long, with a complicated, jam-packed schedule, forging a career in the larger-than-life world of magazine publishing. For me, small was new, and small was good. I finally felt ready to stop going at a dead run, as I had been for so long, to slow down and settle into being happy.

Making dinner every night was a new pleasure for me after years of takeout meals at home or at my desk. I looked forward to putting in the half hour of calming busywork that getting dinner on the table entails, once Chris had come home and was able to take Zack off my hands. I'd stand in the kitchen and feel my brain slowly empty of the zillions of details and to-dos that make up a day in the office as my hands took over, chopping peppers and onions into just-right dice, whisking a vinaigrette, and washing salad greens.

As I poured the water from the salad spinner down the drain that night, I was feeling grateful for everything in my life, but I couldn't ignore Chris's silence pressing against my back. Sometimes people are quiet in a room in a way that feels like company, but today, as with a lot of days in the last few years, and especially since Zack was born, Chris was quiet in a way that felt like an absence. I started to turn around from the sink, wanting to find a way to pull Chris back into the room. I was sure that when I faced the sofa my eyes would find Chris staring blankly into middle distance, ignoring our tiny son, who was playing at his feet. And that was exactly the domestic tableau I beheld. Chris didn't turn to meet my gaze. Instead, as he felt my eyes come to rest on him, he let out a slow, pointed exhale.

I bristled, disappointed and annoyed. "Want to tell me what you hate so much about your life today?" I said, wincing inward slightly as the harsh words came out.

And so, still not turning his face, with its long, aquiline nose, huge blue-green eyes, and those full, pink lips I was delirious to call mine when we were first married, he said, simple as pie, "I'm done." Then he sighed again, and turned slowly to look at me with a flat, empty gaze. "I'm done with this," he said, gesturing with his hand to encompass our living room, our kitchen, our home, our son, our future, our dreams, every single memory we'd ever made together in our thirteen years as a couple, and me, suddenly meaningless me.

I felt my face go slack in shock as my vision narrowed to a tunnel centered on Chris's blank face, and everything else went dark.

Done. Just like that.

From the day Chris made this pronouncement, I felt my whole life click into slow motion as the last moments of my marriage started to slip through the hourglass. Suddenly there was a time bomb ticking loudly in the middle of the house, threatening to smash my life—my family, my security, my entire identity—into unrecognizable bits.

I entered a kind of split-screen crisis mode, shuttling between a panicked search for solutions and the velvety comfort of hiding in denial as I tried to figure out how to defuse the bomb. My mind became a Japanese teahouse: orderly, quiet, with delicate sliding shoji screens to separate my conflicting needs, to make it possible for me to keep on keeping on when it seemed that my husband had just brought everything in our life to a dead stop. As I started to ponder the impossible whys of how he and I had found ourselves here, and the impossible questions of how I would begin again, I slid open and shut the shoji screens in my mind to hide or reveal, a little at a time, what I was feeling—the anger, the fear, the bottomless grief—so that I could keep myself from being overwhelmed by my emotions. In a hush, I tiptoed around Chris and I tiptoed around myself, afraid to glimpse my reflection in the mirror and see the fear in my eyes.

This talk of divorce was coming at a spectacularly bad time. I was the primary breadwinner in our family, and I had recently been fired from a job I loved. Chris and I were still learning how to be parents; our cherubic son was still an infant. We owned this lovely, but needy, house, and the big mortgage that went along with it. And I was interviewing for a big new job, the job of my dreams: taking the helm of *Redbook*, a huge national magazine that was all about women living their grown-up lives—and in no small part, their married lives.

The irony was as rich as buttercream frosting on a wedding cake.

In the end, I got the job. But I lost the guy. The life we'd built together over thirteen years began disassembling itself without my permission as Chris and I started the slow, hard work of breaking up. Then our house began falling apart, too, revealing breaches in the foundation and the roof that the house inspector, my husband, and I had all missed before Chris and I bought it—and, we would find out later, that the couple who sold us the house had maybe intended to hide. On my very first day as editor in chief of *Redbook*, torrents of water poured into the basement of the house. And the floods continued as September-hurricane rains worked their way up the coast and pounded the Northeast, forcing me to undertake a months-long renovation that led to the house's foundation being jackhammered into bits. A few weeks later, the roof and walls of the house started to leak in three or four or five different places, depending on how the wind was blowing.

The symbolism of it all was undeniable: water flooded my house for months, as pain was flooding my life. The foundation of my existence was being rocked, as was the foundation of my house. Water followed me everywhere, and so did the tears. I was running a magazine about love and marriage just when everything I thought I knew about either was being put to the test. And I was reinventing that magazine at the same time that I was going through the incredibly painful process of reinventing myself.

And it got worse. I had to fire two full-time nannies in a row and so found myself scrambling to patch together child-care arrangements for Zack. And then there would be a beach house fire and the two emergency room visits, and all the heartbreaking ways in which my family and friends couldn't give me what I asked for despite their best intentions, because they had to live their own lives, too.

I kept my best game face on at work, desperate not to show weakness either to my staff or to upper management as I spearheaded the magazine's transformation. My friends marveled at how I was able to handle the pressure of the big job while I had such a young son. But the job was, in many ways, the easy part, even though it absorbed so much of my concentration and time: I knew that I knew how to run a magazine, and I trusted my skills and instincts at work. But I was just learning how to trust myself as a mother. And I had absolutely no idea how to handle the crisis in my marriage.

Had someone sent me a short story with a heroine living the events that were unfolding in my life, I would have rejected it for being facile and unbelievable. But this wasn't a story, it was my life. And there was no way to get to the other side—of the divorce, of the house's flaws, of my own weaknesses, which I'd spent a lifetime trying to ignore or exorcise—except to live through it all.

I know that on many days I watched my divorce unfurl from a safe distance, as if I were perched somewhere over my own shoulder, or standing just behind one of my mental shoji screens, my eyes peeled for the flashes of wisdom that would help me to begin to make sense of the end of everything I thought I knew about myself. Friends and family commented on my calm, wondering why I wasn't angrier. But I didn't want the heated blur that comes from anger. I wanted clarity. I wanted *answers*. And eventually I realized that anger—at my ex, at life, at God, at the house that leaked, the dishes that were dirty, the fate that would seemingly send me plague after plague until I started wondering if maybe I had been cursed— would keep me from feeling everything I needed to feel to be able to let go and be free.

That is just one of the lessons I learned on my journey through divorce. I stumbled across these lessons like so many river stones tossed on the shore, quieting thoughts coughed up out of the endless roil and thunder that filled my head in those two dark years. I picked them up and played with them in my mind, the way a hand will worry coins in a pocket. They gave me comfort, even though they weren't the answers I thought I wanted, and the lessons weren't always easy. Like the time I found myself lying on my kitchen floor for the fourth or fifth time, crying away another night, and I realized that even though I had so many people in my life who wanted to help me, no army of friends was going to be able to meet me here in my alone.

But as the weeks, and then, the months unfolded, it slowly dawned on me that I didn't need an army, even though I often felt my friends and strangers and our whole entire culture urging me to make divorce the ultimate battle. What I wanted on the other side of all this pain wasn't to win, to be "right," or even just to be able to claim the cruddy consolation prize of being the one who was "wronged."

What I wanted was peace.

I decided the only way to rebuild was to start to understand who I really was, to love and forgive myself my failures, to move beyond all the dashed dreams to trust myself again. To dare to imagine who I might be on the other side of all this. To hold my best idea of myself in my mind's eye and walk toward her, instead of being distracted by the anger and hurt that threatened to take root in my soul and scar it forever.

And that has been the journey of a lifetime: to decide who I am and who I've been and who I want to be, and to do all of that with compassion, both for myself and for my ex.

Five years later, I can honestly say that my divorce is the best thing that ever happened to me. Because I am at peace, and not just with my divorce. With myself.

Who but an optimist would propose that this is what divorce has to offer?

2

A Partnership Is Not Really
a Partnership

I didn't realize a marriage could just *end*, could just be undone by one of the parties. After almost ten years of being married to Chris, I had slowly taken on the skein of beliefs by which so many marriages are bound: that there are times both good and bad; that that which doesn't kill you makes you stronger as a couple; that you are in it together. My friend Charlie likes to say to his wife when they stumble through the daily difficulties of togetherness, "Honey, from here it's a long, straight road to the sweet respite of death. Just put on the yoke and pull." (Of course, he also talks poetically about how meeting his wife ushered him into a "house of love" and about how having a child built a whole new "wing of love" on that house.) Charlie's workaday sentiment captures the truth of the shared labor even the happiest marriage requires, but it also reflects that what you build with your labor becomes bigger than the sum of the two selves who created it—the magic of marriage. I had felt that in my relationship with Chris. I had started to trust it and lean into it in a way I would never have thought possible, because I spent the first half of my life afraid of marriage, and certain that I would never choose it.

I grew up the middle child in a boisterous family, with a brother on each side of me—the older one rebellious, the younger one cautious—and our parents had big personalities and stubborn temperaments. They had always talked to us as if we were adults, neither of them really connecting to the oogy side of parenting; even as a young child I had a sense of my parents' having barely survived our high-maintenance toddler years. (To this day, my father says that children should be born five years old.) Our parents were wildly interested in our minds, though, and they loved stimulating and challenging our burgeoning intelligence. Every night at the dinner table was a family performance, with each of us, our parents included, showing off how smart and fast and funny he or she could be. There were no rules of engagement, and our wide-ranging conversations— leaping from how the planet Earth was formed to neighborhood gossip to decoding the lyrics of a Carly Simon song—generally centered on proving who was the most *right*, with each of us seizing any opportunity to catch someone in a grammatical or factual slipup. Often a family argument ended with one of us kids leaving the table and storming down the hall to look up a word in the unabridged dictionary that had hallowed place on a stand under a spotlight in the living room. To be right was the greatest prize, but humiliating whoever had been wrong—in a clever way that made everyone laugh—wasn't so bad, either. One thing is for sure: I didn't learn mercy at the dinner table.

I didn't learn it anywhere else at home, either. The emotional weather in my parents' relationship was unpredictable. They clearly both had their ideas of How Things Should Be: My father was an industrial engineer, with a special degree in Should; my mother, a Southern steel magnolia, equal parts Delta Burke and Liz Taylor, with all the queenliness that implies. They didn't argue so much; instead they had contests of will and tried to erase each other. There were many silent family dinners during which you could feel the force of my parents' separate unhappinesses pressing against one another, squashing any of my feeble attempts to jump-start a conversation or get a distraction going. My father ate his dinner on edge (therefore, so did we all), waiting to hear one of us kids chew too loudly so that he could bark at us and vent some of his tension.

I was closest with my mother, who has two speeds: intense and asleep. The two of us bonded in a female allegiance. I used to tease her, to try to make her tell me I was her favorite, but she would say only that I was her favorite daughter. I spent much of my childhood convinced that my mother and I were essentially the same person, and she encouraged that fantasy. We even sent off to get our handwriting analyzed so we could compare what the expert said about the two of us; I still remember my mother sniffing in disagreement when the expert explained that my handwriting indicated I was more "rational" than she was. I, too, was dismayed that we had a difference, but somewhere deep inside me I felt relieved that I had something that belonged just to me.

We used to sit on the big front porch of our house, gently rocking the porch swing as she talked to me about Life. Much of my mother's conversation about her youth and her past was tinged with regret. She struggled with a sense of loss for not having graduated from college, since she'd dropped out to support my dad, and over not having found work that she felt used her smarts and potential. She regretted not having lived out her dreams—the dreams she had for her career, her intellect, her *self* that had nothing to do with having children and a family. She talked about the complicated undertow of her relationship with my father, the ways in which she didn't feel valued by him (and I inferred the converse on my father's behalf, making precocious judgments about the ways people, despite their best intentions, don't quite fit together). She urged me to find my own path, and to make sure my life belonged to me fully before I gave it to someone else. But my mother wasn't doleful; she was very strong, a creative and dynamic personality, interested in everything, whether learning how to cane a chair by hand or taking on a local retailer for bad customer service. I thought she possessed magic,

even though she also carried so much sadness. In these many conversations my mother taught me the power of will.

I learned to put up my radar to sense gathering storm clouds in
both my parents, becoming the air-traffic controller in my family. I
thought I had it all figured out—the set of his jaw that meant my
dad had had a long day at work; the slight sigh my mother would
give when she felt like picking a fight—and I'd play my parents off
each other. I'd reassure my dad that I was comforting my mother;
I'd tell my mother that I was calming down Dad. Meanwhile I'd be
kicking my younger brother, Scott, under the table if he was chewing too loudly, or, with my eyes, begging my brother Gregg—five
years older than me and tired of the family drama—to be quiet
when he talked back to Dad. What my role actually was in all this
doesn't matter; a child's sense of security had been born, based on a
vulnerability I could barely tolerate: *I must be in charge at all times.*

I examined my parents' personalities and decided that what each
needed most the other was simply unable to provide—they did not
meet in their soft places, but instead clashed in their hard places.
I felt sorry for them for being so ill-suited; it was hard to see two
people I loved and depended on not be able to connect. I packaged
up my own loss and fears surrounding their storminess and stuffed
those feelings deep down inside me until they took the shape of a
powerful sense of responsibility. Responsibility for my parents. For
everything that happened in my family. For everything that happened around me. It didn't always feel safe in their marriage, and as
I got older, I wondered what the point of risking an unhappy marriage would be. It didn't seem at all possible to me that you could
find a person who would continue to change with you as life unfolded; life was too unpredictable. But unpredictable wasn't scary to
me, not then. Unpredictable meant the world was full of possibility,
possibility just waiting for me.

What did feel safe amid life's tumult was making plans, being
in control. The upside of being the daughter of two strong personalities was that I never lacked confidence in my own opinions or

my own abilities. I could read before kindergarten, started school early, went to reading classes with the grade above me, and generally got the impression from teachers that I was very interesting, which spurred me on to new levels of precocity. At the age of seven, in second grade, I started telling anyone who would listen that I was going to be a magazine editor when I grew up. When I was eleven or twelve I even interviewed the imaginary adult me for a magazine that I made with white paper, colored pencils, and a stapler. It was the first of many magazines I would make with my bare hands. I drew a picture of me: I was wearing an emerald green surplice-wrap dress and had colored my blond hair a bold shade of red. In the accompanying interview, I spouted all kinds of irresistibly breezy bon mots about how wonderful and fascinating and rewarding my life was. This was the language I had picked up from all the magazines my mother read: *Glamour* and *Redbook* and others she plucked from the racks at the supermarket or drugstore checkouts. There was going to be no time for marriage in this independent, wildly satisfying life. I knew I wanted to be a mother. (I planned to adopt two siblings from foster care.) It was the husband I could do without.

I zoomed through high school on the twin engines of hubris and adrenaline. Thus propelled, I could almost pretend that my lurking doubts and insecurities weren't there. I made good grades, edited the school paper, and participated in way too many extracurricular activities, afraid of missing out on something. But I always felt the pressing anxiety of figuring out what was happening in any room—what motives were at play—intellectualizing the ordinary insults of teen life as a way of surviving them. I searched for what people wanted, whether it was recognition or friendship or humor, so I could give it to them and feel I'd earned myself a place. When I graduated I was entangled in a complicated relationship with a serious boyfriend, but I had serious plans: I was headed off to college to get myself ready for a life that would be big enough to satisfy me *and* my mother. After a few crazy weeks and high-drama, long-distance visits, he and I let each other go.

Four years at Washington and Lee University in Virginia (as a member of the second class of women); a custom-made major incorporating journalism, English, and business classes; a semester in Paris writing a thesis titled *"L'internationalisation d'*Elle *et de* Marie Claire"; a coveted summer internship at *Mademoiselle* magazine in New York City; a senior thesis on magazine start-ups, which included a business plan for a general-interest magazine about design . . . Boom, boom, boom, I was lining up and knocking down achievements. I was a crazed student, working too many hours a week at a part-time job, taking too many classes (I graduated with almost a full year's worth of extra credits), sleeping very little. But my desire to succeed—and my fears that I wouldn't—were so strong, I didn't know how else to do it except to be firing all cylinders all the time. I was fueling the engine the only way I knew how in order to launch my real life with extreme momentum to make it everything I'd dreamed. I did not see marriage in that sparkling future.

And so, of course, in that funny way that life works, I was the first of my college friends to head down the aisle.

I started falling in love with Chris just a year after I had graduated college and moved to New York City. I had met him during the previous summer, when I was interning at *Mademoiselle* magazine. During my internship I was tormented not by the editors I worked for, as in *The Devil Wears Prada,* but rather by the other assistants, who turned up their noses at my wardrobe of full skirts and chinos (which I had adopted when I got to W&L, shedding my 1980s mall chick look). They acted as if I was maybe ten pounds too heavy and a few degrees too uncool to be seen sitting near them. Chris was still a film student at NYU, with the de rigueur longish hair and the clunky black boots of that tribe, and I met him because he was friends with a high school friend of mine. He was terribly cute, but he was also shy, hiding his big blue-green eyes behind wavy strands of light brown hair that kept working their way out of his ponytail.

We didn't talk much that summer, but when I moved back to New York to get a job for real a year later, we began running in the same crowd, catching each other's eye across the room. We started having hours-long phone conversations two or three times a week, me taking the princess phone I shared with my roommate across the living room and into the bathroom, because she was so sick of hearing us talk about everything and nothing. I was completely charmed by the juxtaposition of his quiet, gentle nature and his cleverly vulgar sense of humor, and entranced by all his ideas of what his life would be: screenwriting, filmmaking, sharing his imagination with the world. I said to him one night on the phone before we'd even kissed: "You expect great things, don't you?" As a maker of plans and a dreamer of dreams, I could offer no greater compliment.

A few days later, at a party in his tiny apartment, Chris and I found ourselves alone together in the kitchen. We talked, and mooned, and kissed at last, and then kissed some more. From that night on we were together pretty much constantly, to the chagrin of both our roommates. I was completely attracted to the way that Chris was unlike anyone I'd ever met: he was a just-left-of-the-mainstream guy, but, with his big heart and easy affection, he was no angry, cynical rebel. He was an outsider in the same way my older brother is: smart, determined to be self-determined, uninterested in what people think he should be or in following a typical path. I admired that bravery in Chris, as I always had in Gregg. I wished I could care less what people thought of me.

But even the dopamine rush that flooded my circuits in the first flush of infatuation wasn't enough to mask a constant unease. I was thrilled to be with Chris, yes, but I was also afraid. I couldn't afford to have this distraction now. After three long months spent hand-delivering resume packages to every major magazine publishing house, walking the length and breadth of Manhattan both to save money and to learn the city, I had landed the editorial assistant position I desperately wanted. Even better, the job was at *Mirabella*, a smart and gorgeous women's magazine that had recently launched, and that had been the focus of my college thesis on start-ups. It was exactly the job I had set out for when I moved to New York City! I couldn't believe my luck.

I was working in a glamorous, all-beige office with a swooping, circular reception desk behind glass walls, assisting two brilliant and lovely features editors who were generous in showing me the way it was done. I was living in a teensy apartment in a graffiti-covered building in one of the grittiest downtown neighborhoods, because it was all I could afford. (My college friends who'd been raised in New York's best neighborhoods weren't allowed to visit me at my apartment.) I flitted in and out of after-work publicity events— book parties, music parties, launch parties, beauty parties—where I could eat free meals and drink free drinks to help offset the ridiculously meager wage I was delighted and honored to be earning. I had chopped off my long blond hair and hennaed it flame red (as planned), and saved up my money to buy a pair of thigh-high flat-heeled suede boots like those the impossibly chic fashion editors at the magazine were wearing. I had people to impress, ladders to climb, captions to write. Falling in love wasn't in my plan!

But I couldn't resist. Chris was everything I hadn't known I wanted: a long-haired rebel with a sweet and sensitive heart. A silly guy with serious dreams. Someone grounded and loving and kind. But above all, he was my safe place.

After years of people's being impressed or annoyed or flummoxed by my hyperconfident personality, I thought everything about me was big. I wondered if I was *too* big. But being in love with Chris made me feel small, in the best way, as if he could put me in his pocket to carry me around and protect me from the harsh, mean world. One night as we danced together in my East Village apartment (to Matthew Sweet's alt-rock anthem "Girlfriend"), Chris swooped me up into his arms, something no man had ever dared to do with my five-foot-eight-inch frame, and he made it seem easy, like I was no burden, no trouble.

I had never thought of myself as sensitive or vulnerable until I met Chris. I had no idea that underneath my confidence and braggadocio was a girl who was terrified that life might not turn out okay, that I might find myself trapped in regret like my mother. I hadn't realized that I expected love always to hurt just a little—that competitive pinch in my family—until I felt loved with no conditions by Chris. He peeled away my tough take-no-prisoners exterior and revealed the soft part within—the part of me I would have told to buck the hell up if I'd known it was there—and he loved it, too. Plus, he could play the guitar. And sing! I remember the dizzy feeling I'd get watching him play for a roomful of our friends at parties, unself-consciously belting out "I Like the Way You Walk," by the Hoodoo Gurus, while I sat there in my colored tights and wildly patterned Betsey Johnson minidress. It seemed like a miracle to me that someone could do that, and I felt my body churn with attraction. And he was smart and silly and funny and he thought all my crazy and grand plans for life were great and good and *reasonable*. Nothing I thought was too big for Chris. Unable to keep myself from trying to see the future, I visualized the life we'd live, fulfilling all our creative dreams and making up the rules as we went along, having two or three children with beautiful blue-green eyes, just like his, and building our careers in New York City and becoming everything we were meant to be.

The love Chris gave me was a good, simple thing I could trust. I told friends that it felt like I was a balloon reaching up into the sky, and he was down there on the ground, firm and sure, gently holding on to me to keep me from disappearing into space. With Chris I somehow felt more real than I'd ever been in my life. It became impossible for me not to think about marrying him.

And so even as I was falling head over heels, I was filled with dread, a sense that I was being fooled. I already knew this could never work out.

I shared these fears with my mother, who was my closest confidante and friend as well as my roving unabridged dictionary and encyclopedia. I called her as many as three times a day some days from work, when I hadn't been able to find a fact or piece of information I needed in the magazine's reference library (in those days before the Internet replaced reference libraries as the main resource of editorial assistants). Our conversations, once the business at hand had been taken care of, were always far-ranging; they encompassed the doings of my everyday life as well as our musings on people and love and life in general. I tend to live my life out loud, to share every experience I have as I'm having it, with a full set of emotional footnotes about what it feels like, which I attribute to our shared lack of boundaries.

After about a year and a half of being a couple, Chris and I started to talk about moving in together. We were already spending most of our time together at each other's apartment, standing outside on freezing-cold nights waiting for the bus that would take us on our slow, sixty-block evening commute between my apartment downtown and his uptown. We felt certain we were going to end up together, married or not, but the finances of living in New York City were accelerating our decision. What was the point of paying for two apartments if we were only ever sleeping in one at a time?

I dreaded telling my mother, who had always made it clear that she totally disapproved of living together before getting married.

I also didn't want to tell her because I was embarrassed—embarrassed to let her know that I was someone who had been fooled by love and comfort and company, despite all the proof she'd offered that my independence was my most precious asset. I called her, practically in tears, and tried to tiptoe toward telling her that it seemed logical for me and Chris to move in together (although it wasn't logic that was making me want to do it), and that I knew that he and I would get married, when I was ready, later, down the line. She said, "Stacy, you and Chris know each other far better than your father and I did when we got married. So you'll do what you think is right." It wasn't quite permission, but it was what I needed.

So Chris and I started our apartment search in earnest, and after a few weeks we walked into the apartment I instantly knew would be our future home. It was tucked away on a picturesque block in the West Village, one of the oldest neighborhoods in New York. Normally the area would have been out of our financial reach. But the apartment was teeny-tiny—four hundred square feet, which contained a small living room, a bedroom barely big enough for a queen-size bed and a tiny dresser, an old-fashioned pink-and-gray bathroom, and a galley kitchen that didn't even have a full-size refrigerator and was tucked into the hallway between bath and bed. When we got to the open house, there were already dozens of potential renters there ahead of us. But after a four-second lap around the place with Chris, who agreed the apartment was amazing, I was determined. I walked up to the real estate agent and said, "I am sure that this apartment was meant for me." I handed her my business card, hoping that the fact that I worked for a magazine would make me stand out in her head. She informed me that there was already a taker for the place who had given her a deposit check, and that there were about eight people on the waiting list ahead of me if that deal fell through. I was crestfallen, but I thanked her and said that we had our deposit ready and all our references in order, and we could close the deal in a heartbeat. When Chris and I got home I cried, because I just knew in my bones that that was where we were supposed to start our life together; it fit the storyline in my head.

The real estate agent called me two days later to let me know that the first deal had fallen through. And she said, "I'm not sure why I'm calling you, because there were a lot of people ahead of you on the list, but you just seemed so passionate about living here. . . ."

A feeling of luck and optimism about my relationship with Chris started to replace the cynicism and doubt. And so I fell in love with Chris the way I do anything: full speed ahead and with nothing held back. Every conversation with him was filled with kisses and my trying to express how much I loved him. We talked about getting married all the time, and I was always speculating about when we would decide the timing was right, though Chris insisted that he would surprise me with the proposal.

We fell into some comfortable couple routines, with me cooking dinner on weeknights, the two of us going for gut-busting Saturday brunches at Aggie's down the street with our friend Alix, and Chris joining me for very late nights at the office at *Mirabella,* where I earned some extra money by transcribing interviews for one of the editors, who was writing a book. Chris and I sat near each other in the dark, hushed office, only the bank of lights above us aglow, the security guard prowling the floor every hour. Chris worked on his own writing while he waited for me to finish, and then we'd take the subway home together at 11 p.m. or midnight.

The fact that he wanted to be with me even when I was plugged into headphones, typing away, filled me with comfort. And when I cried listening to the heartbreaking interviews—people sharing their experience of being biracial in America, telling wrenching stories of hate and displacement and the lurking cruelty in humanity—Chris would pat my hand and tell me it was okay, and say he loved me because of the way I loved the whole world. "You have so much love to give," he said. Being able to live fully in the sad side of me, to be the woman who roots for the underdogs and believes that trying hard counts in the game of life, was deeply healing. I had spent years hiding behind being strong, but with Chris I could be weak and soft, too. I was starting to let go of the idea that marriage would hold me back, and to see that Chris's love was building me a foundation and a sense of security I'd never known. From that stable, grounded place, I thought, we would be able to achieve anything.

One night, after we'd eaten a stir-fry I'd made on our tiny stove, I turned to Chris and said, "What are we waiting for?" We'd been a couple for two years, which felt like a lifetime to me then. I was wearing sweatpants and my hair was pulled back in a ponytail; this wasn't exactly the moment for the Big Proposal, but I was tired of waiting, impatient as ever to make my plans a reality. He shrugged and said, "I thought you were waiting until 1997."

It was true. When Chris and I first started talking about getting married, I told him we'd have to wait until 1997—first because I was trying to put it off to an age that seemed "old enough," and second because I'm very superstitious about dates. My brothers and I were born on the twenty-seventh, seventeenth, and seventh of our respective birth months, in descending order; July for the boys, January for me, the girl. And my parents were married on December 17. I may be overconfident, but I've also always believed there's no harm in doing what you can to keep the universe on your side, and 1997 was the first year October 17 fell on a Saturday. But that night I said, "I don't want to wait that long anymore." I snuggled up against Chris on our big sofa—the sofa we'd bought with all the money I'd made transcribing those interviews at night, with him at my side—and said, "Let's pick a date." I got out my calendar and started looking for an auspicious date in October, deciding that Saturday, October 1 of that year, 1994, sounded almost as good. We'd both be twenty-five when we married.

We called both sets of parents that night to announce our happy news. I had met Chris's parents and spent some holidays with them, and I loved them like crazy. In fact, when I met his parents was when I became utterly certain I would marry him. His family was calm and grounded and Midwestern, with none of the hugely competitive spirit that drives mine, although everyone was accomplished in his or her own way. Chris had always said he felt really different from the rest of his family; he didn't want a simple life, and he was always attracted to the fringes of things. But I was seduced by their big-hearted welcome and their warm manner—they seemed very clear and calm about the way they were a family, living in the quiet assumption of connection, without angst or turmoil. When I watched his parents, Cole and Barb, I felt a real sense of partnership between them; the link they shared was gracious and humble, polite and sweet. Instantly I said to myself, If Chris comes from this place of calm, of understated and understood love, then sign me up; he can lead the way.

And lead he did, especially when it came to laying down ground rules for our fights and disagreements. In my family you won bonus points for being clever, and you took home the prize if you drew blood by cutting to the emotional quick.

My habit when I got into an argument with Chris was to be haughty and mean and to turn up the volume until I was in a state I didn't know how to come down from. Which meant that I only knew how to end our arguments by putting on my coat and flouncing out the door, walking the streets in our neighborhood until the adrenaline stopped flooding my circuits and fueling my indignant, unforgiving attitude. But because Chris didn't fight me in that same way, when I came down I felt disgusted with myself. I would call from a pay phone, my head resting against the cold metal booth, my voice a whisper: "I'm sorry. I don't know why I got so upset." In one sense, I did know why I got so upset: I thought I put everything at risk by being vulnerable and soft. But the gentle way Chris reacted to the worst of me—hurt, but forgiving, wanting to understand—showed me I had everything to win. When I got home with my head hanging down and my lower lip trembling, he would hold me and calmly tell me that he really hated it when I left in the middle of an argument, and that it wasn't fair to him or to us.

And so I learned to trust that he wasn't trying to score points in a fight, and each argument was a baby step forward. There was the night I put on my coat, fled the apartment, and then stopped at the bottom of the stairs, leaning against the front door of the apartment building, trying not to open it and leave. "Stacy?" Chris called quietly. I stood there, not breathing, and said in a small voice, smaller than I recognized as being me, "Yes?" "Please come back," he said. And so I did. And little by little, argument by argument, I stopped putting on my jacket, stopped trying to flee, learned to trust him even in our disagreements, and learned to find my strength in the work of being partners, not individuals at war.

I knew that for me marriage was going to be a daily choosing, not a destination. As I started working on the wedding plans with my mother, I kept pointing out to friends that the big day wasn't marking the beginning of my relationship with Chris: it was a celebration of both what we'd already built and what was to come. This distinction seemed critical to me; it was my way of infusing the idea I'd been so afraid of with life and flexibility. As I was going through all the fun and exciting (and banal and endlessly anxiety-producing) motions of having a dress made, finding a photographer, choosing a menu, I was sure that I wanted to marry Chris. But I still couldn't find the place where I was *certain*.

One day as I admitted all my anxiety to my mother on the phone, she said, "I think I've done you a disservice in letting you think you know anything about my relationship with your father." I paused, dumbfounded. How could the years of her sharing all the intimate details with me—the good, the bad, and even the ugly, things no daughter should ever know—mean I knew nothing about their relationship? She went on to say that every couple meets in a place that no one else can see, and that as the years unfold there is more and more created there than the mere sum of life events. "As far as for you and Chris go, you are trying to answer a question you don't get to know the answer to. You don't get to know if you and Chris will make it. The two of you have looked as far into the future as you can and seem to agree about where you are going. That is all you get. And someday you may or may not have to face the question of whether you will stay together, and you won't know that moment has come until it's there."

Well, I certainly didn't like that answer at all. But I had to try to accept its wisdom.

After a few months of planning the wedding and pushing down all my anxieties about making this big step, I had a night where all I was trying not to think about broke through. Chris and I were home in our little apartment, with its casement windows lending it a sense of Parisian romance, and he was regaling me in his sweet way with all the reasons why we were destined to be together, and how he knew I had been put on the Earth just for him. I was sitting in the green

Naugahyde office chair we'd bought from the local Salvation Army, the one that went with his desk, where he did his writing (and I played the video game Doom for hours on end). I felt my heart start to race and my hands go numb. I began to cry softly. Chris scooted over to me on his knees and took my hands and looked up into my face and asked me what was wrong.

I explained that I felt like a liar because I didn't truly believe we were "meant" to be together. I explained through tears that I loved him so much, but it seemed like I was keeping some kind of terrible secret by not telling him that I wasn't so sure about this seemingly magical "forever" thing. I didn't believe in fairy tales—not for anyone, but especially not for me. Being happy has always made me nervous, as if I'm inviting disaster. Walking down the aisle wasn't going to erase my anxiety about all that lay ahead that we couldn't predict. Of course I wanted, I *intended*, to do my best to love him forever, but I could not pretend that I was able to truly make that promise.

He gently gathered my hands into his and told me he understood. And then he said, "I promise if you ever want to leave me, I will let you go." I know it sounds crazy, but those were the most beautiful words I had ever heard. I felt that with those words Chris really proposed to me. I knew then that he really *knew* me, and could accept the part of me that was always afraid. I wept with gratitude for his acceptance of all my anxieties and those parts of me that are broken, and for his confident, gentle way of guiding me through my storms of doubt. He knew what to do with me when I didn't. How could I not entrust him with the rest of my life?

So on October 1, 1994, Chris and I were married in front of eighty-five friends and his parents, who had been high school sweethearts, and my parents, who had just reconciled after a six-month separation. To me, the two sets of parents together embodied all I believed and hoped was true about marriage: I was prepared for it to be both good and hard, complicated and simple. The wedding was a joyous and marvelous occasion, and I had never felt so loved in my life as I did in that roomful of people who knew us so well, standing along with us, their hearts and eyes filled with love.

The ceremony was supposed to take place in a lush, green spot enclosed by trees, but the sky was gray and overcast when I woke up that morning. I sat in my mother's bedroom as she applied her makeup, and I pouted. She said simply, "There's a Native American blessing that says, 'Rain on your wedding day means there'll be no tears in your marriage.'"

So the ceremony took place in front of a plate-glass window overlooking the garden as an early-fall shower rained down. Chris and I promised to love and trust and honor and respect and admire and support each other for all the days of our lives, and we believed it, taking that leap of faith into free space that somehow feels like solid ground, that mystery of marriage. But I'm pretty sure our feet didn't touch the floor once as we walked back down the aisle after the ceremony.

In one of the photos from just seconds after we exchanged vows, Chris and I are standing together, he with his chin jutting out and up and a prideful look on his face, and I'm tucked under his arm, even though I'm wearing three-inch heels, gazing up at him with my eyes wide and filled with glee. I'm using my grandmother's lace hankie to pat away the tears that spilled down my face during the big hug we had shared right after the ceremony. That photo captures everything that we were claiming as ours in our marriage: the mutual joy in discovering and protecting a person as your equal. But in that photo I can also see, just a little bit, how Chris was unafraid to be bigger than me.

With that newfound stability at my back, I threw myself equally into my social life and my career. Chris and I had a large group of friends and we went out a lot, to concerts and parties and bars and movies and just hanging around in a pack in the way that seems so necessary when you're in your twenties. We also had Alix, my friend and fellow assistant at *Mirabella*, over for dinner every Tuesday night to watch *Melrose Place*. My specialties at the time were budget-conscious stir-fries and vegetarian curries, but once in a while I'd splurge and make a warm spinach-and-bacon salad with pears and Stilton. Alix and I would stand at the stove eating "frontier snacks" (the name was a way to glamorize the fact that we were using toast to scoop up bacon crumbs and fat from the bottom of the pan) and catching up on the dramas of the week before we settled, with Chris, onto the giant shabby-chic sofa.

One night when we were all three talking, during the commercials, about boys and couples and love and life, Alix said to us, "You two are the least-married married people I know." Chris and I squeezed hands, smug about the way we were building our life to be a place where we could both flourish, separate and together.

I loved how getting married had changed nothing in our relationship, except that I felt calmer and more secure. The commitment Chris and I had made to each other had taken shape in my mind as a specific image: me and Chris, two separate people, divided by a space between us, but leaning toward each other, our heads resting together, our arms clasped, making an A-frame in which to weather the storms of life together. The divide was the place our conflicts lived, the places we didn't mesh perfectly, the parts of us that belonged to each of us alone. For me, the marriage commitment was a promise to always reach across that divide, to never let go, to never be so wholly in the self that I would drop my hand from his, even in the moments when our disagreements might be so strong that one or both of us turned away. That image, of reaching out, our index fingers always touching, even if we were facing away from each other, made me feel safe. It was a position I felt I could hold forever, a forever I could believe in, because it perfectly captured how the partnership was carried by both of us at the same time. I didn't have to be responsible for the whole thing. It wasn't only up to me.

Fast-forward a decade or so: Deciding he wanted to leave me felt like the first decision Chris had made in our marriage for some time. Well, that's not totally true: he regularly chose what kind of takeout we would order for dinner on the many nights in a row I came home from work too late or too tired to cook. I was so overstimulated from managing the cycle of deadlines involved in putting out a monthly magazine that I couldn't make even that simple decision.

But it is also true that Chris had become a silent partner in the marriage. He was present and absent at the same time, at home in the house, but always secreting himself away into his office on the second floor, the door closed. Inside, he was working away on a screenplay and on film and Web business ideas that had been swirling in his head since I'd first starting dating him. I knew Chris was frustrated that he wasn't where he wanted to be professionally, and so I tried to give him as much room as possible on that front—to not need him, to give him a lot of time alone—but I longed for him to be able to be satisfied with all that we had built together. We'd achieved so many of the dreams we'd talked about when we first met as broke twenty-one-year-olds, scrabbling for success in the pressure cooker of New York City life. We had one of the two children we'd always planned to have, some relative financial stability, and, at last, a house and a beautiful backyard. I wanted all that we shared together to be Enough. So for many, many months I had been learning to live with less and less of Chris, hoping that if he found his footing in the things he wanted for himself, he would once again be more fully present in the life we shared. But having the baby—something we had both wanted for years, and that I had kept delaying as I launched one magazine or another—pushed him further out of reach. He had become depressed after I got pregnant, barely able to stumble through his days at work, practically unable to talk to me and tell me what was happening. I was pulled back and forth between joy about being pregnant and fear about going through so much of it alone as Chris withdrew.

The birth of Zack seemed to draw Chris back out of his shell a bit, and he was in love with his new son. But the realities and demands of life with a newborn were taking their toll on him and I felt like I was on eggshells, trying to take care of as much as I could on my own.

One gray March morning, a few months before Chris pronounced the end of our marriage, I was sitting on the living room floor, playing with Zack as he leaped around in his ExerSaucer. We had just come back from our regular Saturday visit to the gym, where Zack played in the nursery, crawling around on the squishy wrestling mats, while I tried my best to beat down my new-mom anxiety by running on a treadmill. I was getting ready to dash upstairs and take a shower, leaving Chris to watch Zack for a few minutes in that eternal back-and-forth kid-shuffle that couples do, and making plans for the rest of the day.

I looked up at Chris and mentioned that maybe we needed to drive to Home Depot; we were still settling in to our house and the list of things we needed—shelves, dimmer switches, extra trash cans, lightbulbs—was still quite long. He was sitting on the sofa, just a few feet away, and I saw him stiffen at my words. Then he turned to me and unloaded.

"You are always filling up my time with errands, constantly making plans for me. I can't stand it!"

He went on, raging against the way I saw his time as belonging to me. Stunned by his outburst—Chris wasn't given to snit fits or petty anger—I simply sat there, speechless, as waves of shock pumped through my body, trying to gather my thoughts.

I saw clearly for the first time that Chris felt tormented by this new life: the house, the baby, the responsibilities, the demands, the sacrifices, and, worse, the real-live togetherness of it all. For the first ten years of our relationship, Chris and I had been a couple that spent a lot of time apart, pursuing our own work, interests, and friends, but we always reconnected at the end of every day on the sofa: watching TV, vegging, catching up. Now I wanted his help and his presence more. I wanted us to be a *family*.

I took a long breath. Then I said slowly, "You never want to come to the park with us. Or to the playground. Or even just go for a walk. You don't want to do anything with us. Running errands together as a family is the only way I know to get you to spend time with us. What *do* you want to do with us? What? Can you name anything?" Tears started sliding down my cheeks.

This was when I began to see that he had been struggling with everything in our married life, not just his own dreams and desires. I hadn't realized that I'd been trying to "trick" Chris into spending time together as a family. I had no idea that I was terrified by the way in which he was disappearing from me, and had been disappearing for some time. For years I had been standing to the side and waiting for him to be happy, at the same time willing myself to ignore the many signals that he wasn't. To actually begin to speak the truth of that into the room and have it become a real thing between us, instead of a constant presence that we both tacitly agreed to ignore, was deeply unsettling.

Chris didn't—couldn't—answer my question. He mumbled and paused, said something that sounded like "No." And then he said, "You're right." He looked at me, openly surprised and chastened, and admitted that he didn't know the answer. He didn't know what he would enjoy all of us doing together.

The shared realization of the distance opening up between us did not bring us closer. I did not start to connect the dots regarding the struggle we were in as a couple, because I wasn't looking for dots—and because of the ways in which marriage is the triumph of faith over circumstance. That moment declared its importance and snapped into bold relief only after Chris had gathered enough strength to tell me he wanted out three months later.

But the dots had been there, and, yes, I could see them now as we sat on the sofa and he told me our marriage was over. I had grappled with fleeting feelings of hating Chris when he launched into his frequent rants about the irredeemable horror of stupid people, which threatened my own I-love-humanity worldview. We had struggled for months with the every-other-night-sex my ob-gyn had recommended when I didn't get pregnant after six months of trying. He had been miserable during the pregnancy, threatened by the way our son would underline all he'd failed to achieve, undermine all he still hoped to do—and he hadn't even been able to talk to me and express those fears. As I sat on the sofa listening to Chris telling me he was done, I could see that I'd been coiled into myself for a long time, waiting, waiting, waiting for Chris to be happy, for him to want to join me in our lovely life—or, at least, a life that *I* thought was lovely. We'd faced down some demons and the hard stuff of life, standing together as my mother battled cancer and beat it, and then as his father fought cancer and lost. We'd survived the Internet bubble (during which we both lost our jobs), and six months of living apart as I flew coast-to-coast for a job. And we'd been through a round of marriage counseling in 2001 after we'd started living in the same city again. For thirteen years, we'd been learning together, and finding our way together.

So how were we supposed to find our way apart?

I sobbed to Chris, trying to make sense of the fact that he wasn't telling me we were having problems, that we should go to couples counseling, that he thought we weren't getting along anymore. *Hell, tell me you hate me!* But no, he was telling me that our marriage was over. He had decided. Alone.

Along with my panic, I felt disgust. How could I not have understood that this could happen? I had years of experience creating magazine contracts for contributing editors and partnerships, in which pages of legalese explained the commitment being entered into and which "party" (the magazine or the writer) owned what under which circumstances. I knew that buried deep within each contract was a "get-out clause" that gives either party the power to end the partnership with thirty days' written notice, no matter how many pages of expressed legal togetherness came before it.

I didn't realize marriage had its own get-out clause, which could leave one partner standing there, dumbfounded.

I felt hoodwinked. Especially because, finally, our marriage had taken root in me. Just two or three weeks after Zack was born, I'd had my first taste of Ever After: lying in bed one morning with Chris, little Zackie between us, both of us exhausted from the all-night-long feedings, I'd felt the touch of grace, the immensity of what we'd created. My eyes filled with tears, and I looked at Chris and said, "I get it now. This is so forever." I was in. All the way in. It had taken thirteen years of sharing a life with Chris for me to get there, to find the place where shooting for forever seemed possible. Little did I know that Chris was already long gone.

Forever can be undone in a second: once Chris chose to enact the get-out clause, the magic of that leap of faith we'd taken together instantly evanesced. Sitting there with Chris that night on the sofa—the sofa we'd chosen because it was the only one big enough for both of us to lie on at the same time, the one we'd had to have disassembled and rebuilt three times because it didn't fit through the doorways of three different apartments, the sofa I'd had recovered in red fabric for the price of a new sofa when we moved back to New York after our year in San Francisco because it was worn but I couldn't bear to get rid of it—it was utterly impossible not to feel like a fool for having been caught believing in that leap of faith.

3

You Don't Get to Know Why, But Ask Anyway

The world did not come to an end the night Chris told me he was "done." Somehow I moved through the evening's regular paces: dinner was cooked and eaten, dishes were washed, Zack was carried upstairs and put to bed. Somehow, I came back downstairs to finish a conversation I'd never wanted to start, a conversation I had never even had the foresight to dread. I sat on the sofa next to Chris, not touching him and barely even looking at him because I was so afraid, and I cried. He talked, and I talked. I reasoned and begged and pleaded and sobbed and wailed. I tried to manipulate. I tried to convince him I would die That Very Second if he didn't realize the total wrongness of his thoughts. I didn't yet understand that these tactics would no longer work, that I was already out of the equation.

At first I blamed the whole incident on the Memorial Day barbecue I'd thrown the weekend before. I knew Chris hated it when I threw parties. (Was that why he was leaving me?) He thought that they were too much work, that I wore myself out, that I was miserable in the days of busywork before the big event. The truth is actually that I am never happier than when I am in a swirl of creating anything (Reason #2 that he was leaving me?). He hated the way I needed him to help me: to run to the store to get a forgotten item; to watch and entertain Zack while I boiled the Red Bliss potatoes for the potato salad; to prep the asparagus for grilling, chop up apples and oranges for the sangria. But I had planned the party anyway, inviting twenty people to our beautiful backyard as a belated housewarming. I've always thought that having a house aswirl with all the people you love most is the only proper way to bless it (Reason #3?). The party was five months late, but with the baby, and then my getting fired from a job I loved just two months after we'd moved in, we'd been in no position to celebrate much of anything, worried as we were about paying our bills. We had been in survival mode.

For me a party isn't just a party; it's an opportunity to express hospitality and love to everyone who attends. I learned how to put together a party from my mother, a fantastic cook and even better hostess, whose approach to entertaining could be reduced to the simple motto "Too much is never enough!" And so for every party I'd ever thrown, I'd made everything from scratch. But too far into the planning for this party, I discovered I was in over my head. I had picked recipes that were overcomplicated. I was making too many dishes. I also had become consumed with decorating the pergola and the deck just so, seeking out new outdoor pillows and lanterns and strings of lights. I asked Chris to go to Home Depot to buy galvanized tubs to hold the sodas and beers the day before the party because I didn't want to use the coolers we had in the basement. At some point, I realized that trying to do this much when I had an infant son was impossible; that the difference between eight for dinner and twenty for a barbecue was bigger than I had figured. I kept apologizing to Chris the day before the party as we worked nonstop to get everything ready, but he was beyond assuagement. Irritated, he marched around the house, taking orders from me. I winced whenever I needed to ask him to head to the deli up the street to pick up another ingredient, and I breathed a sigh of relief anytime he left the house.

But the barbecue the next day was totally enjoyable. Friends and acquaintances from all different phases of our lives showed up, and they mixed and connected easily. Our green backyard was at its best. Zack, all beaming blondness and supersocial to the core, charmed all the guests, crawling on the lawn and the deck, raising his arms to ask people to pick him up. The food was delicious, and everyone was amazed that I'd made it all myself. Still, my closest friends, like Alix, could tell that Chris was withdrawn; they'd become used to his disappearances over the years, the way he would be in a room and yet somehow not be there, eyes cast down to the ground. But after some of the early guests had left and the grilling was done, Chris managed to relax, drinking beers with his friends and laughing under the stars and the twinkling metal lanterns I'd strung up among the pergola's grapevines. The last man standing finally headed home around 11 p.m., ten hours after the festivities had started. As Chris and I cleaned up the dishes, sorted the bottles, and dumped the melting ice from the tubs, I apologized to him, with a formal, full-on admission that I had been wrong. We sat down on our red sofa and I agreed with him that the plans I had made were too big. That things were different now that we had a son. That I was sorry. Really sorry.

And here we were, just five days later, back on the sofa, with Chris telling me our marriage was over. It had to have been the barbecue, right? If I could just take that whole weekend back, this wouldn't be happening.

Or maybe it was the stress of the new house? And having a baby? And the fact that I'd just been fired? And that we were in tight financial straits? Plus, there was the pressure I was feeling about trying to land this big new job, heading up *Redbook* (Reasons #4, #5, #6, #7, #8, and #9). I mean, Chris, think about it, I urged. Everything has changed in our lives in the past eight months. We wouldn't be normal if we weren't having some adjustment issues!

I was trying to tell him a story about why he was feeling this way, filling the air with my words because I was terrified to have Chris speak his reasons. What if Chris was getting ready to tell me some terrible truth about me that I couldn't deny? What if the end of my marriage was really all my fault?

I don't remember much of what Chris said to me that night on the sofa, other than that he was unhappy (Reason #10) and I was unhappy (Reason #11) and he thought that this had been true for both of us for years. No, he hadn't fallen for another woman, but he admitted that a brewing crush he had at the office was one of the many signs that he knew he was done. I can't recall many of his exact words, but I do remember the awful *feeling* of it all, of being sucked down a black hole, and the nausea in the pit of my stomach, and the vertigo. And I remember Chris trying to be gentle with the dozens of ways he must have said, "I don't want this anymore." I believed that his kindness surely meant there was enough love left that maybe I could fix things from here. I just needed to untangle the logic that had led us to where we now were and start the repair work. How could he mean we weren't happy? I thought we were as close to happy as we'd ever been.

Yes, we had been through some hard times, and challenging times, and busy times. It was true that for the past ten years I had been more work than play. Shortly after we married, I had helped launch a new weekly magazine in a job where I worked literally around the clock—and it was my job, as managing editor, to make sure everyone else did, too. I was coordinating the work of thirty editors and writers who created the hundred or so pages that made up the magazine. For weeks the editor in chief and I left the office together on Wednesday nights at 5 or 6 a.m. the next morning after having spent the final hours of the night with our feet up on the table in her office, handing the last pages of the issue back and forth between us, her edits in red, mine in blue. We'd share a cab home, sleep for three or four hours, and then come back, bleary-eyed but not beaten. Saturdays and Sundays I went into the office to sign bills, figure out issue costs, finesse the coming issues' article lineups. I logged in ninety hours a week at that job for the first six weeks, twice hallucinating from lack of sleep.

I thought it was the most thrilling thing I'd ever done in my life.

And so I did it again, joining another launch team and getting another magazine off the ground. And then a year later, I stepped into my first editor-in-chief job, at *Modern Bride*. An editor in chief! At twenty-nine years old! Ahead of plan! Three years later, I was asked to head up a general-interest magazine and Internet company all about design, an idea I'd been carrying around in my head and desperate to bring to life since I wrote the business plan and created the mock-up for it in college. Chris dared to say yes to my dream; he pulled up stakes and moved to San Francisco, and he telecommuted to the Internet programming job he'd worked in for the last few years but didn't love. One year later, after the dot-com bubble burst, my company was out of business and Chris had been laid off.

The dot-com/magazine job had pushed me to my limits, both physically and mentally, with the constant travel between New York and San Francisco, and the pressure of trying to stay in business, close another round of financing, and persuade my team to work another week or two or three in very uncertain conditions, sometimes without pay. I was starting to understand that I'd been subjecting myself to these successive tests of will not just because I wanted to build my career, but also because I was trying to prove my worth, to find the safe place I'd always dreamed about since I was a little girl.

A colleague in the business who had been following my career called me up and asked, "Are you ready to calm down now?" Yes, I said, I was. He pointed me in the direction of the job of executive editor at *Marie Claire*. In just three days, I packed up our San Francisco apartment (Chris had already moved back to New York) and completed my proposal for the *Marie Claire* job—story ideas, marketing ideas, "big" ideas—as I sat on a single plastic chair in an empty apartment. I e-mailed the test and got in my car and drove across country, back home to Chris (who'd been rehired by the same company that had laid him off) and our new apartment in Brooklyn. I was totally thrilled when I was offered the job: happy to pull up a chair and see how it was done in the big leagues, happy to have a mentor, happy to give myself permission to focus a little bit on my whole life instead of just my career, and to think about having the baby Chris and I had talked about for years.

So Chris and I had the baby, and we bought the house, but then I got fired, and now I was sitting on the sofa and my husband was telling me he wanted to leave me.

After three hours of Chris's talking and my crying—I got up from the sofa only to turn on the lights and draw the curtains closed when it got dark—nothing was any clearer to me about why this was happening. Once I had moved past the begging and the trying to give him easy reasons why we were having a hard time, I gave in, balled-up tissues all around me on the couch, on the coffee table, on the floor. I let it sink in that he had told me he wanted to leave. I flashed back to the flare-up we'd had the day I wanted him to come to Home Depot with the baby and me. I realized that Chris wanted to be anywhere but here, and worse, that my absence in those past years had suited him more than my presence. Our metaphorical little A-frame house, me leaning into him and him leaning into me, had ceased to be weatherproof. And what was worse, I had no idea when the rain had started coming in.

"Please help me understand," I said. "If you really think this is over and you are done, I beg you to help me get it, to explain it to me enough so that I can see what you see—why we can't be together—so I have half a chance of being able to move on and let go." *So I can breathe again someday. So I can be a good mother to your son. So the entirety of these years we shared is not thrown into doubt. So I don't have to spend the rest of my life with a black spot on my heart, hating you for destroying everything we built together.* I knew I might not ever agree with his reasons about why we

couldn't be together anymore, but I also knew that without understanding at least part of it, I would spend the rest of my life asking
the same questions, wondering what I could have done differently to
avoid this terrible outcome.

Exhausted and finally empty of words, we went upstairs to sleep
in the same bed we'd been sharing for years—in the bedroom across
the hall from where our nine-month-old son was asleep in his crib.
My heart was sick at the thought of Zack's losing his family so
young. I was sick for myself, too, and worried about Chris and what
was happening to him: the man I married, the man I thought I knew
so well, whom I still wanted to take care of and love and protect
and honor. I lay curled into a ball, my back toward Chris, the way
I'd always slept next to him, and wept silently into my pillow until
I fell asleep.

The next morning, when I opened my eyes to the sounds of Zack's
cries, the room still gray with darkness, I felt a heavy thud land in
my chest. I couldn't imagine what I had done to make myself feel
that way. Did I run over a cat with my car? Not hand in my college
term paper? Then the events of the previous night registered, and
a split-second later I shifted into the coping mode I know so well.
Don't think about the big picture, I told myself, swinging my bare
feet out of bed and onto the bedroom floor, gently sliding shut the
shoji screens in my mind so I could pad across the hall and greet my
infant son with a smile on my face.

One thing at a time. Gotta get Zack up. Feed him. Spend some time
playing on the carpet with him. Take a shower while Chris entertains
him for a few minutes. Avoid meeting Chris's eyes. No, meet his eyes
and give a gentle, forgiving smile (which he returns). Okay. It could
be worse. Feel the flutter of anxiety flapping in your chest, and will
it to calm. Open the closet doors, pick out an outfit. Get ready for
the nanny to show up. Hopefully she won't be late today (the way
she's been late every day). Get out the door. *Do you have your keys?* Get

on the subway, slide through the turnstile, fold into the masses of people who don't know what's happening to you. Get to the free-lance job in the office tower you're working in while you're looking for another full-time job. (I was working with an editor to help inspire and direct her team to dream up the next evolution of her magazine, work that had come to me out of nowhere when I needed it most.) Those morning tasks completed, I could get my morning coffee, sit down at my desk in my temporary office, and then think about my problem, Chris's unhappiness, and think about the Why. Why was he doing this? What was he trying to escape?

I am the queen of Why. I have lived my whole life looking closely at people's actions, searching for the little clues that they can't help but put out, like fine threads sticking up from their clothing. I tug on those loose filaments and follow them until I can suss out the motivation each is attached to. I don't think people do inexplicable things. I think they do things with reasons and rewards attached that I can't immediately see, because I am not living their lives, their fears, their dreams. I started following the whys when I was grow-ing up in my family full of drama and personalities, and riven with quiet currents of discontent. I refined that skill as a magazine editor, imagining the complexities of my readers' lives and defining their core emotional desires to direct how each magazine I've worked for connects with them, those millions of people I'll never have the pleasure of meeting. How is it that we become who we are? How do we know what we want? This is my daily daydreaming.

As I sat at my desk and thought about Chris and our marriage, I felt as though I were staring into a washing machine, watching all the events of our life whirling around, my eyes straining to pick out a single detail from the churn. I felt the thrum of anxiety somewhere behind my breastbone. If I thought about it all too long, it felt like I was in the washer myself, flipping over and over, no way to know which way was up or how to get my feet back on solid ground. I kept trying to slow my thoughts so that I could wrap my head around the situation and come up with the exact reasons why Chris was feeling like he had no choice but to leave our marriage. If I could do that, I could sort out this mess and get our relationship back on track.

After having to admit to myself that it wasn't just the barbecue that had brought us here, I clung to the notion that Chris was having an extended panic attack in response to all the new responsibilities in our life. Everyone has some post-baby panic, right? That explanation seemed logical. More important, it made the problem seem solvable. It meant I could alleviate the pressure on him, I could make room for him in whatever way he needed. I might not be the smartest or the luckiest woman I know, but I have always been willing to work harder than anyone else. I could do more, I could learn to live with less, even though I'd already been learning to live with less for so long: less help, less partner, less love, less him.

And so for weeks after the conversation on the couch, for weeks after my first subway ride trying to figure out Why, I tiptoed around in my life, trying to be the perfect wife and mother and to protect Chris. I tried to show him that this life could be good (not yet accepting that it was exactly this life that he didn't want, even though he had told me that quite clearly). I cooked dinner almost every night that summer, standing at the grill. I did as much of the child care on my own as I could, taking just two or three hours on weekends to run errands without Zack. I gardened and grew five kinds of heirloom tomatoes in our backyard. I mowed the lawn and cut back the grapevines that were engulfing our pergola. I prepped all of Zack's weekday meals and did our laundry and ran the nanny schedule. I kept working on little details in the house, making it more comfortable and more beautiful, without asking for his help. I was always suggesting to Chris that he go upstairs and into his office after dinner, to work for a while, to be with just himself, to see how that could fit into our family life.

But even amid this wifely martyrdom, I failed: I forgot to water the lawn (all six-by-ten feet of it), creating a dust bowl in our backyard—and yet another time-consuming task (reseeding the lawn) that I would need Chris's help with. I threw a big family party for Zack's first birthday and, apparently not having internalized the lesson of the barbecue (although I did order absolutely every single other scrap of food for the party), I decided to make a birthday cake, in the shape of four baby blocks that spelled out Z-A-C-K. My mother had always made the most amazing cakes for me and I wanted to do the same for my son. I took shortcuts to simplify the process, but it still took the better part of two days to make the cake, and I was ashamed of my bad judgment. As I frosted the cake, Zack whined at my feet, wanting some of my attention, and my mother-in-law, who'd come into town for the party, wondered aloud why I was making the cake because all Zack really wanted was me. Chris sat stonily silent next to her. I knew what he was thinking. I could feel it all the way across the room. He was hating me. I wondered how it was possible for Barb not to feel the force of it, too, as she sat smack dab in the middle of the psychic pathway running between Chris and me.

The last thing I wanted to be doing was giving him new reasons to hate me.

At night, I could feel other reasons sneaking into my head. I caught glimpses of where Chris and I didn't see eye to eye, the parts of me that I didn't necessarily even like myself, the instances in our marriage in which I had been selfish or mean or ungenerous, the moments when I had doubted our relationship. Maybe I was a bad person. Maybe I wasn't who I thought I was. Maybe I was unlovable.

It turns out that the first weeks and months (and, let's be honest, even *years*) of breaking up are about unearthing all the whys that might have paved the hidden path that has led to the end of your marriage. First you dwell in the whys you create for your husband. And then on those that he serves up, which you instantly try to bat away. The whys offered up by friends and neighbors and coworkers, which come at you unbidden before you are strong enough to hear them. And even the whys of strangers you run into in your daily life, the curbside prophets and checkout-line shrinks, people to whom you blurt your story, in that strange intimacy that being strangers affords. Because such people know nothing about me, I find it easy to bestow upon them the power of oracles, as if their insights into my situation had been handed down from the heavens.

The whys are like hats: deep down, I know I don't look good in one, but I can't resist trying them on, seduced by their power to flatter and conceal. I was hoping that maybe one of those reasons would reveal the best and nicest and prettiest me. I was looking for the hat that would sit just so, and would hide some of the scars and ugliness I knew were hidden in the story of my marriage, stories I didn't want anyone else to know, that I myself wasn't ready to see.

At first I was afraid of what my friends might say to me, of what their insights might reveal to me about my relationship. If I hadn't had any sense that my marriage was falling apart, then how did I know I knew anything about anything? Maybe I really was an over-bearing, miserable, unhappy shrew that no one could love. Maybe Chris was some kind of freak and we should never have married. (But that would be my fault, too, for choosing him.) What if my friends had, for years, been quietly commiserating and wondering just when the hell Chris and I were finally going to admit we were a bad match?

It was upsetting enough that I apparently hadn't known what Chris was thinking. But if there were people all around me who had a more accurate sense of my life—of *me*—than I did, I was definitely going to fall apart for good, because my sense of self has always been based on being able to read a room right, to know what people are going through. And to read myself correctly, too. I'm fa-natically dedicated to the idea of striving to be honest with myself, to be fearless about knowing and voicing my motivations, desires, complaints, fears, to be in touch with the whole of me. The habit makes it easy to be forgiving of people's failures, your own included. I've always believed it's the only way to have half a chance of achiev-ing happiness in this complicated world.

Now I could feel that there was actually something worse than watching my happy life disappear, something worse than getting up and going to my freelance job and trying to be the happy-happy wife, trying to cajole and comfort Chris out of what I was sure was just a momentary insanity. It was the empty, sinking feeling of watching my entire sense of self break into a thousand pieces, in the same way that the spaceship breaks up in the Asteroids video game, four little tiny lines just . . . drifting . . . away . . . from one another, disappearing into outer space, becoming so much cosmic junk.

I've always thought I was a loving person. But I can remember dozens of times I wasn't as loving as I could have been with Chris, starting with that moment at the sink when I was washing the arugula. I believe I have a generous spirit, and I can be generous to a fault, always lending people money or an ear and my time when they're in need. But had I been generous with Chris in the last few years as he started to disappear from me? No, not always. Sometimes I was short with him, and sometimes I was just flat-out pissed that he didn't want to do what I wanted to do, be where I wanted to be. Direct, honest, truthful, even about the hard stuff in life? My friends have always said that I am the bravest person they know, because of the ways in which I am unafraid to see who people really are, and not judge them. Or that had been me, before I started to feel threatened by Chris's impatience with me, and began folding into myself, turning away from him as he turned away from me. Simple exchanges and misunderstandings Chris and I had had in our years together seemed suddenly, ominously important. Every single piece of who I thought I was was being called into question as I sifted through our shared history, looking for my answers.

But that sifting only awakened more agony because so much of what I knew about myself I had learned with Chris. I had found my way into a career I'd wanted since I was a child. I had realized that it wasn't my job to be in charge of my family's happiness and that I couldn't fix every crisis that hit my parents or my siblings, whether it was my mother's colon cancer or my older brother's nihilistic worldview. I had learned that my way of getting angry took more from me than it helped me. I had started to accept Chris's version of me, that I did have "so much love to give" to the world, that I really loved people, all people, and wanted them to love themselves, too. I was learning to live in my own quiet spaces, take deep breaths, and slowly accept that even if every dream I ever had didn't come true, I would be fine; that it didn't mean I was a failure. Chris had helped me take those lessons in, and now I was going to have to give it all back.

At one point when Chris and I were talking about the logistics of breaking up, I couldn't stand the exhausting pressure on my brain anymore. I stood up and screamed at him: "How are you just going to get up and go? You have half of me in your brain! How is it possible that you get to just walk out the door and take that part of me with you?" He had shared ownership of so many of my memories. He got to live my youth with me. He was the person who—besides me—knew my family best, and who could read its underground tremors almost as well as I could. He had been with me as my older brother careened through a crisis that started with the high-risk birth of his daughter, Anna, and ended years later when her mother passed away suddenly, leaving Gregg and his girlfriend, Melissa, to become full-time parents to a grieving child. He could do a perfect imitation of my father. He knew that my younger brother, Scott, was a real softie with a big heart. He was the person who knew the scared, sad girl who lived inside me that I didn't let anyone see. He was the only person in my family who could out-talk and out-argue my mother as the two of them lamented the fallibility of the world's politicians and business leaders. He was the man I had a secret language with, the weird half-words we'd made up that meant "I love you" only to us.

I was going to have to start over and remake myself from scratch. The very thought of it gave me a tingling sensation that fizzled somewhere deep in my chest and right out to my fingers and toes, as if someone were taking an eraser and starting to blur my edges. Whenever I felt that zing creep into my consciousness, I would get up and dance, shaking my arms and jumping up and down to keep myself from disappearing into fears that were so big I couldn't even name them.

For a woman who has lived her life in words—in endless conversations with myself and anyone around me, in dreaming up my own big, minutely detailed plans for life, and in decoding and predicting people's motivations and actions—the big, blank, indescribable blackness of the fears I was feeling was worst of all. I wasn't sure I was strong enough to strain to see into the dark, into the things I didn't want to know, to find out the Why of my divorce. But I didn't have a choice. The why was the only thing I could try to understand in a world where everything I had come to trust and thought I knew had been torn from my grasp and ripped to shreds.

In June, Chris and I were invited to go out to Amagansett on Long Island for a weekend at our friends Rose and Scott's beach house. Four couples would be there, all the people with whom we'd spent much of our time before marriage and babies had pulled us into different orbits. Two of the husbands, Charlie and Paul, had been my very best friends for my first decade in New York, and we'd spent many long-winded evenings at the Old Town Bar, eating chicken wings, downing pitchers of beer, and generally amusing ourselves. I missed those days: having a baby had separated the boys from the girls, and I didn't really see Paul or Charlie that much anymore.

I was very excited to get Rose's e-mail. A weekend at the beach sounded great. It would be a small, sunny reprieve from the grind of what we were trying to live through. I told Chris when I got home from work and he shrugged and made a face. "I don't like the beach," he said.

My stomach sank in disappointment. "I know, but it would be so fun for Zack. And to get to see all the other babies . . ." I trailed off, embarrassed to be caught in thinking that we had been doing kind of okay, sailing along even though we had a cannonball hole gaping in our prow. I had thought it might be good for Chris and me to be with old friends. I said so to Chris.

"They're not my friends, they're your friends," he said.

"Oh," I said, surprised and confused. I dug back into the memory banks: I'd met Charlie when I started working at *Mirabella*, and Chris and I started dating just six months later. Chris was already my boyfriend when I met everyone else. He'd spent plenty of nights at Old Town with all the guys and me, and then later with the girlfriends who became wives: Rose and Lisa and Marnie and our friend Steffi. We'd shared a summer house in upstate New York for two or three summers with different combinations of the couples. The whole extended group of us had vacationed together in the South of France one summer, renting a farmhouse and sharing big, communal meals of foods we'd bought at the markets. These friends made up most of our social life, so of course I thought they were "our friends." Chris's comment made me see that he was already shrugging off pieces of the life we'd shared, like a snake shedding a skin, revealing the new him.

Then I thought about all our other friends, and realized that yes, there was a group of them I would have called "Chris's friends." They were his best friends and roommates from his NYU college days: Matt, who'd been the best man at our wedding; red-haired Bill; and Eric Voelker, whom we always referred to by his last name only. Those were the guys we spent all our time with when we first started going out, trolling the Lower East Side and the Upper East Side for cheap bands and cheap beer. But we saw them less and less together, because I didn't want to go see cheap bands and drink cheap beer anymore, although we still had homemade dinners and movie nights at our place with the three guys from time to time. Usually I'd go out to dinner with Alix or Eric, and Chris would go out for beers with Bill and Voelker. It seemed like a good, smart way to maximize our time apart; it hadn't occurred to me to think of that division as a fault line in our relationship. I wondered how it is that you live a life and don't see it clearly until a threat brings it all into focus.

So I let idea of the weekend at the beach drop, confused by all it had brought up between us. But the next day Chris told me he'd changed his mind and thought that it would be great for Zack to get to see the beach and that we should go. Zack was at this point a chunky ten-month-old, but it's amazing how much personality can fit into a baby of that size. He was a fast crawler and an avid explorer, and was really gregarious and outgoing. Every morning as I sat on the sofa and put on my makeup, he would pull himself up by holding on to the windowsill and wait for the garbagemen to come down our street. The days they did he waved furiously at them, slapping his fat hand on the window to get their attention; they rewarded him with funny faces and waves of their own. Zack's happy spirit made the after-work hours in the house bearable. Chris and I had a ray of light to focus on together. It was only after Zack went to bed that I felt the discomfort between Chris and me flood back into the room.

The eternal optimist in me thought it would be good to be away, to be in a group of friends who all had babies the same age: four kids under a year old. We would share the hassles and hilarities of parenting, be unified in having to troop back to the house from the beach for naps, and be able to tolerate the occasional tantrum, because we'd all been there. I thought it might help Chris see that our life wasn't any different from anyone else's, that this is what the first year with a baby is like. So we took a Friday off from work, packed up our swimsuits and sun hats, and headed out to the Hamptons—immediately finding ourselves in slow-moving traffic along with thousands of other New Yorkers who'd had the same idea.

I've always been the driver in our relationship, because Chris doesn't like to drive, and doesn't particularly like or trust cars. (Well, actually, what he doesn't trust is the other drivers.) Chris had to drive us all home from the hospital after the baby was born, and the stress of that trip alone—as Chris negotiated packed Manhattan streets, painfully aware of the precious cargo in the rear—aged us all. As the daughter of two avid car fans, and a sister of not one but two mechanics, I know and love driving. Unless there's a lot of traffic. Unless I get lost. Unless Chris is sitting in the seat next to me, stewing because he knows I'm tense, tense because he knows I'm stewing.

We inched our way out of the city, finally merging onto the highway where we could go a little faster, but the mood in the car was frozen and hushed. By the time we made it to Long Island, traffic had slowed down again, and Zack was starting to get antsy, complaining in his car seat. Halfway to Amagansett, we decided to try to take a shortcut that Paul had suggested, using the back roads, but a few minutes into the shortcut we were weaving in and out of residential neighborhoods, with their tidy green hedges and gravel driveways. We were lost.

Chris was on edge. I was on edge. I willed myself to stay calm and keep the anxiety out of my voice. I asked Chris to read the directions again, but he threw them down in frustration because they made no sense. I asked him to call Paul, since I was driving, but Paul's instructions didn't help because we didn't know where we were or how to get back to a main road. Zack had started to whimper a little, picking up on the tension in the car. I could feel hot tears begin to sting my eyes, because I was starting to panic about Chris's being upset with me and upset with himself for being there.

I was driving around in circles in an empty, manicured neighborhood, not another car in sight. Chris finally snapped at me, asking just what the hell I was doing. I pulled over without even thinking, put the car in park, and opened the door and got out and turned to him and screamed, "I don't know!" Then I walked off, leaving the car door open, the bong-bong-bong alarm mingling with the sound of Zack starting to cry. I kept walking to the end of the block, pounding my fists on my head, trying to think of a solution as I gasped for air and tears streamed down my cheeks, but all I could feel was that I wanted to lie down in the middle of the street and have a car drive over me and end this misery. Not the misery of being lost, but the agony of being wrong, of being the problem, of trying so hard to be careful and diligent and think good things and wish me and Chris to a better place, but being unable to get us there by sheer force of will. When the strange politeness between us was stripped away—as it was now—we were left with just us, two people standing on opposite sides of a divide.

Zack's cries pulled me back toward the car. I wanted to comfort him; I wanted at least to be a good mother if I couldn't be a good wife. But I was still hysterical. Chris started to get out of the passenger seat to get Zack, and I said, "No!" He sat back down, his hands up, as if I had a gun. I knew I was out of control, but I didn't know how to calm down. I was back to being the young woman who had stormed out of the apartment when Chris and I had our fights more than a decade earlier. I could feel it all slipping through my fingers: my marriage, my foundation, my self-respect.

Lifting Zack out of his car seat instantly centered me. I stood there and shushed him and hugged him, bouncing him slightly, saying "There, there" to him, and saying it to me. And I turned to Chris and said, my voice shaking from the effort of not crying, "I am trying, so, so hard. I am trying to make this all okay."

Chris said, "I am, too. I am trying, too." Then, more quietly, "It shouldn't be this hard." We just looked at each other, our gazes empty and sad.

There we were, all three of us, lost in a beautiful neighborhood, green lawns and perfectly trimmed hedges and sunlight all around. The place we were supposed to be, the life we were supposed to be living, was somewhere nearby, but Chris and I had absolutely no idea how to get there.

Back in the car, we eventually came across a sandwich shop and got directions, and then we were on our way to our friend's house. But we couldn't shake the vision of what we'd seen in each other on that back road: that even when we were on our best behavior, our personalities sparked against each other in a way we couldn't steer around.

The weekend was a long and grinding struggle. Even though

it was so adorable to see Zack with the three other babies—all playing together at the beach in big dishtubs we'd filled with ocean water—he was still a baby, who, of course, required a lot of work and attention. I felt that labor pulling hard on Chris, even though I was trying to do everything myself. Zack was charmed by the texture of the sand, but he kept eating fistfuls of it, despite our efforts to get him to stop. As Chris got more and more uptight about it, I finally hissed at him to just go away and let me take care of Zack. Later that night, when the sand worked its way through Zack's system, he was miserable and inconsolable, with a flaming diaper rash added to the mix.

Our friends did their best to ignore the tension simmering between Chris and me, even when he had to disappear from the beach or the evening dinners to take walks by himself to clear his head. I just said, "Yeah, we're having a hard time," trying to keep my lower lip from trembling as I spoke, and my girlfriends nodded in commiseration, lending me the luxury of pretending that what Chris and I were going through was just part of the normal ups and downs of married life with a new baby. I couldn't tell them anything more than that. And I certainly couldn't have told them how, exactly, we had found ourselves here.

Since the night it all started to end, and the day, three years later, that we were pronounced divorced, I have unearthed and sampled and tried on and been offered at least 316 reasons why Chris and I didn't make it. Many of the reasons would be familiar to anyone, divorced or not. They're like Muzak you hear on the elevator: you didn't even know you knew the tune until you catch yourself humming along. Here's a sampling:

Reason #12: Because he is a total idiot, just like all the other guys my girlfriends know who simply can't deal with grown-up life.

Reason #13: Because I married the wrong person. It was all a terrible mistake.

Reason #14: Because women just want to catch a man and change him and keep him from becoming his true, coolest self, so he has to bust out and be free.

Reason #15: Because he/she is not capable of having a relationship.

Then there's Reason #16 (my go-to favorite, especially in the middle of the night): Because I am essentially unlovable.

Or Reason #101: Because he/she is and always has been a loser/jerk and I was an idiot ever to fall for him/her in the first place.

Or Reason #102, the useful converse of #101: Because he/she is a liar/fraud/con (wo)man who did this just to hurt me.

The list is, of course, endless, and it can be customized to suit your particular situation.

When I was still under the impression that I was happily married, I encountered a memorable case of someone who had framed her life in terms of Reason #102. I'd met this woman at a work event, and I spoke to her at some length. She was wearing a ring with a remarkable rose-colored oval diamond on her right hand. "Wow," I said, "that's a beautiful ring." Without hesitating for a second, the woman presented the ring to me for my examination; the stone must have been at least 2 carats.

"Yeah, can you believe it?" she said. "Can you believe a man would love me enough to give me a ring like this and then leave me?"

I was startled by her instant revelation (and it's pretty hard to startle me with that stuff, since I have so few boundaries myself) and by the intensity of her rancor. Wow, I thought, all that must have happened pretty recently for her to be so raw and be wearing the ring still.

"Oh," I demurred, "I'm so sorry to hear that. Was it recent?"

She snorted. "Five years ago we married, and he left a year later. Can you believe it? Men are just unbelievable."

He was four years gone and she was still bleeding like this, in public. She put that ring on every day and thought miserable thoughts about what she believed she'd been promised. It was impossible not to see that she was in love with her loss, in the same way she'd probably once been in love with her husband. By the time I walked away from her, her unhappiness and anger had settled on me like a fine dust blown in through the windows during a storm, and it took me a few days to shake it off. Months later, the woman and her ring came up in conversation with some friends, each of whom had been told the same story in the same manner by her at one time or another. It made my soul ache to think of someone being stuck in her life like that, forever tied to a single moment.

I desperately wanted not to turn out like her, not to hold on to the shell of what something had been as if the mere fact of it (and the artifacts of it, like that ring) somehow meant more than the feelings and the memories themselves. I wanted to dare to imagine myself whole again.

The first part of being whole was for me to get a new full-time job. I felt brutally exposed by my life's circumstances, like a turtle walking around in a hailstorm without a shell, dealing with my unstable marriage, freelance work, a house Chris and I could barely afford, and a baby. Plus, I was still reeling from having been fired from the job at *Marie Claire*, a job I'd really loved.

Marie Claire was owned by the same company that owned *Redbook*, which was a good news/bad news kind of thing: on the one hand, the company knew my talents and my leadership ability very well; on the other hand, the editor in chief of *Marie Claire* was going to be my main character witness as I tried to land the job at the helm of *Redbook*, and she would be free to elaborate on all my faults.

I think I knew my boss was going to fire me before she knew it. After all, it was my job, as "Number Two" (as the position of executive editor is often described) to her "Number One," to know her inside and out, to know which ideas would please her and which wouldn't, and to constantly react to whatever shifts she made in the magazine's voice and content, so that the articles and story ideas produced by the team of editors I managed would be on target. She and I had shared ideas about what made *Marie Claire* special—it was a freewheeling, truth-telling fashion magazine with a social conscience and a love of surprises—but we came to that mission from very different thought processes and leadership styles. Our first year together, she wrote me a note at the holidays that said, "I just love the way you think!" Unfortunately, over time that became less and less true, and what had made us good and dynamic partners was now making her pull back: she disagreed with my editing decisions and started chafing at the suggestions I made. She wanted someone who thought more like she did. After two years at the magazine, when I was seven months pregnant with Zack, I was riding home on the subway with the managing editor, Kim, my partner in crime in managing the staff and running the magazine. I looked at Kim and said, "I think she's going to fire me." At first she said, "Nooooo." But I started to explain why I thought that my boss was talking herself out of her enthusiasm for working with me. Then we looked at each other, and we both knew it was true.

Nine months later, I was fired.

So, yes, the *Redbook* job would help stabilize my life and my sense of security in my career, but that's not why I wanted it. I wanted it because, even on my darkest days, I am always up for the next challenge. And I wanted it especially because I saw very clearly in my head what the magazine could be. I wanted to make *Redbook* reflect the rich, optimistic ways that women are facing the complexities of twenty-first-century womanhood, creating and finding our own rewards in our too-many-choices-and-not-enough-changes world. I wanted the magazine to help women focus less on her to-do list, and instead help her focus on her to-be list. I knew how busy I was since my son's birth, but that in no way meant that I'd stopped having dreams for myself. I knew I couldn't "have it all," but I also knew there was still so much out there for me—as well as a nation of women who were looking for the same kinds of answers, ideas, and support as I was. There is comfort to be had in other women's experiences with the hard choices women face every day, and I wanted to make a magazine that shared that.

Being in the running for the job of editor in chief is a job in itself, and the process takes months. In April I had handed in a twenty-eight-page proposal that detailed my vision for *Redbook*. Then I had worked with a friend who was an art director to create some sample covers, calling in photographers' portfolios and spending hours looking for just the right images that captured the vibrant, fulfilled mood and spirit I wanted to show on the cover. Now I had to make it through the series of interviews that led to the president of Hearst Magazines, the famously tough Cathie Black, and convince her that I had what it takes to lead a "legacy" brand (*Redbook* was 102 years old at the time), despite the fact that most of my experience was in magazine launches with circulations that were dwarfed by *Redbook*'s audience of ten million women. It was a lot of work and a lot of pressure to add to a life filled with a full-time freelance job and a young son, and I had to rely on Chris to make it possible for me to do all those tasks, the way I always had in the past.

Chris and I kept eating dinner together every night. We kept sleeping in the same bed, and daily we discussed all the logistics that come into play when managing two jobs, one son, one full-time nanny, and one house. I was partly lulled into thinking that maybe we were going to ride out the emotional storm. But at the same time, I could also feel something silent in Chris, something that was *waiting*, pulling for me to get the job in a way that felt different than in the past. I imagined that he was doing some kind of math in his head, figuring out that if I got the job I'd probably make enough money to be able to carry the house on my own. Then he would be able to up and go; then he could be free. I didn't want to make it that easy for him. Despite how hard it was for us right now, I didn't want the marriage to end. I thought the job would make it possible for us to stay together. Chris could stop working and spend all his time on his own dreams. Then we would be okay. Then we would be happy.

Finally I was called in for my first interview with Cathie Black. I had met her once a few years before, when I had come in to pitch an idea for a new magazine at the same time I was launching the design magazine in California. That previous experience didn't make this interview any less intimidating. Cathie's incredibly smart, instinctual, and very direct; she always gets right to the heart of the issue at hand. Adding to the intimidation factor, she has great taste and style. I spent a good two days shopping for just the right interview outfit, spending more money on a new pair of shoes—nude lizardskin stilettos—than I usually spend on an entire outfit. I justified the purchase by figuring that the shoes were classics and were an investment in my future, whether I got the job or not. (Yes, I still have the shoes, and yes, I still wear them.) I bought a new bag that looked far more expensive than it was, though it wasn't cheap. I found the perfect pair of white pants and a bright fuschia jacket—to me, the color of optimism and confidence. Done.

It was a hot and steamy summer day when I made my way to Cathie's office, splurging on a car service to take me on the long drive from Brooklyn to midtown Manhattan so I wouldn't turn into a sweaty mess on the subway. Eliot Kaplan, the man who had drafted me for *Marie Claire* just three years before, met me in the plush reception area of the Hearst Corporation headquarters. My heels sank into the thick carpet. When I was shown into Cathie's office on the forty-second floor, I tried to ignore the sweeping views of Central Park from the windows. I sat down at the large round table, my heart racing with excitement. She and I had a long conversation about women, about marriage and motherhood and what women wanted from those institutions today, and about what they needed from the institution of *Redbook* itself. I nodded, feeling the metallic tang of dread in my throat. Was I misrepresenting myself? Would I not get the job if she knew the truth about what was happening between Chris and me? (But wait, I reminded myself, even *you* don't know what's really happening.)

As we were wrapping up, Cathie said, "You may not think so, but this is a big step up for you." I was surprised by her comment; I knew this was a big step up for me, even though I'd been running magazines for years, and I said so. I also told her I was absolutely sure that I was ready and that all my experience to date, even though it had been at smaller magazines, had prepared me for *Redbook*.

As I stood up to shake her hand and leave the room, she thanked me for my time and complimented me on my handbag. I smiled to myself, thinking the bag had just paid for itself. As I walked down the street in the summer heat, grinning from ear to ear, I called my dear friend Eric, who worked for Hearst, though his office was in another building. I asked him to meet me for coffee. Eric has been my best friend since we were in college, and has stood on the sidelines and rooted for me at every turn. He knew how long this particular dream had been in the making. In the coffee shop I picked at a sandwich, not yet able to eat because of the adrenaline rush, and he and I allowed ourselves to imagine for a few minutes that I might actually get the job.

A week or so later, I got the call that told me it was down to me and just one other candidate. I was excited, but now I had to face the fact that this might actually happen, and all the things it might set in motion—or bring to a halt—in my marriage. That night I came home from my freelance job and sat in the corner of the living room I'd painted a dark plum six months earlier. I'd picked the color because it was dramatic and daring, a bold gesture that set off the collection of black-and-white photographs I'd hung from ceiling to floor. But sitting in the small purple chair in the corner I felt dwarfed by the darkness of it all. I told Chris I was afraid to take the job, that I didn't want to disappear into an all-consuming job at the same time our marriage was under so much pressure. I begged him to let me choose our marriage over my work, to give me some hope that we were going to work things out, and I burst into tears. I cried not just for that day, but also for every other time I'd signed up for a new work challenge, because now I wondered if I'd been putting nails in the coffin of our marriage all these years. Maybe my work was the reason we were in such trouble, after all (Reason #159). I told him I couldn't take the job, because I simply wouldn't be able to do it without him, without his support, his love. Chris shook his head slowly, staring down at his hands, and said, "No. You don't need me." (He sounded so sure that I didn't need him. Not true; but still, yet another reason.) "This is where you are going," he went on, "this is what you have been working toward all this time, your whole life." And I started to sob, face in my hands, because I could hear in his words that he was already letting go of me, and I couldn't bear the sound of it; he was talking as if he were putting me and my luggage on a train and knew he'd be staying behind on the platform. Apparently I hadn't changed anything with all my well-intentioned housekeeping and cooking, all my keep-my-head-down tactics. I could feel his eyes on me, I could feel him feeling bad for what I was feeling, and in that moment I suddenly got a very clear glimpse into what he was thinking: he'd gotten me to where I'd been headed all those years, even before I met him. And now he felt as if he had to leave me to have his turn.

That couldn't be the reason! I wanted to shake my fists at him and say "No! No!" I know I wanted Chris to have his turn in our marriage. I had been trying to help him make his own dreams come true all along the way. But I was too afraid to say all that, now that every conversation we had felt like a game of Jenga, every word another small block of wood placed on top of the tower that's leaning, threatening to topple over and come crashing down. Besides, I wasn't allowed into the place where his dreams lived and hadn't been for a long time.

Back in the days just after we were married, *Mirabella* folded. I didn't find a magazine job before my severance pay ran out, so I took a job at the J.Crew catalog, which at the time loved to hire magazine editors. I was fascinated by the inner workings of the catalog—I've never met a glossy-paper product I didn't like—and was hired to be the managing editor for the women's pages during the busiest time of the year, when the fall and holiday catalogs pour forth in an endless stream. But since the catalog doesn't have stories that need to be dreamed up or edited, the job didn't demand the same amount of mental real estate that my magazine job had. So I had more time to enjoy myself. More time to be with friends, go to the gym, play video games, carouse. More time to focus on Chris.

One night, as Chris and I were having a conversation about his temp job, and I was suggesting other jobs he could try that might get him closer to his true love, film, he snapped and said, "I'm not your latest project. Don't try to solve me." He went on to say that since leaving *Mirabella* I'd had too much time on my hands and was spending too much time thinking about him, and that *he* was the one in charge of his life.

Oh. And *ouch.*

This was the beginning of Chris's making clear to me that the part of his brain that focused on what Chris loved most (or at least needed most in his life)—his creative work, his ideas and plans for the future—belonged to him alone, and that I wasn't allowed in. I spent the next nine years of our marriage longing to know that part of him, and at the same time trying to train myself not to ask questions, meddle, or offer suggestions, a mode that cut so deeply against the grain of my entire personality it was almost like asking me to hold my breath forever. I created a story that made it acceptable to me: Chris would share more about his plans when he was further along; he didn't want to let me in until it was all more real. And I guess that this was the moment in our marriage—just a year after we'd married, in fact—that I started to put my head down and wait for him to want to be with me.

Three years later, when I became the editor in chief of *Modern Bride,* I suggested to Chris that he could stop working. His frustration at not working on his own projects full-time had turned into a deep hatred of his job; its politics and intractable communication challenges had become a central force in our lives together, a constant low-thrumming background noise, in the same way that the pace and stress of my jobs had. I told him it was all about choices for us at this time: we could move out of the city to New Jersey and get a place we could afford on one salary, or choose a totally different New York City neighborhood in one of the outer boroughs, or make other concessions, have children even later, although I was thirty-one, then thirty-two, then thirty-three and starting to hear the ticking of my clock. But his reaction was the same: "Stop managing my life." But wait, wasn't it our life, or our lives? Weren't we committed to drawing the road map together, commingling dreams and goals, and practicing the act of compromise all along the way? Clearly Chris and I had very different ideas about how that shared path gets built (Reason #164); we were pretty far into a marriage for me to be discovering this now.

But the fault line didn't feel obvious then. Even in hindsight it still doesn't seem that clear. Every couple struggles; coupledom is a constant renegotiation of agreements and boundaries. How are you supposed to know which of the little emotional pebbles that trip you up is the one that's actually the tip of an iceberg, something huge and immovable lurking beneath the surface of your relationship?

The pressure and excitement of almost having the *Redbook* job was starting to mount. Magazine publishing is a small world, so some chatter had started that the current editor of the magazine might be replaced, and my name was appearing on the gossip-generated "short list." To everyone who asked I denied I was in the running but one day, my name made it into a published item in one of the trade newspapers that cover the publishing business; I flinched, hoping it wouldn't hurt my chances.

My office phone rang, and I picked it up. It was Eliot Kaplan from Hearst, calling to ask me casually what my plans were for the upcoming Fourth of July holiday weekend. Where would I be? Would I have my cell phone with me? I had no plans, except to be home with Chris and Zack, enjoying the backyard and pretending we were doing fine. I assumed he was asking so that Cathie would be able to reach me, so I spent the entire weekend with my cell phone in my hand, staring at it and willing it to ring with what I hoped was an offer, not a letdown. Nothing. It went on like this for almost ten days, with me literally jumping every time the phone rang. Then, finally, I picked up my phone at my office on Wednesday morning the next week, and it was Cathie Black. I excused myself to stand up and close my office door, and then, after a few pleasantries (and me trying to stay calm and cool), she said, "So, you ready to have some fun?"

"Definitely," I said.

And then she offered me the job. I was grinning so wide I thought my bottom jaw would drop off and clatter onto my desk, while I took furious notes on a scrap of paper as she explained when the announcement would be made, when she would introduce me to the team, and when I would start—which was essentially as soon as I could realistically wrap up my current work commitment, in less than two weeks.

I hung up the phone and leapt up out of my chair, punching my fists up into the air as I jumped up and down, silently hissing "Yesss! Yesss! Yesss!" Then I stopped. Who to call first? Chris? I felt sandbagged by the thought that he wouldn't be coming along with me for this ride. I pushed it out of my head and dialed him. "That's great. That's so great. Good for you. Congratulations," he said warmly, genuinely. When I got home that night he gave me a big hug. It felt so good, to be held by this man I trusted, who'd been with me through so much. Did we still have a chance?

I was a magazine editor who had revitalized a bridal magazine shortly after she herself got married—as the press release the company issued the day they announced my hiring said. And I was going to do the same thing for a magazine that was largely about marriage and the grown-up life that goes along with it. What it didn't say, of course, was that my own grown-up life was falling to pieces.

✣   ✣   ✣

Two weeks before I was named the editor in chief of *Redbook*, I had made an appointment for Chris and me to go talk to my shrink. I had seen Dr. Glassman when I started having panic attacks after my mother was diagnosed with colon cancer, but when I got pregnant with Zack, I felt a lot of my issues fade into the background, and I stopped seeing her. But now I suggested to Chris that we go talk to her: that we couldn't, just shouldn't, consider breaking up without talking to someone to help us clarify what was coming between us.

Chris and I had tried marriage counseling before, when I was the one having doubts about where we were headed. After living mostly apart for the year that I worked in San Francisco, Chris and I had reunited in New York City in August 2001. We were already trying to adjust to coming back to New York—to living together full-time again, to Chris's trying to find work after he'd lost his job in the AOL–Time Warner merger—when the 9/11 attacks happened and turned everything in the world (and especially in New York City) upside down. Chris was really angry at the world for all its stupidity, and I, as usual, was coping by trying to forge ahead and define the future; for me this translated to becoming obsessed with buying a house or an apartment. And we were arguing—a lot. We agreed that we wanted to buy a home and that we wanted to start a family, but everything else was up in the air.

I wanted to buy a big place in a developing neighborhood: a brownstone in one of the neighborhoods "in transition" in Brooklyn, possibly in Clinton Hill, or a big, family-size apartment almost anywhere except the fancy neighborhoods we couldn't afford. Chris didn't want to live in a fringe neighborhood; he wanted to be somewhere central, but at the same time, he was insisting on an extra bedroom he could use as an office. I kept trying to explain that we couldn't have both the nice neighborhood and an extra bedroom, but I failed at being nice about it (Reason #176). Chris told me I was a snob (Reason #177), that it mattered too much to me what the place looked like. I was confused by how I could be the snob in this scenario, and after another one of our circular arguments, I remember screaming at him—something about if he wanted to go back to the East Village and Dumpster-dive for his dinner because it was so bleeping glamorous to be poor and cool, then fine, he could go hang out there with his friends. I didn't understand what was so bad about having Nice Things. What was so bad about having made some money and wanting to buy a nice apartment?

One night as Chris was heading down into the bedroom in our apartment after another real estate discussion, I said cautiously, "I think we want really different things. I think maybe this is a problem."

He stopped dead on the stairs and spoke up at me, his voice rising in pitch. "What do you mean? You think we shouldn't be together?"

I said I wasn't sure, but that it seemed clear we were not in agreement about what was next. So I suggested counseling, and got a name from Dr. Glassman. In the first two sessions, Chris was practically silent, giving one-word answers to the therapist's questions. He kept focusing on whether my unhappiness was his fault and what he had done to trigger it. I focused on telling him it wasn't about whose "fault" it was, it was just that maybe we imagined such different lives for ourselves that we wouldn't be able to find the middle ground. But after those two sessions, the therapist stopped plumbing our disagreements about our shared road map and started investigating my complicated relationship to my parents' marriage. She said point-blank to me—as I tried to tell her that I was perfectly aware that my parents' relationship had shaped my sense of the world, but that Chris and I didn't think that that was at play in the dynamic between him and me right now—that until I was ready to be really married to Chris instead of my mother, she didn't see how it was possible for the two of us to find a way to work things out.

I cried in Chris's arms the whole way home on the subway as he comforted me, telling me that I was fine and she was wrong. I was mad and sad and angry and disbelieving that somehow the therapist had collected enough information in three sessions to decide that this was all my fault. I'd always feared that everything bad in my life was somehow my fault, my responsibility. I had spent a good piece of my adult life separating my sense of my own relationships from what I'd seen in my family when I was growing up. I had a lot of empathy for both of my parents for not getting what they needed, and for not being able to figure out a way to make their relationship more satisfying at that phase in their lives. I had prayed for them to break up and free each other when I was in high school and college, and beyond. But when they did break up, at my mother's insistence, the year Chris and I got engaged, my mother was surprised to find that she slammed headfirst into a wall of grief. And my father, after a few short months of enjoying bachelor life and the quiet in his apartment, decided that maybe life was too quiet. My parents came back together because, it turns out, the life they'd built—a home they both loved, a shared appreciation for a good meal and the rewards of entertaining, a love of antiques, and a bottomless passion for exploring small inns up and down the East Coast—seemed bigger than the sum total of all the reasons they rubbed each other the wrong way. Because sometimes the marriage built over time is bigger and stronger than all the Why-Nots. I wanted this to be true for Chris and me now. As Chris kept rubbing my back and smoothing my hair on the subway, I felt the gentle "click" of why I was with him, of why I trusted him and loved him, and I felt him reconnect with me as well. It was because he took care of me when I needed it most, and I took care of him by running our life and making the plans. We went to the counseling session the following week and told the therapist that we were past our crisis and didn't need to see her anymore.

So now, three years later, we were heading to counseling together again to try to come to an agreement about all our why-nots. When I met up with Chris in the reception area of Dr. Glassman's office one night after work, he was brusque and short with me, clearly unhappy to be there. I felt a twinge of guilt that I was torturing him by insisting that we try to find ways to stay together. But when we got into the office, Chris didn't need any prompting to get started. He had plenty to say, enumerating all the reasons I wasn't a happy person: Nothing was ever enough. I had never been happy in any of my jobs. I was always looking for the next thing, the next opportunity, the next project, whether at home or at work. I didn't know how to just be happy. I was always creating conflict. I didn't get along with people. I just sat there, mute, stunned by his picture of me, and not really recognizing the person he was describing. I've always been known as a team builder. I'm a boss people like to work for because I don't create drama. Yes, I'm a dramatic personality, but what I want is for people to focus on doing great work, not waste energy on office politics. Wasn't this the man who knew me best? I got that strange, awful feeling again of having no idea who I was.

When Dr. G. asked me what I felt about all he was saying, I didn't know how to respond. I started to cry. I said, "I don't know who he's talking about." I talked about my sense of our marriage: how Chris had been disappearing from me, that he didn't want to spend time together anymore, that he didn't even seem engaged with Zack. Chris responded by sharing his total sense of fatigue at our life. He said that he felt overwhelmed by everything, and that he hated that I always knew what to do, as a mother, as a homeowner, "even though I know she doesn't know any more than I do. She just does it."

He hated me for being capable. For dealing. For buckling down and handling the stress of life. For being someone who attracted stress into our life. For being someone who liked challenges. For being the person who would step in when he had to step out.

I'd been feeling optimistic when we walked in—*Okay! Here we are! Let's face our problems together!*—but now I was feeling the sick weight of something else. I was afraid. Afraid of *Chris*. Somewhere deep inside my brain, I'd been having this thought for a long time; it felt familiar, like a spot I'd rubbed shiny over the years, and yet it was the first time I had brought it out from behind the shoji screen where I stored the things I didn't want to know, the feelings I didn't want to have. I had been afraid that he was going to do exactly what he was doing now: walk away from the life we'd made together. I had felt his gathering unhappiness for many years, and I'd hunkered down and tried to wait him out. As I began to describe the fear that was engulfing me, Chris snorted in derision. He thought of me as the one in charge (Reason #225). But I had fallen in love with him because he had been bigger than me, and he had loved me in a way that made me feel small. It was why I believed I needed him if I were to get the job at *Redbook*: after days at work being the one in charge, I needed the balance of coming home to him and being a person with needs and uncertainties, being life-size.

At the end of this long, hard hour, Dr. G. summed up what she'd seen. "You two are pretty far apart," she said. "And I'm not sure that joint counseling will really help you where you are right now." I was stunned. Somehow Chris and I had ended up in two totally different countries, even though we had shared the same zip code, the same home, the same bed for more than thirteen years. And there were a hundred reasons that had led to that. Not just #1, or #2. Or even trusty old #102.

4

You Can Handle
More Than You Think
(But a Little Denial Helps)

At first I told no one. Not even my closest friends, the ones who already knew everything about me, where the bodies from my past were buried. I was trying to keep the secret of what was happening even from myself.

I imagined the changing shape of my life in tiny, superficial slices, as if I were trying on the idea of being One of Those People Who Are Divorced. I let out a sigh of relief that I hadn't changed my name, so I wouldn't have to change it back and live with that public expression of my failure. Then I felt suddenly dismayed that my son didn't have my last name. I made casual mental lists of what furniture Chris would want and what furniture I would fight for. I thought of myself as a statistic, and counted the number of divorced people I knew. I mused over the fact that I had been the first of my college friends to marry and now I was going to be first to divorce. This did not make me feel like a pioneer in a way that I liked. All these thoughts were a way of dipping my toe into the waters of change as if I were getting ready to slip into a warm bath.

But sometimes I would instead drop directly into a raging river of anxiety: How was I going to carry the mortgage on my own for the year and a half until we could sell the house without a tax penalty? Where would Zack and I be able to afford to live next? How was I ever going to share custody of my baby and let him go away and sleep somewhere other than his home? But how could I deny him his father? These questions were so impossibly large, I could barely see them whole.

Amid all this roiling, I would occasionally catch myself living a moment of normalcy and I'd panic, chastising myself for dropping my guard. *Who are you to be walking down the street enjoying the sunlight? Your marriage is over! Who do you think you are, daring to lose yourself in a book for twenty minutes before bedtime? Your husband is leaving you! Why are you running on that treadmill? You should be running for your life!*

The temptation to get down on my knees and succumb to the vicious power of what I knew was coming next was immense. The twenty-four-hour vigil probably wouldn't keep the serious, scary stuff from coming, but because I had missed all the signs that my marriage was unraveling, a relentless, unforgiving focus was my punishment. I had to get hard, close off, get strong. This attitude helped me be removed from it all, so I could handle the weight of everything that threatened to push me underwater.

Take a deep breath. Slide the shoji screen shut. Hear the calming message in the "shhhhhp" sound as you gently push aside the thoughts that are too big to be looked at right now. Step back into the small and simple order of what must be done today, and do not stray.

A friend of mine had seen her own marriage draw close to the precipice just a year or so earlier. It was awful to hear about the confusion and the threats and anger and acrimony and sheer nastiness that her husband was doling out. Yet she was still going to work, still being a mom to her two kids, spending weekend days together as a family with her husband, exploring Chinatown, going to beaches, whatever. I remember when, at one dinner, she casually made reference to "when we were fooling around this weekend." My fork stopped midair.

"You mean you guys are still having sex?"

She looked at me levelly. "Yeah."

"How can you *do* that, the way he's been treating you?"

She shrugged. "You just do."

I said, "Gosh, you *want* to?" I had been struggling for years with not wanting to have sex with Chris. I'd chalked up my ambivalence to four or five different things—health issues, stress, nothing having anything to do with our relationship.

"Yeah," she said. And she shrugged again, as if to say, "Of course."

At that time, I had the huge luxury of hating her husband full force on her behalf. But now that I was myself living this life of In Between, I began to understand that she too had been drawing the shoji screens open and closed, doing the intricate dance of protecting herself and trying to stay connected, daring to stay open, in the hope it would all work out. (And you know what? It did.) I was floored, months later, by the depth of her bravery. And it wasn't too late for me to be inspired by it.

The distance between my brain and my mouth is very, very short. If I'm having a feeling or a new experience or a thought, any kind, really, then you are having it, too—whichever "you" is in the room with me at the time. When I was pregnant and working at *Marie Claire*, I would amble down the hall every day to declaim for the articles department about how creepy and fascinating it was to be pregnant, all the ways in which a woman's body prepares her mentally for the work that lies ahead in being the mother of a newborn: the craving for a midday nap; the nights lying awake in your bed, hands on your belly, wondering just why you are up at this hour; the way that you lose control over what you do and don't eat because the body's in charge, reminding you that you (and your will and whatever big ideas you had about what you were going to accomplish today) are damn secondary to what's happening inside. My coworkers teased me for being a walk-ing science experiment and an oral report wrapped up into one, but I couldn't help myself: I was so moved by the way everything made sense in some grand, life-writ-large way.

And making sense of it all—life, who we are as a culture, why *Lost* is so popular, my abiding emotional connection to Cheetos—is really what all the talking is about, anyway, even if it sounds like a running monologue on my life. This habit is at the core of how I do my work as a magazine editor, focusing the magazine's vision and sharing it with the team. When I helped lead the launch of *TimeOut New York*, there were thirty-eight people, more than a dozen sections, and about a hundred pages for me to manage in closing the issue every week. That's a lot of talking, cajoling, prodding. And there were definitely days I was totally overwhelmed. One of the funniest wiseguys on staff would catch me on the days I was on a slow-burn silent freakout about some looming crisis or another and say, "I get worried when you're quiet. Means something no good is going down."

Yeah, something no good was going down in my life now, all right. I was being quiet, even with myself; the constant chatter in my head had been replaced with a heavy silence, a protective baffle between me and all I was not yet ready to face. It didn't help that I was at the freelance job, with no longtime friends and colleagues to aid me in puzzling through the riddle of my messed-up life. I spent a lot of time with Krissy, a savvy, funny assistant on the staff who'd been assigned to help me with the huge project I was managing, and we spent hours poring through research together, or through stacks of back issues. She had a crazy love for babies, and so she always asked me for the latest story about what Zack was up to; he was just nine months old, and so there was plenty of cuteness to share. But one day, talking about how sweet and funny Zack was just bumped into the part of me that was so sad and disbelieving that Chris was willing to walk away from all that. I blurted out to Krissy what was going on, instantly wishing I could take it back.

Oh, great. I had a breach in my nice, solid wall of denial. Now I was *leaking*.

A day or so later, I gathered the strength to tell a friend what was happening. I closed the door to my office and sat down at my temporary desk at my temporary job, my sense of displacement in my life utterly complete. I picked up the phone and dialed my longtime friend Mary Rose, whom I'd worked with at three different magazines through the years.

"Did you hear anything about the job?" she asked right away.

Mary Rose was my confidante (and confidence-builder) in my efforts to get the editor-in-chief job at *Redbook*. We'd first met as assistants at *Mirabella* more than a decade earlier. She's the person I've relied on in every job transition I've made. She's the one I called in tears when I was sure that the proposal I was writing to land the *Redbook* job (a proposal that at one point I'd believed had been filled with really good ideas) had turned to total crap in my mind in the final stretch. She's the one who reminded me that all my proposals turn to dust, or worse, in my mind just before I hand them in, and that, in the end, I almost always get the job.

I told her I wasn't calling about *Redbook*. I lowered my voice and told her that Chris had told me he wanted to leave me. I whispered not so much because I was afraid someone in the surrounding offices would hear me, but more because I still didn't want to know it myself.

"I'm so scared," I said. And then instantly regretted saying it. Telling her what was happening was reporting on an event. Telling her how I was feeling meant it was really happening to me. Saying it made the fear real.

She just said, "Oh, Stace, I'm sorry." And then she sat there on the phone with me for a minute, silent, while I breathed in the pain of letting it all be real for the first time, tears rolling down my face.

In our many conversations about *Redbook*, Mary Rose and I had kept circling back to the point that what we craved most was honesty and truth-telling from other women about the joys and challenges of grown-up, mom-and-wife life, along with all the good tips and info about how to get stuff done that was already in the magazine.

She and I had talked about the power that comes from knowing that there are other imperfect women just like you—women who didn't want to have sex with their husbands or had yelled at their kids or had ordered a pizza for dinner for the second time in a week or didn't manage to make the laundry's whites whiter (or didn't even care that they were supposed to want to make the laundry's whites whiter). There's strength and comfort in being able to admit your small daily failures and then move on. I wanted to steer women away from the reflexive guilt that comes along with being a wife/mom/friend and instead help them focus on what living their lives feels like: Do you like your life? Do you love it? Are you taking care of yourself? Or are you running like a hamster in a wheel and forgetting to put *you* on that list of things to do?

I wanted to encourage women to dare to become the woman they were meant to be, even as their new roles and responsibilities put so many demands on their time. But I thought I was meant to be a woman who was married, with a child—children!—and a career I loved, and now that was all changing and I was so afraid. How was I going to help other people love their lives if I couldn't even do that for myself?

When Mary Rose and I hung up, I dried my cheeks, took a deep breath, patted my red nose with some powder, and tucked all the fear and the dread and the utter, shattering grief somewhere down deep inside. I gathered my folders to go head up a meeting with eleven young magazine editors who thought I had answers, at least for their magazine.

By the time I got to the conference room, I had set the heartbroken girl aside and was leaning into my saving grace: confidence under pressure. Every time I felt the lick of panic start up in my chest, I reminded myself that I was good at this, that I had always sailed through turmoil with the stoic calm of a ship's carved figurehead cutting through the stormy seas. I can sort out the noise and instead focus on the Things That Must Be Done First, and Next, and not get lost in the tumult. This trait had always served me well in getting magazines off the ground, in managing the bumpy road of continually changing plans to accommodate the many expected unexpecteds that knock well-laid plans off course. Now I just had to apply it to my life.

At that time I had no idea how much harder life was going to get, how much more roiling water was headed my way. But it was good practice for the months and years of living on two tracks simultaneously—one where I was broken and flailing, the other where I was in charge and had to come up with the answers—that lay ahead.

Krissy kept my secret, and so did Mary Rose. And then Eric and Alix, and, soon after, Kim and Melanie and Holly, the handful of friends I told in the following weeks, all people in my day-to-day life whom I felt I couldn't avoid telling because of the many days my heartbreak was written all over my face. They all inherently understood the unspoken rules of having this piece of information that was my own personal kryptonite: they weren't allowed to bring up the topic first, because it might be a day I wanted, *needed,* to pretend my life was fine; they didn't tell me what they thought—about Chris, about us, about whether we would make it—because at that time I still knew so little about what *I* thought about these things. They treated me like a normal friend, not like the hospital patient I felt like; they followed my lead and did the dance of denial with me. I know how hard it is to do nothing and say nothing when a friend is hurting; after all, I had failed my own friend in that manner myself when she was struggling with her marriage. Their stepping into the cone of silence with me was inaction of the most loving kind.

Once I was announced as the editor in chief of *Redbook,* my life switched into overdrive. Only days after I took the helm, I had to fly down to Washington, D.C., for an exclusive interview with President George Bush and First Lady Laura Bush in the White House, three months before the 2004 presidential election. In September, I was slated to host a big luncheon at Lincoln Center celebrating women's strength and spirit and their charitable work, and Democratic presidential candidate John Kerry was to be the keynote speaker. And of course there was the ordinary work of taking over a magazine: deciding where to stick your finger into the engine of a magazine in progress and pause it so you can begin rebuilding it, without bringing the full-forward motion to a screeching halt. (You have four weeks to build an issue, and the printer doesn't care that you're the new kid in town.) There's the work of defining and conveying the new vision to the staff, over and over and over, and showing them exactly how to express it; deciding which new sections to introduce, which old ones to kill; and all while helping a staff of creative people manage their fears about not making the cut to stay on the team.

I had done most of that before. Thank God I had done it before. But renovating a magazine that is already running is very different from starting one from scratch. Launching a magazine is a little bit like building a shiny new racecar and getting it out on the track as fast as you can: it's all adrenaline and zoom and spark. Taking over *Redbook* was like steering the *QE2*: fast changes were more likely to be punished than rewarded—with longtime readers, say, canceling their subscriptions because they didn't like the new typefaces. My boss had been quite clear with me during the interview process: "*Redbook* isn't broken." Move slowly, she was saying. Be patient. This is a big magazine, with ten million customers. Learn about your audience before you wow them with your own big ideas about who they are.

At a launch the trick is to get people's attention and get them to buy into the franchise. At *Redbook*, Job One was not to scare away the women who were already reading the magazine. Slow was a new speed for me.

I went home from my first day at work—so much to learn, so many people to meet—with a stack of manuscripts and story lineups and budgets. Chris disappeared into his office after dinner, as he did most nights, and after I put Zack to bed, I started reviewing all the paperwork I'd lugged home. I was essentially trying to stuff as much of the magazine into my head in a single night as possible; the first few weeks at the helm of a magazine are like trying to see every tree on a mountain just after you've stepped onto a hiking trail. A heavy rain had started earlier in the evening, and the way it cloaked the house in its muffle helped my concentration. But then I heard a sound that made the hairs on the back of my neck stand up: I heard water running freely, somewhere in my house.

I stood up, took the three steps to the basement door and yanked it open, and the sound rushed up the stairs to greet me. I bent over, craning my neck to look down into the basement. Water was pooling at the bottom of the stairs. My heart jumped in my chest; I kicked off my flip-flops and ran downstairs. Dirty water was pouring in from under the basement door that led to a stairway up to the street, and it was burbling up out of the drain in the middle of the floor. I started screaming for Chris as I pulled boxes and toys off the floor, putting them up on shelves. The water was almost covering my feet by the time Chris ran downstairs, and it wasn't slowing down. The sump pump in the corner was firing, but there was no way it would be able to keep up with the gallons that were gushing in. After fifteen futile minutes splashing around in the basement trying to decide what to do, I realized we needed a Shop-Vac to suction the water out. I hopped in the car and raced to Lowe's, straining to see through the driving rain. When I got home, it took almost five hours for the two of us to suction up the water, with a hose snaking up the stairs and out the door and draining into the backyard. And then we had to clean up the leaves and the dirt and the garbage that had come into the house: the water was backflow from the city storm sewer system. When we bought the house, the basement walls and floor had been painted a cheery, bright chartreuse, which had made the basement seem like the perfect playroom for Zack. But the flood created fetid boils in the floor's paint, the ancient, stained linoleum floor underneath showing through in patches, the fine silt of sewer dirt settling into the ruined surface. Chris and I mopped once, mopped twice, then gave up on the project for the night and headed upstairs, exhausted and dripping wet. We plunked down on the sofa, not believing what had just happened, and somehow we ended up in an embrace. I still remember the heated "survival" sex we shared that night, clinging to each other on the sofa, united in our battle against the elements. The strength of our physical connection in that moment gave me false hope about where we were headed.

The storm had been the aftershock of a hurricane that had battered the Caribbean and Florida coasts. Unfortunately for us, the forecast for that fall promised the worst hurricane rains in the Northeast in years. My life was leaking, I was leaking, and now so was my house.

A little over a week after I'd started at *Redbook*, I boarded a shuttle headed for Washington, D.C., on a hot, humid August day, for my one-on-one interview with President Bush. It didn't occur to me until I'd landed in Washington that I should have brought someone from the magazine with me; for an interview of this importance, an editor in chief would usually surround herself with a small entourage: someone to take notes while she does the interview; someone to be in charge of meeting everyone in the room, collecting and handing out business cards; the group all there together to fully embody the strength and power of the magazine and the millions of women we represent. It was a strange oversight on my part (and I'm sure it was truly confusing to all my new employees I'd left back in the office, especially Janet, the executive editor of the magazine and the woman who had moved mountains to secure the exclusive interview), but I didn't spend any time dwelling on my error. I just approached the first of three security gates, pulled out my credentials, and began the process of getting admitted to the White House.

This was the first time in my career I was running a magazine that didn't have a solely liberal perspective, and I wanted to honor my readers' diverse perspectives by coming to this interview with the President with a totally open mind. To prepare for it, I had talked to my older brother and his wife—both big supporters of Bush at the time—for almost three hours, asking them every question I could think of about what being Republican meant to them. I needed to shake the Democrat out of me enough that I could emotionally connect to their point of view. My sister-in-law Melissa, frustrated that she and I saw the world so differently, tired of the conversation after an hour, but my brother Gregg was able to lead me to the place where I could totally see and *feel* what President Bush represented for him. He said, "You know, Stacy, at the end of the day I live in a different world than you do, and that's the way I like it." Got it: he wanted his world to be him and his family and his farm and his decisions and he wanted to be left alone. As for me, I loved living in a complex, incomprehensible world. Through his eyes, I could see why maybe that wasn't so appealing, and so I took that perspective and tucked it in my pocket when I went to Washington, D.C.

That steamy August morning, the Senate had released the 9/11 Commission Report, and as I walked the curved path that leads up to the White House after clearing the second security check, I could see dozens of press people standing in clumps outside the press room, their TV cameras and equipment weighing them down. Inside the White House, press aides greeted me and led me from one public anteroom to another in the progression that leads to the White House residence. They let me know the President was running a bit behind schedule for our interview because of the press conference, so I would first interview Mrs. Bush. This gave me plenty of time to go over all the careful prep work my brand-new team and I had done for this interview, and more time to get nervous and wonder why on earth I had come here by myself.

After a bit, I was ushered into the private White House elevator that leads to the residence—the top floor of the White House, the one with the big, arched window you can see from Pennsylvania

Avenue—and then into the Green Room, a long room lined with bookshelves and furnished with gleaming wood furniture and toile-covered armchairs. Two recording secretaries were already seated. I said hello, pulled out my two portable tape recorders, and set them down on the coffee table next to their official transcript recording machines.

Mrs. Bush came in, dressed casually but with an air of relaxed formality. She led me over to the window, which seems small as you see it from the street, but which is actually at least twelve feet tall, and pointed down into the Rose Garden, where the President was speaking. Through the window's wavy glass I could see the pha-lanx of reporters and cameramen. I wanted to ask the President some tough questions about why it was getting harder for families to make ends meet and make life work in America, and how he saw his role in helping relieve that pressure, but I was reminded by the scene unfolding below I was here for a casual chat as befit my publication, not a policy talk.

After a few minutes, Mrs. Bush and I sat down and started talk-ing, first about her daughters (one of the twins, Barbara, was mov-ing to New York City later that day) and her hopes for them, and then about her hopes for women in America and the world, because she had recently been to Afghanistan and met with women there.

Just then there was a stirring over by the elevator, and the Presi-dent bounded into the room with a group of a dozen or so people around him. The deputy press secretary greeted him and talked di-rectly into his ear for a minute, telling him my name, my affiliation, and what his wife and I had been talking about. Mrs. Bush said, "Hi, George," and drifted over to the other side of the room, standing behind an easy chair as the President marched over to me, extended his hand, and said, in his easy cadence, "Hi, Stacy, howya doin'?" He plunked down right where Mrs. Bush had been a moment before.

The President's minders spent most of the interview sitting back in their chairs, quietly chitchatting with one another. But when I asked the President a question I'd asked Mrs. Bush—"What is the one thing you think people most misunderstand about you?"—the room woke up and sat forward, leaning in toward us. President Bush laughed and repeated my question. "What is the one thing I think people most misunderstand about me?" He paused, then said, laughing and grinning, "Just one?" He cast his eyes up to the ceiling. Mrs. Bush casually said, "You want to know what I said, George?" He started to turn toward her, but then he turned back toward me, and leaned forward as he said, with a strength and resolve in his voice that wouldn't return for the rest of the interview: "That I long for peace."

I *felt* it as he said it, and I thought, Point, Bush.

It was the highlight of the interview, the one moment that I felt I got to see George Bush as he really was, rather than the man who was saying what he was supposed to say. When I moved on to the questions I really wanted the answers to—questions concerning the ways in which women's shifting roles have changed this country so dramatically in the last four decades, and the fact that the government and corporations haven't helped in any meaningful way to address what those changes have meant for society and the American family—the President offered only platitudes and statistics I already knew very well myself.

As the interview drew to a close, President Bush ambled over to the console table where one of his aides was laying out documents for him to sign. As I started packing up my recorders and my notes, the press secretary came over to get my e-mail address so she could send me the Official White House Transcript of my interview, which, she informed me would be ready in less than an hour. President Bush, looking down as he signed the papers, said to me, "You look pretty young to me. How long you been running that magazine?"

I laughed. I was thirty-five, in fact, and not sure whether that was young or not young to be running a magazine.

I said, "Well, actually, just nine days, sir."

President Bush looked up at me. "No foolin'?" he said, his voice turning up high at the end, like the voices of all the Texas boys I went to college with did when they found something amusing. He broke into a big smile and came around from behind the table, marching toward me, hand extended. "Well congratulations to you. What a start, huh? That's just great."

I nodded and laughed and shook his hand. And then he asked who, exactly, was *Redbook* for. I answered him—saying young women who are just starting to establish themselves as wives and mothers and workers and homeowners and more—and then added, "I'm doing my best to help couples stay married and get the divorce rate down."

Oh, God! Now I was leaking in front of the President of the United States. I was making my problem bigger than my problem. I was making *myself* bigger than my problem. I was grandiosity in action. I was doing anything I could to get away from the feeling of being a small, scared girl in a life turned upside down.

But what I really was that second was embarrassed and suddenly deeply grateful that there wasn't another *Redbook* staffer there to hear my strange statement. After the Official White House Photos were taken, I scooted out of there, still cursing myself for my slip, which, thankfully, hadn't been recorded. My weakness would not make an appearance in the Official White House Transcript of that afternoon's conversation.

By the time my cab pulled up at the airport curb, I was tightly wound with denial. All that was left for me to do with this day was to get home and open the door and walk into my almost-broken life and my kind-of-broken house, and figure out how to get through another day of this In Between without leaking. I tried to be strong and batten down the hatches, fearing that the leak would turn into a gushing torrent that I would simply disappear into.

But my house was continuing to leak. In the weeks after the White House interview, three more hurricanes ripped through the Northeast, and the force of the winds was helping water find new ways to come into our home. Leaks appeared in the third-floor guest room and in the second-floor hallway. At night, as the rains lashed our house, I'd lie in bed, awake and electric with attention, counting the seconds between lightning and thunder as a way to gauge whether the storm was moving on. Most nights, I'd get up and pace the house while Chris slept, checking all the sites where water was coming in, placing buckets and towels underneath the drips, opening the basement door and peering down the stairs. One storm passed with no water coming into the basement. I prayed that the flood had been a bizarre fluke, some backup in the sewer system that had unclogged itself. But I knew this wasn't true from talking with the neighbors, some of whom had been born and raised on this street. Maryann, a feisty, nosy sixty-year-old with short silver hair, was one of them. She'd seen owners come and go in our house for the past ten years. It had stood empty for a long time, been boarded up and condemned by the city, and then discovered by a series of people who'd bought it, done a little bit of work, and then flipped the house. Maryann stopped me on the street after the first storm and asked if we'd taken in any water. Then she said the young couple we'd bought the house from had borrowed her Shop-Vac more than once to clean up after a flood, and they'd even borrowed it once after the house had gone to contract with us. Maryann told me she'd seen Chris and me going in and out of the house, with Zack in his carrier. She told me she asked the husband if he'd fixed the flooding problem, and he'd said it wasn't his problem anymore.

"I feel so bad for you, with a young kid like that and all," she said. "I don't know how they could do that to you." I couldn't know if Maryann was telling me the truth or not, but yes, I felt bad for me, too.

The second time the basement flooded, Chris and I were up for hours pushing the water toward the sump pump with a big push broom having given up on the Shop-Vac. The next morning, I went to work exhausted and devastated. How were we ever going to fix this problem? My mind could barely compute that someone would sell us a house with a "finished basement" knowing the house took in water in such a dramatic way. It made me sick. This had been our dream house, and now it was turning into a nightmare.

Chris and I had put every single penny we had into buying that place, and now we were going to have to sell it, but I would never be able to sell a flawed house and pretend it was fine. If we sold it as is, we'd lose a lot of money, but if we lost money on the house, then we would have nothing to divide.

I'd been running a sprint since I was twenty-one, thinking that saving money and gaining a foothold in a competitive career would make me feel that I'd found my safe place, and that I'd found a partner to share my life and grow old with. And now everything was going to be taken away from me. Balance sheet: zero.

As I walked onto the *Redbook* floor the morning after the second flood, I passed Janet's office. I'd recently confided in her all that was happening with me, because I didn't know how *not* to tell her: my looming breakup with Chris, our upcoming tenth wedding anniversary, the problems with my house. She looked up as I walked by and said, "How'd it go last night?"—referring to the storm. I broke down in the hallway, crying about the flood, about being exhausted, frightened, alone, worried about losing all our money, disbelieving that so much could go wrong at once. She got up and steered me into the privacy of my office, saying gently, "Let's not do this out here." I sat down on my sofa and sobbed. My home wasn't my safe place. My marriage wasn't my safe place. But work was still my safe place—in fact, my only safe place.

So after a few minutes of giving myself permission to wallow in all that was falling apart, I pulled it back together. I dove headfirst back into the comforting rhythm of meetings to attend, decisions to be made, story ideas to approve, photographs to edit, focusing on bringing my readers the best ideas of what life can be, to inspire in them optimism and comfort. This, in turn, comforted me as well. I have always believed in what I sell, and I sell only what I believe in. And so I spent those long, busy days at work making the magazine more honest and real as well as brighter and happier.

But even though the work was comforting, it was a *lot* of work. Every night, I was taking home a stack of manuscripts an inch or two thick, so I could read and edit every single word once, twice, three times or more before the issue was published. In addition, I needed to get up close and personal with the magazine's budget, to be sure we were spending our money in the right places for the greatest impact.

I also had a coming-out party of sorts on the calendar: *Redbook's* annual luncheon gala, a celebration of women and celebrities who have made an impact on the world with their charitable work. All the top executives from Hearst would be there. This year, Democratic presidential nominee Senator John Kerry was slated to be the keynote speaker. This meant we'd have a full house, and it also meant we'd need twice as much security. Having our guests scanned with metal detectors as they arrived would add almost an hour to the tightly scheduled proceedings. An event of this size—350 guests, a cocktail hour, a luncheon and an awards ceremony with a keynote speaker—takes months to plan, and I'd come on board just seven weeks before the scheduled day. There were menus and décor to approve, and speeches to write: my own short speech and those that would introduce all the winners.

Making things a hair more complicated was the fact that the event was scheduled to take place the day after the wedding of one of my best friends—in Camden, Maine—in which I was supposed to be a bridesmaid.

Tina and I have been friends since we were roommates in college, and when I first moved to New York, she'd let me stay with her rent-free until I got settled and found my job at *Mirabella*. I lay awake every night in her living room for three months, yearning for my big New York life to start and staring out at the Empire State Building until its lights snapped off at midnight. Years later, Tina lent Chris and me the down payment for our first apartment. She was someone who, like me, had given her all and more to her career, logging insanely long hours on Wall Street as she launched an index for the Latin American emerging markets and later the Asian emerging markets. After leaving Wall Street and New York banking and moving to Boston in search of a more reasonable lifestyle (although she was also trying to make the Olympic rowing team at the time), she'd met what seemed to be her perfect match: she was a libertarian financial type who was a hard-core competitive rower; he was a conservative oil commodities broker who was a hard-core amateur sailor. It's the kind of partnership you pray that you and your friends will find. And I've always believed that you have to show up for life; I couldn't imagine not being at the wedding. There is always a way to figure out how to manage the fallout at the office.

Being in Camden, Maine, right before the *Redbook* luncheon meant making the hard last days running up to this event even harder. I would have to oversee and approve all the final details, edit and practice my speech after the speechwriter had handed it over, and edit and approve all the celebrity speeches, and do all this from a part of Maine known for being beautiful and remote—i.e., treasured specifically because it's not electronically connected to the rest of the world.

Then there was the matter of Zack. I was torn about whether I should take my son: I wanted all my college friends to meet him; he was dazzlingly blond and outgoing and cute, just starting to speak, still refusing to walk because he could crawl like greased lightning. The last time I'd seen them was more than a year before, at another friend's wedding, and I'd been hugely pregnant. I couldn't imagine not taking Zack and showing him off; I couldn't imagine being away from him.

But what I could imagine, quite clearly, was how miserable taking this trip would make Chris. He had never cared much for travel, while I love change and new places and not knowing exactly where I'm going. Since Zack had been born, though, Chris's mild dislike of travel had turned into full-blown anxiety. Zack was a pretty good traveler, but of course he was still a baby, and so there were inevitably times where he couldn't be entertained or wouldn't be quiet or couldn't fall asleep on a flight, and all three of us would emerge from the airplane after we landed throbbing with exhaustion and covered in smushed snack foods. To me, the mom, this is Just The Way It Is. Traveling with a toddler is hard, but you simply have to take it in stride, because the end result—visiting relatives, taking a vacation—is always worth making the journey. But traveling with both a toddler and someone who has scant ability to manage the realities of traveling with a toddler? That's a fresh hell for sure.

So I suggested to Chris that he stay home with Zack, especially because I was going to have to fly back from Maine on Sunday, the day of the wedding, since I had a 6 a.m. call time for the event on Monday. Chris was torn; he'd known my friends from college for many years, and he wanted to show off Zack, too, as crazy in love with him as he was. Plus in trying to make our marriage work, he was trying to do things he knew were important to me—and neither Chris nor I ever got good at realizing that this was almost always a mistake for both of us, even after the weekend in the Hamptons. So we booked tickets, making arrangements for Chris and Zack to fly home Monday with my friend Eric and his partner, Dave, so there would be some extra hands to help Chris, and got ready for the hard, long trip.

Well, there's long and hard, and then there's epic. The trip to our wedding destination itself was fine: after a two-hour flight, we landed, got into our rental car, and drove two hours to where we were staying with the group of my college friends—a big house across the street from the main inn. But finalizing all the details surrounding the event was more intense than I could have imagined, and I was greatly hampered by the fact that my cell phone reception was very spotty and there wasn't a phone in the guest house, so I couldn't hook up my computer. I couldn't rely on being able to get through to my office, and I couldn't count on keeping the line while the conversation unfolded, either. The inn had an ancient fax machine, but it took almost an hour for the twenty-page document containing the luncheon's "run of show"—a minute-by-minute breakdown of the event—to come through. I skipped most of the prewedding activities and spent the better part of the two days before the event seated at the long dining room table in the guest house, rewriting the speeches because the speechwriter's drafts had come in way off the mark. I needed the words I said in my first public event to be exactly right, to capture the shift I was making in the magazine. Adding to my anxiety was the fact that it had been raining cats and dogs on and off the entire time we were in Maine, as hurricane rains swept the full length of the East Coast. I knew that the rains had already made their way through Brooklyn, and I couldn't keep myself from worrying about what was happening in the basement at home. I'd let my mind touch on it, and then push it behind the sliding doors in my mind, keeping that empty space of calm in my mind's eye. *No point in thinking about that until you can do something about it later. Move on to What's Next Now.*

The wedding was scheduled for Sunday, and by Saturday night what was done was done as far as the *Redbook* event was concerned. So Chris, Zack, and I went off to the rehearsal dinner, which was being held in a barn. I was genuinely happy for Tina and Matt, but also filled with sadness, remembering my own wedding day, when I was surrounded by many of these same friends I love so much. I had felt so confident that Chris and I would clear life's obstacles together. Trying to put a good face on things between Chris and me exhausted me more than I would have guessed. I was desperate to have my friends' comfort about what I was going through, but I simply couldn't tell them yet. I couldn't afford the luxury of falling apart because I was taking care of Zack, and taking care of Chris, too.

Chris hates social gatherings like these. He's a world-class talker; get him started, especially on the topics of film, TV, and underground humor, and he is an incredibly detailed conversationalist, and a hard one to stop once he gets going, but he's a little shy. He is also harshly judgmental of most social conventions, because he considers them fake. For years I'd been scooting to his side at parties to introduce topics of mutual interest to help grease the wheels when he was meeting friends and acquaintances of mine. And so much small talk in New York City, a town in love with achievement above all else, inevitably starts with the question "And so what do you do?" That is the question Chris hates above all, not wanting to be defined by someone else's idea of success, not wanting to be defined by the jobs he's held simply to make money and not because they were his passion. One time I saw Chris talking to Tina at a party, not looking at her, but staring down at the ground. I approached just in time to hear Chris saying, "I sleep, I eat, I work. Then I eat and then sleep and then work. Eat. Sleep. Work. Eatsleepwork. *That's* what I do." *Uh-oh.*

So I had my radar on high alert, especially because Chris had been prickly and unhappy for most of the weekend, annoyed that I was busy with preparing for the *Redbook* event. I worked hard at the rehearsal dinner, checking in on him often, to save him from people or conversations that might annoy him, to give him a break from Zack when he needed it, or to hand Zack off to him when he needed the distraction from the party around him. When we got back to the guest house that night, he and Z went right to bed, and I sat downstairs with Eric for a late-night catch-up. I confided in Eric that trying to keep Chris in a good frame of mind while also running the event back in New York was stressing me in the extreme, but that I didn't know how not to feel responsible for making Chris happy. I thanked Eric for being willing to help Chris get Zack home, but in my heart I knew the trip was going to be a nightmare, no matter how much help Chris had, because he was so angry that he was at the wedding, surrounded with exactly the kinds of things he doesn't like and tries to avoid. For the ten-thousandth time since all this had started, I felt guilty for being me.

The next day, the wedding was beautiful, despite the fact that a steady drizzle dampened the proceedings. Tina and Matt exchanged vows by the marina, small craft bobbing in the water in front of them. The bride and groom were beaming as if the sun were shining, even though I could see the tiny drops of water plink-plink-plinking off the end of Tina's nose from where I stood at her side, clutching my bouquet. I was going to miss all the fun and festivities after the ceremony; as soon as we got to the restaurant where the reception was being held—by which time the sun had broken through the clouds, offering its glorious benediction—a car arrived to pick me up for the long drive back to the airport. It's decidedly unfun to have to leave a party that hasn't started and know that everyone will have a blast without you—in this case, of course, everyone except my husband. I got into the car, feeling sick again that I had no judgment, and that clearly this whole uncomfortable weekend was my fault. But after a few minutes on that nauseating train of thought, I just slid the shoji screen shut—*shhhhhhp*—and snapped into gear, thinking about what lay ahead the next day.

When I pulled up at my house six hours later, I was exhausted. I dragged my suitcase into the front hallway, picked up the mail off the floor, and turned on the living room lights. I walked over to the door to the basement, opened the door, and flicked on the light. My stomach dropped. Water was up to the third riser of the staircase, higher than I'd ever seen it. Worse, it wasn't even raining outside. That meant the drains hadn't drained and the pump hadn't pumped. I crept down a few steps and peered into the room: the sofa was floating several feet away from the wall it had once stood against; the downstairs refrigerator was pitched sideways and bobbing on the black water, its door wide open; leaves and gunk clung to the walls four feet from the floor, marking the height the water had reached in the three days of storms. The pilot lights for the furnace and water heater would have been extinguished, and there was no way to get them relit with two feet of filthy rainwater still in the room.

I padded up the stairs, turned off the light, and gently closed the door, deciding that I would think about all that another day. I was learning that I could handle the truth of my life, the bigness of it all and the disaster unfolding within it, only in small pieces. Getting the water out of the basement tonight was not going to solve the larger problem, and so it would have to wait. You can handle more than you think, I told myself. You can handle more than you think by not thinking about things all the time, by not thinking about things all at once, by not being all-or-nothing—which had been my favorite way to be until all this had started to unfold.

I didn't love having to learn a new way to be, but it looked like I didn't have a choice.

I crawled into bed in the dark alone, the crib in the room next door empty for the first time since Zack was born, and I felt that emptiness in my heart and throat. I was spending my first night away from my son, except I was home and he was not. Everything in my life was backward. I let out a long sigh and willed myself to sleep.

The next day I got out of bed at 5:30 a.m. and woke myself up with a cold shower, since there was no hot water to be had. I got in a car, carrying my outfit in a garment bag, and was driven into Manhattan in the dark, to kick off the final hours of prep for the event—hair and makeup, speech run-through, microphone checks, place card adjustments—while a team of caterers and florists put everything into place. Two celebrities didn't show at the last minute, but John Kerry's presence in the room was electric. I spoke, telling the crowd that some of the grandest victories and achievements in life—rebounding from rape to become a spokesperson for sex crime victims; extending a helping hand to terminally ill children in hospitals—start with the smallest steps.

That speech was for the room, of course, and to honor the brave actions our honorees had taken. But there was a message in it for me, too: Take small steps. Do one thing at a time. Be a hundred percent where you are when you are there. That afternoon, I was fully in that room, and very proud of what we were celebrating. At that moment I was also proud of me, and all I'd done to get here. The next morning, the front page of the *New York Times* carried a huge photo of John Kerry at Lincoln Center, standing in front of the magenta backdrop at our event, arms outstretched.

Chris and Zack came back from Maine that night, Chris exhausted and undone by the trip, as if he'd had to fly Zack home on his back. He basically handed Zack into my arms and stomped up the stairs, leaving a trail of dissatisfaction and blame that I could tell had my name all over it as he disappeared into his office. I'd known this is how this trip would turn out. When would I stop waiting for Chris to become somebody he wasn't? When would I stop failing as a human being?

I was slowly learning the truth that would get me through the process of having my life and house fall apart around me: I could keep two opposing thoughts about myself in my head at the same time and know they were both true.

I am a Mess. I am Fine.

I didn't have to choose one idea and dwell in it. When I tried, I would only find myself seesawing wildly between the two, anyway, as I collected evidence for the alternative. *I came to work crying today; that means I am a Mess and I should quit my job before someone discovers what I wreck I am.* Or *Wow! I actually really just had a fun two hours playing with Zack in the park even though we are surrounded by two-parent families that make my heart ache. I can do this; I can be a single mother and figure out how to live on my own and be Fine!* Since I didn't know what to believe anymore, I decided I would just give myself permission to believe it all, and try to learn to live in the quiet balancing point of In Between.

The only problem was that resting in the In Between felt like slowing to a halt. I just hated feeling stuck, not knowing where Chris and I were going, as if I were a butterfly whose wings had been pinned. I tried to remind myself that the calm of not moving, of being in the balance, was the reward, and that trying to flap my wings against all I didn't know didn't get me anywhere. I had to find a way to set aside my most trusted coping skill—charging into tomorrow by sheer force of will—and learn how to be still.

It doesn't matter how many times we hear the aphorism "Want

to make God laugh? Make plans" and knowingly chuckle at its bittersweet truth, because making plans is what we humans do. Now the plans Chris and I had made as a couple were being undone as Chris pulled away from me. I felt every single withdrawal, like an octopus releasing its grasp, one suction cup at a time—pop! pop! pop!—leaving dents in my spirit, signs of what once was there.

Especially because Chris *was* still there, eating dinner with me most nights, spending weekends with Zack and me, sleeping in our bed. We didn't talk about breaking up every day, and sometimes we didn't talk about it for two or three weeks; it was easy to be lulled back into the normalcy of day-to-day life.

October 1, our tenth wedding anniversary, was looming large on the calendar. I couldn't stand the thought of limping across the finish line, making it to ten years of marriage and not acknowledging it, even if we didn't ultimately stay together. I cautiously asked Chris after dinner one night if he thought maybe we should go away and try to celebrate the anniversary, since not everyone makes it to ten, even though we didn't know what was going to happen with us; my voice rose at the end of every phrase like a teenager's. As I asked the question, I felt like I was standing there naked, covered in Sterno, and Chris had a lit match. I said we could take off one day from work, have the nanny stay for the weekend, and go up to the mountains somewhere, be alone together for the first time since Zack was born. "Okay," he said. I couldn't read what was in that "okay," but it seemed straightforward enough.

And so I hit the Internet in a whirlwind of research and tried to find the perfect place for us to go. Most places within easy driving distance were booked already, so I ended up choosing a breathtakingly beautiful hotel in the Berkshires that still had rooms available—probably because the rooms were breathtakingly expensive. For me, rationalizing the cost was easy. If the weekend away gave Chris and me a chance to reconnect and remember all the reasons—heck, even *some* of the reasons—that we'd married, then it would be worth it. And if it failed, then at least I'd tried, and hadn't let this opportunity slip through our fingers.

I made the reservations and had my assistant send out an e-mail to the staff letting them know I'd be out of the office next Friday "celebrating my tenth wedding anniversary." It looked good on e-mail, I thought. I could almost will myself to believe that we were going under circumstances as happy as they seemed. I leaned a little bit more into my denial and crossed my fingers. Kim, who'd left *Marie Claire* and joined me at *Redbook*, came into my office later that day and said, "That e-mail was weird." I was too embarrassed to tell Kim that the wording was mine. Sometimes it still felt good to pretend.

My denial manifested itself in other ways as well. I kept buying tickets for Chris and me for theater and concert events that were months in the future, unable to stop myself from living in the Maybe. *Maybe we'll still be together by then, and wouldn't we be sad if we didn't have tickets.* I also stopped writing in my journal, in which I usually jotted brief updates about what was happening in my life and in my head. In the two years leading up to the divorce, I made only one entry, just days after that first conversation with Chris on the sofa. The entry is written in a whisper, in light pencil, and my handwriting is this small. Now *that's* denial. Everything that was happening seemed so big I didn't even attempt to write about it. How could I have made sense of it in a journal entry? Especially since circumstances kept getting more and more challenging. After Chris and I had made our plans to go away for our anniversary and I'd made arrangements with the nanny to stay for the weekend, suddenly she asked me for a cash loan, intimating a complicated personal problem. This tipped my personal-crisis scale into overload: I can handle a lot of pressure, but to be uncertain about my son's daily care? It was unsettling beyond words. So maybe a diary entry for that moment would have looked like this:

> *Dear Diary,*
>
> *My life is a sick joke. I am living a literary allegory, having the foundation of my house give way at the same time that the foundation of my very life is crumbling. Chris is leaving me and the house is falling apart, taking in sewer water in the basement and leaking*

tears from the roof. Boo-hoo-hoo. And just when it seems things can't possibly get any worse, they do! To wit: I had to fire my nanny today, after giving her an envelope stuffed with cash. Cash I need to fix my messed-up house, but oh well. This nanny loved my son like crazy, but I think she hated me. She was late every single day, no matter how I begged and pleaded and bribed her to be on time. And then she asked me if she could borrow a large sum of money to help her with a personal problem. Very uncomfortable. So I decided to just cut my losses and move on. Yes, dear Diary, I did.

Unfortunately, I had to fire her the day before Chris and I intended to go away to "celebrate" our "tenth" "wedding anniversary," so now I don't have anyone to take care of Zack. Of course, that's how these things go. I called my parents to help me, but that meant that I was subject to my engineer father's running me through seventeen alternate scenarios in which (1) the nanny would not have needed the money, (2) she would not have needed it by today so that I wouldn't have had to let her go today, and (3) my wedding anniversary would not have been October 1, this weekend, so that (4) I would not be asking them to step in and take care of Zack so Chris and I can go away. It's not that Dad doesn't want to do it; it's just that he would have liked a few more days to mentally prepare for taking care of my son in my house (my father likes surprises even less than Chris, but that's an engineer for you). Right, I should have gotten married October 8. I'll get right on that, revise history. That will fix everything.

Oh, and did I tell you, dear Diary, that I'm running a magazine all about women and love and marriage and stuff? Isn't it rich?

My parents did come to the rescue, along with a consortium of friends, and Chris and I did get to go away. We drove four hours without incident or traffic, and as we pulled into the crushed-stone driveway of the hotel, a grand mansion that had been refurbished by two modern architects, a fleet of bellmen descended upon the car, greeted me by name, and whisked away our bags. I was entranced by the hotel and its manicured expanse of green lawn, but I tensed up. This place was too fancy for Chris; he had a hard time feeling like himself in posh surroundings. So before we even got into our beautiful room with its view of the lake and the trees starting to don their fall colors, I was on guard. We managed to drink the champagne that was waiting for us in our room and lavish some sexual attention on each other and eat our gourmet dinner. The next day, we took in the view from our stone balcony overlooking the lake and walked through picturesque towns, but the undercurrent of tension was impossible to ignore. It wasn't miserable, it wasn't awful, we didn't fight. In the end, I thought it had been a good thing to do.

But just a few weeks later, after another night of my cooking dinner and Chris's putting the dishes in the dishwasher, and the two of us settling down into our evening routine after I put Zack to bed—TV and the sofa for Chris, reading manuscripts at the kitchen table for me—I tried to start a conversation with Chris about where he thought we were as a couple. He was dismissive, and didn't turn his attention away from the television. It was clear I was annoying him. I started to get upset and snapped at him, "If we are supposed to be trying to work on our marriage, do you think you could take part in this conversation?"

He whipped his head around to face me. "I'm *not* trying. I am done trying. I am waiting for you to be finished trying." And then he turned back toward the television, raising the volume to erase whatever I might say next.

It was as if he had slapped me across my face.

"You are still coming home and eating dinners I cook for you?" I gasped, as I stood up from the kitchen table. "And sleeping next to me in our bed? When did you decide you were finished trying? When were you planning on telling me?" I backed away toward the stairs, my old habits of self-protection kicking in now that I knew for sure I was sleeping with the enemy. Why did we go away for our anniversary if we weren't still trying? Why had he agreed to take the trip? Why had he made love to me all those days?

"It was goodbye," he said simply.

I was shaking, I was so angry and so completely humiliated. "It isn't goodbye if the other person doesn't know it's goodbye," I said, crying. I kept backing up the stairs, desperate to get away from him and find some way to protect myself. I started throwing out rules. I told him that he should start sleeping in the guest room, and that we wouldn't be having dinner together anymore, and I asked when was he planning on moving out, now that I knew he was already gone.

"I don't have any money to move out," he said. "I need a few months to save enough money to rent a new place."

If I'd had the money to give him I would have run to the ATM to get it and thrown it at him. I didn't have it; what I had was a credit card bill for a romantic weekend away that would have covered his first month's rent. I couldn't believe I was being left by a husband who wouldn't quite leave. That night I lay in bed in the dark and cried jaggedly, deeply, feeling something dark in my gut break loose with the cutting finality of his rejection. As I cried, I heard Chris moving around the house, collecting the blankets and pillows he'd need to make his bed in the third-story guest room.

Time began to move very slowly, even as each day passed in an instant, crammed with the pressing requirements of being a mom and running a magazine and trying to figure out how to fix the house. I started living by what I called the Rule of One like a fervent convert to a new religion: You can do only one thing at a time, no matter how much you have to do. Every day, many items on the gigantic list of Things That Must Be Done—calling plumbers; calling my insurance company; calling lawyers to find out whether I could sue my house's previous owners if they had misrepresented the property; figuring out where to get the money to start fixing the house; finding a lawyer to talk to about my divorce; finding a nanny agency and hiring a new nanny for my son, then firing the new nanny—went undone, even though I was desperate to move everything forward. My workdays were made up of back-to-back meetings, and it was a challenge to squeeze in any of these phone calls. For both better and worse, tomorrow was another day, and that day was coming no matter how much or how little I had accomplished.

I wheeled Zack into the office with me for a few days in a row, sneaking him through the lobby and rushing his stroller into an empty elevator so that no one outside of my staff would see him with me. One of those mornings, I ran into the vice president for human resources in the lobby, and I wasn't surprised when I got a phone call from her later that day, reminding me that one of my benefits as an employee was emergency day care. I thanked Ruth (a genuinely wonderful person, and the person I had on my radar as someone to call if I truly reached some kind of limit with what I was going through), but admitted to her I hadn't had time to do all the preregistration paperwork that one must do in order to take advantage of that benefit. I added those tasks, which included taking Zack to the doctor for an exam (oh, God, when was I going to have time for that?), to the to-do list.

I stayed sane with the Rule of Two, for keeping conflicting thoughts in my head at the same time: *I am a mess/I am okay. A lot of things are falling apart/A lot of things are going fine. I am totally incapable human being/I am a perfectly capable boss.*

That last one was a doozy. I struggled mightily with the feeling that I was unworthy to run the magazine because my life was in such disarray. It's not that I thought I had to turn in my Capable Person card just because my marriage was failing. I knew I could still lead—but would people want to follow? I motivate my teams by selling them a shiny new bandwagon, describing the larger goals that drive the content they create as a way to inspire them to really connect to the mission, and get them to ride along with me. But who was going to follow me, with the shape I was in? *Hello there! I'm dying a painful death by a thousand little cuts. Want to be on my team?* I tried to keep reminding myself that the team didn't know (and didn't have to know and didn't need to know) what I was going through, but that gave me a different headache, of feeling inauthentic. As a live-my-life-out-loud kinda girl, not being able to talk about this complicated, challenging, gigantic struggle with my editors—especially the editors who edited and created all the content about sex and love and marriage—felt creepily fake.

I needed to figure out how to be at peace with this conflict. And I found my inspiration in a surprising place: in having been fired from *Marie Claire.*

I had been devastated to lose that job for a host of reasons: I loved the job and had brought a lot of passion to it; I had never been fired before and thought, of course, that it said terrible things about me; I hated feeling that I had been misunderstood by the boss who fired me; I hated feeling like I had been *disliked* by the boss who fired me. But since it wasn't a hostile or hurried termination—I hadn't been escorted out of the building that day, but had instead been given time to wrap things up and try to find a new position— I'd had some time to work through my initial disbelief and embarrassment. My company wanted to try to find a new position for me, my team was sorry they were losing me, and on my last day my boss said to me as she was walking out the door, "Go be an editor in chief." Okay, so maybe I wasn't getting fired because I totally sucked. But it was still hard to handle.

As I was packing my boxes on that last day with my assistant, Holly, my mind was tick-tocking like a metronome in pairs of thoughts:

I disagree with a lot of what my boss said about me in firing me . . . but she made some points that I need to think about and learn from.

This whole experience has really hurt my feelings and made me feel like a loser . . . but I will not let it change my hard-earned sense of what my skills and talents are.

I find all of this extremely embarrassing . . . but I am very proud of the way I handled it with my company, the staff, and my boss, with dignity, directness, and grace.

In fact, I was the one who went to my boss after she'd written a less-than-flattering performance review that described a person I didn't recognize as myself and said, "It's clear you need to move on. Let's talk about how we're going to do this." I was in no position to change the writing on the wall, so I didn't see any point in trying to fight it.

My assistant, Holly, and I had become close in the three years we'd worked together, and on my last day, as she helped me tie up loose ends, she was crying. I looked up at her and said, "I'm going to miss you, too! I'm sorry I'm not crying anymore. I'm just realizing that this is all fine, and I'm going to be fine. That's where I am right now."

The day I walked out of the *Marie Claire* offices, I didn't feel defeated at all. The fact was, my boss and I were not a good fit. And in the work world, the boss gets to be in charge of the fit.

I had been petrified about finding a new job, and petrified about being able to pay my bills. But I also felt that in the firing I had started to take possession of who I was. I could accept that there was truth in a lot of the justifications for my firing, and some not-necessarily-truth, too, and that I didn't have to exist wholly in either one. And now, less than a year later, I could shake my head in wonderment that my firing—which I thought had been the Worst Thing That Ever Happened to Me—had taught me a lesson I needed to help me survive the Actual Worst Thing That Had Ever Happened to Me.

In the end, my firing had been a master class for surviving my divorce. So *namaste*, Lesley, and thank you. But even more than that, my firing had been the beginning of my learning who I really was. The last thing I said to Holly before I left the office was, "I'm starting to get the sneaking suspicion I might be turning into the person I've always hoped I might be." Someone who could be honest with herself and others. Someone who wouldn't get stuck in life's hard stuff. Someone who trusted herself, and trusted life. An optimist.

That learning experience hadn't made me a genius, however. Even though I was starting to be able to see and accept the big picture of my life—Chris and I were going to separate, and I had a lot of big problems on my plate—I still took mental vacations to Denial Fantasyland, that wonderful place where nothing bad happens. Chris and I had tickets for a huge reunion concert for the Pixies, one of our favorite bands. Even though I now knew definitively that we would not stay together, I was sure I could handle going to the concert with him, because a handful of our friends were coming, too. And also because Chris and I still were living our day-to-day lives in much the same way as we had before he moved upstairs to the guest room. I didn't cook dinner for the two of us anymore, but we had an amicable enough flow to our weeks: two nights a week he went out with friends or worked late, and two nights a week I could do the same, attending events for *Redbook,* staying at the office for late meetings, getting to have a dinner out with friends so I could talk about the confusion of this here-but-not-here life Chris and I were living. The schedule was a way for us to test out being separated and start sharing the child care, and having some scheduled time apart had seemed to lighten our load a little. It felt familiar, like our days of being the "least-married married couple," the days when it felt like our marriage was working.

A few days before the concert, Alix said she couldn't come, and I wasn't able to find another friend to come with me. Which meant that I would be going to the concert with just Chris and "his friends," Bill and Voelker. I hadn't seen either of them since the barbecue in May. When I asked Chris if he'd told them both what was going on between us, he said, "Well sure, yeah, of course." Oh, God. Telling my friends was one thing; it had been my secret to share. But to be with people who had heard all the reasons why Chris was leaving, straight from him? I felt panic rising in my chest. But I just pushed it down. I wanted to go to this concert—I loved the Pixies! It was probably my last chance ever to see them live.

The day of the concert, I sat at work, watching the hours tick down to showtime. But as I thought about being at the concert and listening to the sound track of the years when Chris and I first fell in love, I knew I couldn't do it. I called Chris up at work and told him I just wasn't going to be able to be there with Voelker and Bill and keep it together. Chris felt really bad, and tried to talk me into going. He said they'd be fine and would know not to say anything to me about our imminent breakup. This made it worse; it made me feel like a charity case. I told him I was sure and that he should come by my office and get the tickets.

When he walked into my office at the end of the day, I started to shake a little. Chris was wearing his long winter coat and sporting a goatee that he'd started growing at some point after our anniversary. He'd also begun growing his hair out after a few years of keeping it short. He looked so much like the young guy I fell in love with, it made my heart ache. Something in my brain's compartmentalization was breaking down; I could feel something tearing in my Pollyanna outlook that maybe there was still a way to save our marriage. I started to cry as I stood up and walked toward him with the envelope of tickets in my hand. Chris just said, "Oh, don't do that," quietly and gently. When I got to him, he reached out his arms and wrapped me up in them and let me sob, my face pressed against his black coat.

"It's so hard," I said. "It's so, so hard. I don't know how to do this."

He said, "I know, I know. It's hard," and smoothed my hair. He wasn't trying to erase me. He was comforting me, as he always had. It was exquisitely painful, to have him take care of me and be hurting me, both at the same time. But I couldn't step away from him. I needed his kindness; I wanted to be able to let go with grace.

Chris and I agreed we would tell his mother we were breaking up when we were in Illinois for the holidays. Even though I knew we'd be delivering bad news, I couldn't wait to go out there with Zack, now that he was old enough—sixteen months and walking—to experience all the excitement of Christmas, instead of just chewing on wrapping paper while he sat in his bouncy seat. And I was looking forward to a week's break from the dead run of work.

I was also harboring a last secret Fantasyland wish: that Chris's mom was going to be able to snap her fingers and say some magic words that would make Chris change his mind. I trusted Barb and felt very close to her, and not just because she knew Chris as well as I did. Open and loving, she had always made me feel like I was a part of her family. Just two Christmases earlier, Chris and I had surprised Barb with the thrilling news that we were all of fifteen or sixteen days pregnant and the three of us had hugged and cried in her living room. She'd put her arms around me and declared, "I'm going to take such good care of you!" I wanted her to be able to take care of me now.

We had a wonderful Christmas, enjoying the chaos of six cousins, Chris's two sisters and their husbands, and wrapping paper flying everywhere in the delightful gift-opening melee. Later on Christmas Day a powdery white snow started falling, and all seven kids lined up on their knees on the couch, looking out the window at the flat Illinois landscape as it donned its holiday finery. I dressed Zack in his navy blue snowsuit, and Chris and I took him outside for his very first sledding adventure, riding in the cherry red plastic sled his grandmother had given him. I captured the whole sweet moment on video. And later that day I took the last official family portrait of the three of us, reaching my arm out to get us all in the frame: Zack in his striped sweater, Chris with his new goatee, and me, uncertain and trying my best, still, to believe that what the camera would capture was real.

The vacation wound down, and Chris hadn't said anything to his mother yet, even though all the nieces and nephews and aunts and uncles had disappeared. As he and I drove through our final round of errands the night before getting on the plane to go home, Zack at home with Barb, I asked Chris if he was going to say anything. "Yes," he hissed back at me, irritated. When he said it, I felt my last hopes deflate; I hadn't realized I'd had my mental fingers crossed that maybe being with his family and all the kids together had made him rethink his decision. We drove back from the drugstore in silence, walked in the door, took off our coats, and sat on the couch while Barb gave us the updates on Zack's activities of the night before she'd put him to bed. I sat there, hearing my blood pound in my ears, looking at my lap, waiting for Chris.

"Uhh, Mom, we have something we need to tell you, and it's not good," he began. As he went on speaking, Barb started to cry. She said, "But you two? You two always *talked.* I never thought it would be the two of you to break up!" I started to cry, too. Because I realized then, as Chris sat next to me and stared at his folded hands on his knees, trying to find the words to explain, that it was really ending. No fairy godmother-in-law was going to be able to wave her magic wand and make it all okay.

When we got home from Illinois, I printed up our family portrait—in an act of denial or defiance or wistful regret, I'm still not sure which—and hung it on the fridge; it always made Zack laugh when he saw it.

I wasn't able to bring myself to tell my parents for another few weeks. We had been to see them for the holidays before going to Illinois, but I just played my role and so did Chris. At night after I'd put Zack to bed, I would pick up the phone to call them, and then set it back down in the cradle. Then Chris picked a move-out date, the first weekend in February, and I couldn't delay any longer. I called my mother on January 17, my thirty-sixth birthday. It was Martin Luther King Jr. Day, so the office was closed. I was home with Zack, and I had just put him down for a nap. I picked up the cordless phone, dialed her number, and sat down on the same stairs I had backed up when Chris told me he was done trying. When my mom picked up the phone, she wished me a happy birthday, and I said thanks, trying to steady myself.

"Mom?"

"Yes . . . ?" she said cautiously, sensing something in my voice.

"Zack's fine and I'm fine, but I have to tell you something," I said, my voice shaking.

"Yes . . . ?" she said, getting concerned.

I opened my mouth and tried to speak, but instead I cried in an open-mouth wail, as I hadn't for months.

My mom just said, "Shhhh, shhhh, there, there, baby. It's okay. You're okay. Tell me what's wrong."

In my family, we have a history of saying exactly the wrong thing at just the wrong moment because we are so busy being clever. But when my mother sensed something big was happening and reflexively comforted me as if I were still a small child, I wanted to crawl through the phone line and curl up on her lap, to get back to that place in time where you believe your parents can make everything okay for you.

I managed to get out the words. I managed to tell her how little I knew. I remembered to ask her not to tell my brothers yet, and to tell my father not to be angry at Chris, that it would put me around the bend to feel that, because I still loved Chris, I was worried about him, I needed more time to decide what I was thinking. This was all already hard enough without having to do the work of assimilating anyone else's opinions, at least until I had my own.

She told me they would do anything they could to help me, and I believed her. She told me that I would be fine, and I tried to believe her. I hung up the phone and slid down the stairs and lay down on the couch and stared at the wall for an hour, feeling in my gut, as I hadn't before, that this was really going to happen. Chris was going to leave me. And leave Zack. And leave the shell of our life and the shell of our house behind. I would be left there, listening to the echoes of our dreams.

Chris was slated to move out February 5, but I was scheduled to fly to London earlier that same week to attend a three-day management conference of our parent company, Hearst Magazines. I had been asked to make a presentation about what I was doing with *Redbook*. It was an honor to be asked to present, and a little high-pressure, too. I wanted to impress everyone in the room with my vision; and my audience would include not only my boss, Cathie Black, but also three former editors of *Redbook*, including the woman who'd fired me from *Marie Claire*.

I settled on a theme that felt both safe and true. "Reinventing *Redbook*: Changing Everything and Changing Nothing." I concentrated on explaining that *Redbook's* core mission hadn't changed, but that the women the magazine served had changed dramatically in the last decade or so. I crafted a PowerPoint presentation that showed some of the changes, and mentally I prepared for the trip, which would be the first time I was away from Zack since the night I'd left him in Maine with Chris. I would be away for four entire days.

Every working mother knows that business trips are a strange combination of guilt and pleasure. It's hard not to be the one putting your baby to bed, but there's no denying it's nice not to be the one waking with the baby at 5:45 a.m. Plus, you can go to the gym without asking and have some time for yourself, some time to just be. I talked to Chris and at Zack every day while I was there. It was easy for Chris and me to be focused on talking about how Zack was doing. We had just hired a new nanny, Sezi, who was already changing our lives with her heart and good-naturedness and her sweet, loving personality. She and Zack were a match made in heaven, so hearing all about how wonderfully the two of them were getting along was music to my ears. It all felt very normal.

After my presentation, I called the office to check in with Kim, the magazine's managing editor as well as a great friend. After I had related the highlights and shared a few people's positive responses, she said, "Cool, sounds great," and then paused.

"What's next?" I asked, figuring she was going to tell me what pieces of copy had been faxed to me at the hotel and needed to be approved by me right away.

"Have you thought at all yet about what you and Zack are going to do Saturday?"

Oh, God. Saturday. Saturday, Saturday, Saturday. I hadn't thought about it at all. Chris was moving out on Saturday, the day after I returned home from London.

"You can't be there when he moves out," she said. "You don't want Zack to see that."

No, I didn't want Zack to see that. Zack was so young that we hadn't had to explain anything to him yet; Chris was going to be around almost as much after he'd moved out as he had been when he was living with us. We planned to stick to our weeknight schedule of Tuesday and Thursday nights being Chris's nights to come home and relieve the nanny and put Zack to bed, and now Sundays were going to be Chris's, too. We'd been sort of living this schedule for a month or two, so not much in his schedule would actually change for Zack right away.

I was still thinking about all this when Kim said, "You guys just come over to our house in the morning and play"—she had a daughter, Julia, who was about two years older than Zack; they were pals and look-alikes, with blond hair and big blue eyes. "Plan to spend the day with us."

I thanked Kim and hung up, more than a little thrown by the fact that the date had slipped through the cracks, had gotten lost among all the openings and closings of the shoji screens in my mind. I wasn't even sure there was a way to prepare for the day your husband backs a truck up to your house and loads it before driving away for good. Thank goodness Kim got there first.

On that Saturday, Zack and I got up and had our breakfast as if it were a normal day. Chris was on the phone, rounding up the friends who were going to help him move. I dressed Zack in a red T-shirt that said "Mom Rules," as a small act of defiance, and I packed a diaper bag. "I'll call you when it's all done," Chris said, as if he and I were running separate errands and would meet back at the house for dinner. "Okay," I said, and Zack and I left the house before Chris went to pick up the truck.

Zack and Julia spent all day playing in Julia's playroom, while Kim and I sat on the sofa and alternately talked and didn't talk about what was happening. Chris finally called just a bit after dark and said, "I'm out." I hung up and let out a big exhale, not really sure what I was thinking or feeling. I started packing up Zack's toys. Kim's husband, Stephen, walked into the room and suggested that we all head out to dinner and then to the Brooklyn Museum for one of the free activity nights called First Saturdays. I didn't live far from the museum, but I'd never even heard of First Saturdays. We drove over and entered the museum in a happy throng of parents and children, spiced up with hipsters with complicated hair (which made me feel old) and a good smattering of old folks (which reminded me I was young), and were greeted by music. Up on the third floor was the Beaux-Arts Court, a huge square space lined with pillars, the surrounding walls hung with art. Stationed in the middle of the square was an Afro-Brazilian band, blasting happy music through big speakers. Zack immediately began running around the big square hall, sprinting past the paintings and the sculpture, and egging me on to chase him. I bought a plastic cup of red wine and sipped from it between jogging spurts, trying to keep my eyes on my blond bomber, letting the music get into the space in my chest that was tight.

Julia caught Zack and took him with her to the dance floor. She whirled him around, her blond hair flying out behind her like ribbons, her black dress with hearts on it flaring at the hem. Zack had a huge grin on his face as he absorbed the energy in the room. He has always loved to dance, and when he turned toward me I called, "Do the chicken dance!" This dance was one of our favorite jokes. Zack promptly put his hands on his waist, bent his knees, and began flapping his legs open and closed, open and closed, all while trying to keep himself from cracking up. When Stephen caught sight of it, he burst out laughing, and Zack followed suit. I sat on the sidelines loving my son and watching other people love his big spirit, too. I could see that almost before my eyes my baby was turning into a boy, that time was indeed marching on, even though life felt stuck.

Kids were spinning around with their parents, or wiggling in big groups with their friends. Couples were dancing together, impressing each other with their moves. I was caught up in the sheer joy of it all, the delight of sharing in a public spectacle of celebration for no reason in particular.

As I looked at the mosaic floor my son was joyously dancing on, I was reminded that what you see in your life isn't one thing, one picture, one thought. Life is a thousand little pieces, sliding and moving, like bits of glass in a kaleidoscope. You may get a moment of suddenly taking in a pattern whole, and then it's gone again in a flash, changing, shifting into something else. As I sipped my wine, I felt calm and . . . happy. There was no longer any denying that my marriage was coming to an end. But being able to feel so good and so loved on one of the saddest days of my life gave me strength to face whatever might be coming next.

5

Anger Hides Everything You Need to Feel to Get Past the Anger

The first few days after Chris moved out, I waited for sadness to come rushing into the empty place where he used to be, but what I mostly felt was . . . quiet. After eight long months of being on guard in my own home, it was a relief to have an hour or two every night to be by myself, and not be the object of Chris's rancor or indifference. A soothing silence was starting to take shape in my mind in the place where my self-criticisms and self-admonishments had lived, the voices that had been trying to help me save my marriage—a tentative blank spot where I was just me.

Weeknights after I put Zack to bed, I'd sit at the kitchen table and do my work and enjoy the hush of the house, the television dark for the first time in years, since Chris wasn't there to turn it on. I'd grown up in a house where the kitchen radio was always on, then lived with roommates who always had music playing, then married Chris, who felt the TV noise was a good constant companion. I felt guilty for enjoying the silence because somehow that meant I was pushing my marriage even further away, but it was liberating anyway. At night at the table, with my stacks of manuscripts around me and that quiet spot in my mind, I felt focused and industrious, as if I had tidied up my messy life and put it into those neat little piles.

Mornings were a little less orderly. I'd get up when Zack awoke at 5:45 and take him downstairs to feed him breakfast, while I nursed the coffee that I needed to get me started. Then I'd take him back upstairs with me into the bathroom so I could hop in the shower, trying to wash my hair or shave my legs at the speed of light, while entertaining Zack at the same time. We'd play hide-and-seek with the shower curtain, or we'd slap the curtain to make the water droplets jump. This part of the morning routine reminded me every single day that I was now a single mom, and I felt achingly alone. Once out of the shower, it was back downstairs to station Zack safely in his ExerSaucer so he could watch *Sesame Street* and I could blow-dry my hair and put on my makeup while I ran up and down the stairs in various states of undress to keep tabs on him and Bert and Ernie & Co. Promptly at 8 a.m. Zack's nanny, Sezi—upbeat, cheerful, and seemingly unfazed by the chaos in the basement and in my relationship with Chris—would come in the door and head directly to Zack to lavish him with hugs and kisses. I would give Zack a final squeeze and shoot out the door, heading to the subway, falling into the rhythm of the week, one day at a time.

But I dreaded Friday nights, which set me apart from the rest of the world. During the week cashiers and coworkers constantly referred to the coming weekend—"It's almost Humpday"; "Just two more days to go"—counting down the hours until they could be released into the freedom of two days off. I felt trapped by weekends, tied as I was to the house due to the cold weather and the realities of a toddler's schedule. Zack's early rising, three meals, two snacks, two naps, and early bedtime defined the shape and schedule of each day, permitting us only short sorties into the neighborhood, a neighborhood where none of my friends lived. On weeknights

I was busy with work; on weekends I was busy with nothing, and couldn't even remember what I'd done for pleasure before Chris and I were married. I had no hobbies, no outside interests; I didn't watch TV or listen to music, and I didn't have the attention span for movies or books anymore. I would waste two or three free hours surfing the Internet, drinking wine and trying to avoid feeling the dullness and depression that were creeping into my psyche. I'd mindlessly fill online shopping carts and abandon them, or search for words on Text Twist until I had replaced that feeling of anxiety that was always present with a flattened boredom. But despite my best efforts to numb my senses, there were many nights when I'd curl up on the couch for a long cry, wondering how many days in a row I could keep on feeling so empty.

One weekend I decided to try to take a break from this sad monotony, and Zack and I headed down to my brother Gregg's place outside Philadelphia. I love being at Gregg and Melissa's house, filled as it is with Melissa's big, welcoming spirit and Gregg's no-frills, no-nonsense demeanor—as well as all the delicious snack foods I normally don't allow myself that are tucked away in every cabinet. I feel a hundred percent at ease with them, free to be in whatever mood I am at the time, and I can talk to them about anything. Gregg and I are close, in an indefinable way not created by long phone calls or constant e-mails, but rather by a deep trust; I feel my connection to my family most strongly through my brothers. And feeling connected to something, anything, was what I needed now.

Gregg and Melissa's three dogs made every arrival a coronation, a lunging, rumbling wagfest that was the opposite of walking into my silent house. Just minutes after Zack and I arrived, I could feel myself relaxing into the easy comfort of being in a house full of people, all of them wanting to spend some time with Zack, hold him, make him laugh. And Zack is a child who thrives on attention, who was performing for crowds before he could even crawl.

He pulled all the pots and pans out of a cabinet and spread them around the kitchen floor, making music of the clatter. He found a box of cereal on a low shelf and sat right down on the floor, stuffing his chubby toddler hand into the box and feeding himself. Upstairs, he and I played around on the guest room bed, rolling back and forth and giggling. Zack was aiming to impress me; he got a glint in his eye, rolled over and over and over, and—ack! Before I could get to him he rolled right off the high bed, bonking himself on the night table and giving himself a big lump over his right eye. I scooped him up and rocked him as he cried, soothing him. I calmed him, feeling calm myself, musing that all of this dailiness-of-life with a child—the bumps and bruises, the snacks and naps—was so much easier to handle with other bodies in the house. I tipped so easily into a crisis when I was alone, reeling as I still was from the grief of what was gone. Parenting is hard stuff, and it needs a witness, I thought, not for the first time since Chris had left. Not being able to share Zack's small moments with someone on a daily basis was feeling like one of the greatest holes in my life.

After Zack was safely ensconced in the crib that night, Melissa and I settled into an epic conversation about what was happening with Chris and me. She peppered me with questions: When did I first know this was happening? What did Chris say when he started the conversation? What did *I* say? Did I think there was any chance we would get back together? We talked for three or four hours, over many glasses of wine. I kept waiting, hoping, for that nice, fuzzy detachment that three or so glasses of wine can offer, but I felt stone-cold sober as I walked Melissa through everything I was feeling: the loss, the grief, the confusion, the total emptiness, the financial panic, all of it. I told her everything I thought I knew about why Chris felt he had to leave me. He had told me some things himself, I said. And so I shared the story of the Christmas card he'd handed me a few weeks before.

Chris and I had given each other Christmas presents, exchanging them awkwardly under the bright light of the kitchen lamp one random weeknight. I hadn't intended to buy him a gift, even though it felt strange not to. But I had been in a bookstore shopping for Christmas cards, and I'd stumbled across a blank book with a beautiful quotation printed on the cover that had stopped me in my tracks. The words really spoke to me about Chris and where I thought he was in his attempts to get answers in his life, but after I bought the book, I hid it in a drawer, feeling like maybe it was too personal a gift to be giving a man who was leaving me, and definitely feeling that I didn't know what any of the rules were anymore. But when I came home one December night when he had been at the house with Z, there was Chris with a huge wrapped present sitting on the kitchen table and a tentative smile on his face. I said, "Oh, I . . ."

He said, "I know, I know, it's weird, but I wanted to get you something."

I said, "Me, too. I have something for you, but I didn't wrap it. I wasn't sure I should get you anything."

I ran upstairs and found the notebook, still in the bag from the store, and I brought it downstairs and handed it to him.

"It's kind of personal," I said. "But I thought it made sense for you. And for me, too."

He took the notebook out of the bag and read what was emblazoned on the cover in tight rows of ocean blue type against a black background. It was this quote from Rainer Marie Rilke, one of my favorite poets:

> Have patience with everything unresolved in your heart and try to love the questions themselves as if they were locked rooms or books written in a very foreign language. Don't search for the answers, for they could not be given you now, because you would not be able to live them. And the point is to live everything. Live the questions now. Perhaps, then, someday far in the future, you will gradually, without even noticing it, live your way into the answer.

I had written the quote down for myself on a piece of paper and put it into my wallet after I had bought the book for him, since the words suddenly seemed to relate totally to my life as well. I stood across the table from Chris, holding my breath as he read it, wondering why I was making myself vulnerable to him like this. When he finished reading it, he looked up at me, nodding, with soft eyes, and said, "Thank you." I exhaled.

"I got you a book, too," he said. I tore the wrapping paper off my present to reveal a gigantic volume of *New Yorker* cartoons. I had read the magazine cover to cover every week for years, and had always shown Chris my favorite cartoons so we could laugh about them together: a man on the phone looking at his datebook and saying, "Tuesday's no good for me, either. How about never? Is never good for you?"; or two elephants standing in a field, one of them saying, "Does this field make my butt look big?" I even used the cartoons to express complicated things about our relationship, like the one that showed a couple in bed, both reading, the man saying to his wife, "Sometimes I close my eyes and pretend that someone else is denying me sex." Chris and I had laughed knowingly about that one.

"Wow, thanks," I said, paging through the volume. Then Chris handed me a card.

In the thirteen years we'd been together, Chris had been buying me the goofiest cards. Ones with dogs, and punchlines with exclamation points, or cartoon characters with oversize teeth and pithy observations. I'm an introspective, emo kind of gal myself, and so I tended to hand-make valentines or write out bits of poetry on blank cards. But since Chris has always prized his own "silliness," I had gotten used to receiving anniversary cards in primary colors. And so I was surprised when I opened the envelope he'd handed me to find a plain ivory note card embossed with flowers. And even more surprised when I opened the card and saw that it had no preprinted message, just Chris's angular, uneven handwriting. I could feel him standing and staring at me as I started to read it, and the room suddenly felt too small. As I read the first line, my breath caught in my throat and I had to turn away from him to finish reading the note, not able to let him see what my face might show.

> *Stacy,*
>
> *I will always be your friend and I will always be Zack's father, and so I hope someday you will be able to forgive me. I have to try to become the man I am meant to be. I will never forget the love we shared. It will stay with me forever.*
>
> *Love,*
> *Chris*

No, no, no, no, noooo! I felt myself recoiling in my mind, and I bit down on my lip to try to keep from crying. It was so painful to get such a beautiful note from him, a note filled with honesty and love. It seemed impossibly cruel that he was able to find words for sentiments like these only now, as he was walking away from me.

I turned around with tears in my eyes and begged him: "You can't do this! You can't give me a card like this! You can't show me that you are the man I know you are, the man I always knew you were when we met"—generous and loving and big-hearted, and not the resentful man that he had become in the last few years—"and then tell me that the only way you can become that person is by leaving me!" I sat down at the kitchen table under the bright hanging light and put my head down on my crossed arms and cried. Chris just stood there, hands in his pockets, staring down at the ground.

And now here I was telling this whole story to Melissa a few months later. "I hope he's right," I said as I walked back into the kitchen with Melissa to refill our glasses. "I hope he finds out who he was meant to be and lives it. It's the only thing that will make all of this okay."

Melissa was at the sink, rinsing a plate, as I finished this thought. She stopped cold and put down the plate and looked up at me and said, practically yelling at me, "Stacy, *where* is your anger? I mean, come on, I know you're a big thinker and you can explain anything, but are you even *human?*"

Her outburst stopped me short. Was I a freak? I know I'm a ru-
minator, always tinkering around in what other people do and why,
but why was that not "human"? To want to understand how my
husband could just walk out on me and our son? I wanted, I *needed,*
to get inside his head and see what was so impossible for him to
tolerate in our life that he believed he had to get out of our marriage
to survive. He was my best friend, the person who knew me better
than anyone else in the world. Why didn't people understand that
that was a very hard thing to give up? Melissa was angry at Chris the
way I'd been angry at my friend's husband when they were struggling
in their marriage; Melissa didn't have to know what it felt like to be
living in this amorphous In Between.

"Uhh, I don't know where my anger is," I offered in a small voice.
"I'm just trying to get through this, and feel okay about it. I'm angry
sometimes." I had been angry that night when Chris gave me the
card; for a split second, I'd felt indignation rip through me. But the
anger had been washed away instantly by a flood of grief, grief that
I still loved him and that clearly part of him still loved me and yet,
somehow, we weren't going to make it anyway.

I didn't think I could take that love and just stuff it down inside
me, or wave a magic wand and turn it all into anger. I needed to see
why Chris felt like he was dying in our marriage to able to break up
with compassion—in the same way that understanding why Gregg
and Melissa supported Bush had helped me interview the President.
But that night at the sink with Melissa, I so much wanted to borrow
her certainty. Her tone made me feel like there was a grand prize
that I had forgotten to look for, that maybe I had the winning ticket
tucked away somewhere. But as I thought about it, I couldn't imagine what I would cash it in for. I simply couldn't believe that anger
was the prize.

But I did get angry sometimes. Really, really angry. In the weeks
after the house started to take in water, when Chris and I were trying

to figure out how to handle the crisis, I had spoken to some lawyers to get counsel on whether we could sue the people who'd sold us the house. We'd discovered that aside from what the next-door-neighbor knew, the real estate agency that had represented the sellers was also aware of the house's flooding problem. In talking with various lawyers, I discovered I had made some dumb mistakes in the closing process, such as using the house inspector that was recommended by the seller's broker. Chris was being a jerk about it, telling me that the lawyer who had represented us in closing should have caught those mistakes, that the lawyer wasn't any good, had never been any good. Of course, I was the one who had found that lawyer. I was the one who had handled the closing. I had done the whole deal for buying the house: figuring out how much we could afford, making the bid, getting the mortgage, figuring out how to scrape together the money to cover our cash shortfall in making the down payment, booking the movers and the painters. And now I was the one who was trying to figure out how to get out of this mess without our losing everything. Chris's criticisms felt like attacks against me. I could feel my blood starting to boil as he sat there on the sofa, being angry at the world, and insinuating that he would have done things better or differently.

I lashed out at Chris, cursing him for his attitude, especially considering that he had done nothing—nothing!—to make this deal happen. Soon we were in the familiar ruts of marital discord. Chris's take: I'm a know-it-all; I'm hostile and unhappy; I don't let him do anything; I'm hateful; he's aggrieved. My take: He's a discontent; he's useless; if I ask him to help me I get punished by his misery; he can't function in the real world; he can't *deal*. I am holding Zack on my hip as this familiar fight is taking its course, and he's started to cry. Chris reaches over and takes him out of my arms, and as he backs away from me to take the baby upstairs, he fires off his final words: "You are crazy and this is why I can't stand to be with you!"

I screamed at him as he was walking upstairs, "I hate you! And when you leave you will get nothing! Nothing! Not a penny of my money!" I was bent over at the waist, so that I could propel as much volume and power into my screaming as I could, using every cell in my body to attempt to erase him and this terrible feeling of being unseen, misunderstood, of having my good intentions turned around and thrown in my face. I screamed until I was depleted, and when I stopped, I was trembling. I plopped down on the sofa, spent.

I was humiliated by my loss of control, and by the fact that I'd implied that the money meant anything at all in this mess. I tried to forgive myself, understanding that I was trying to take something—anything—away from him, to find a way to stand up for myself and say "I reject *you*" in a way that was deeper, bigger, wider than his deciding to walk out on me. But I could see that my rage wasn't going to let me do that, because as I sat on the sofa, my self-righteousness was replaced with disgust. This can't be who I am, I told myself.

Anger like that has its seductions. The times I was really angry at Chris, I felt as if the anger hid everything I didn't want to see or feel, just as when, as a little girl, I would clean my exploded-closet of a bedroom by getting on my hands and knees and pushing all the discarded clothes and belts and shoes on the floor under the bed. Of course my parents were going to look there, of course I knew I was still going to have to put everything away in its proper place, but it was such a fast and easy solution it was impossible to resist. And anger is the same thing. In the white heat of anger, I feel right, I *am* right! He's a dumb bastard and I am the queen of the desert! But after the anger, I inevitably come crashing down and have to face all the confusing feelings that a breakup leaves on the shore after the tide of love has ebbed: *I am to blame, I am worthless, I will never be loved again.*

Once, in the middle of the night, during yet another relentless rainstorm after Chris had moved out, I heard the dread sound of drip-drip-drip coming from one of the leaks on the third floor. I'd had roofers in to fix the leak, but they hadn't succeeded. When I stepped into the cursed guest room to review the scene, I saw the sodden towels that were already on the floor under the drip, but I also saw another puddle in the middle of the room. And then I realized that our fat cat, Stumpy, had peed all over the photographs that lay on the floor in messy piles after having been rescued from the flooding basement. They were precious images of my high school and college years, not saved in any digital file. I sank to my knees and started separating the photographs, sorting them into piles of ruined and not-ruined ones. I tried to gently pry the damaged photos apart, to try to save these images of my younger self, the girl who thought she could make anything happen in her life, the girl who thought she could protect herself with her fierce will and bottomless drive. I cried for her, for all she had believed, and I was devastated by the knowledge that everything I had hoped was true about life was false: there was no way to create your own destiny. Fate did that for you instead.

I found myself filling up with a fury that had to be directed somewhere. Why was I was the one stuck with the aging cat and the broken-down house and the full burden of the mortgage? And Stumpy was Chris's cat; Chris should have taken him when he moved out.

We had adopted two furry gray kittens the week we'd returned from our honeymoon, and MeMe, the girl cat, had been "my" cat. Thinking about how sweet and tender Chris had been two years before when he'd had to tell me she had died now made me unspeakably bereft. After a wedding, I had run into a deli to buy some beer and he'd gone home and found MeMe lying on the kitchen floor. As I left the deli, I saw Chris standing there in the pouring rain in his tuxedo, his hands crammed into his pockets, a look on his face I'll never forget: love and sadness and responsibility. He'd come to tell me so that I wouldn't walk in, unprepared, and see her cold and dead. We'd walked home, his arm around my shoulders, me crying into his chest. MeMe was gone and now the man who'd known her funny, girlish mews and little paw dances was gone, too. I feared I'd never be able to stop making the list of things only Chris knew, I'd never stop feeling dizzy at the parts of me that were being taken away.

I got the phone and went back to the third floor, calling Chris even though it was 2 a.m., my hands shaking because I was so angry. It just had to be his fault that everything was gone. My voice echoed in the empty room as I screamed at him, tears streaming down my face: "Why do you get to leave it all behind! Why am I the one with everything on my hands! Your son! This goddamn leaking house! And the cat, who's peeing all over everything! It's bad enough you leave me. But you just get to walk away? From everything? And leave me with this whole mess?" Chris tried to calm me down, assured me he'd take the cat, but I knew it wouldn't be enough. Nothing would ever be enough to make up for what I was feeling.

After I'd hung up the phone and put fresh towels under the infernal drips and washed my face, wiping off the tears and the dust, I stared in the mirror for ten minutes, looking at my sad eyes, the hollows under them, the blotchy skin, the way my mouth turned down. It was 3:45 a.m., and I would have to be up with the baby in about two hours. I felt empty and sick, gutted from the screaming and the crying, and ugly inside and out. I had to like *something* about myself, but in that moment, I couldn't think of anything. Living in my anger in that way had erased it all.

Melissa wasn't alone in looking for my anger. As I started telling more and more people that Chris and I had separated, I was overwhelmed by the number of people who wanted to warm their hands in the heat of my rage. Their instinct was a convivial one, a way of joining me and supporting me, but I didn't understand at all why people had a reflexive instinct to link arms with me in outrage, to fan the flames of my anger and assure me of my "rightness."

Friends and strangers alike were inspired to do their own forensic studies on my relationship, with a breathtakingly similar methodology. Almost everyone asked me the same three questions:

"Is it because you married so young?"

"Is it because you made all the money?"

"Is it because you worked too much?"

I know people meant well, but these questions told me everything I never, ever wanted to know about how they saw my relationship. At first I tried to beat these reasons away, taking each as it was offered and trying to flick it away like a Frisbee. I'd remind people that only in New York City is getting married at twenty-five considered crazily young—the average age of a woman getting married in America is 26.5! And Chris liked my money just fine! We spent it together. And he made plenty of his own money. It's not like I emasculated him! (*Or did I? Did I? Have to file that one away to think about later, when I'm alone in the dark staring up at the bedroom ceiling praying for sleep.*) And as far as working too much goes? My goodness, no! Chris had always needed a lot of alone time. After all, he was working on side projects that he wanted to be the main event in his life, important stuff. It was good I wasn't always around, mooning over him and wishing he wanted to go curtain shopping with me.

I gave a slightly different answer each time I was asked, but the weird, disconnected sense of culpability I felt was always the same, as if the questioner were pointing a finger at me.

I'd gone from being a woman of definite opinions to being a nervous, uncertain little girl, defending actions and pathways taken that I shouldn't have needed to defend—that the old me would never have stooped to defend. But now, whatever anyone offered me, I would feel an automatic flinch and I'd have to look at whatever reason they were holding up to me and think: "Are they right? Do they know more than I do? Did I do this to myself?"

And then there was the question that, in one form or another, every single person asked—which, I learned, means it's the question that counts the most:

"Did you have any idea?"

"Were you surprised?"

"Was this out of the blue? Or did you . . . ?"

What goes unsaid in that last iteration is ". . . know you were having a hard time? Did you know you were in a bad marriage? Did you know you weren't going to make it?"

Did you see it coming?

Bit by bit, I started to realize what was happening. People were trying to puzzle out what had led to the end of my marriage in the same way I was, and they wanted to know what I knew. But not because they wanted to know if I could have saved my marriage: they were asking these questions because they wanted to save *their* marriages.

At first the fact that people had seemed to have instant sympathy for me kept me from seeing that this was what these exchanges were actually about—them, not me. I desperately wanted to be comforted and assured that I was the Good Guy. But after a while I started to feel nauseated by their comfort, as if I'd eaten too much cotton candy. A lot of these people were essentially strangers, who'd never met Chris, who didn't even know *me* that well. For all they knew I was a screaming shrew, an unabashed adulterer, a cold, dead fish. How could they know whether I was right or wrong, how could they know who was to blame? With each new conversation about my separation, my vision became more clear: I could see the questioner trying to put all the pieces regarding the end of my marriage into place; he or she barely even needed to talk to me to come to a conclusion. Asking me these questions and steering me toward their own answers was a way for people to keep what was happening in my life at arm's length, just in case divorce proved contagious.

But divorce is no virus; it's lung cancer: We live in a world where people believe that *somebody* has to have caused a divorce. Someone smoked those cigarettes, was the unbearable wife, the unfaithful husband; someone worked too hard, nagged too much, didn't like sex enough—whatever your personal anxieties about your own relationship are, feel free to project them onto me. My divorce has to be somebody's fault, because making that so means the rest of the world can go around believing that Forever After remains a viable promise, no matter how high the numbers of failed marriages climb. People didn't need to know my story, because they already had The Story in their heads, the simple narrative arc that apparently defines every single divorce story in America: "till death do you part" turns to "due to parting, you battle to the death." A promise is being stolen, dammit, and someone's gotta pay.

But the details matter. The life I'd lived was still alive in the details. The person I had become was created by those details, thirteen years of becoming me that I did not want to give up. When I found myself faced yet again with the same questions (that are, confoundingly, personal and impersonal simultaneously) I had to bite my cheek sometimes to keep myself from screaming. *This story may sound familiar to you,* I would think, wishing I felt brave and strong enough to speak it aloud, *but it was mine once.*

People wanted me to be angry at Chris, but I was starting to get angry at them.

I didn't want my marriage to be so easily reducible to a cliché or, worse, a statistic. I wanted people to help me honor my marriage. I didn't want to tie it neatly and attach it to a brick and then toss it to the bottom of the river along with everyone else's.

At first it had been tempting to accept the easy commiseration people were offering, I needed company so badly. But I started to realize that in doing so, in letting others shape my story, I would be emptying my marriage of its contents. And that would mean emptying myself as well. I had to find a way to hold on to the best things I'd ever thought about myself and not give them away. I had to imagine that woman I wanted to be on the other side of all this—calm, whole, forgiving, healed, wise—and keep her image in my head and walk toward her. I couldn't get distracted by what other people were trying to solve for their own lives; I needed to stay focused on whatever was true for me. And I would have to learn to separate myself from whatever Chris was trying to solve in his life, too. He didn't belong to me anymore.

But we did still share Zack, which made it difficult for me to learn where to start putting up boundaries. I kept stumbling over them when they appeared in places that surprised me, and I'd feel the cutting hurt all over again.

On an early-summer Saturday evening, I'd invited Paul and Marnie and their son, Luke, who was six months younger than Zack, over to the house for a backyard playdate, so that the two boys could crawl around on the lawn. Zack and I started playing a game we called "Boiiing!" that entailed my lying on my back and pushing him away from me with my feet and followed by his falling backward in a fit of laughter. After a few rounds of this, Zack started screaming in pain. Eventually I figured out that he had hurt his right foot; he couldn't stand on it, and couldn't stop crying. I tried to ice it; more screaming. I called the pediatrician, who predicted a diagnosis of "toddler fracture" and said he'd need an X-ray. So I strapped Zack into his stroller and the five of us headed out to the local emergency room nine blocks away.

I called Chris en route to tell him we were heading to the hospital. Judging from the background noise that enveloped his voice, I'd interrupted a boozy outing with his friends. As I pushed the stroller as fast as I could, I detailed what happened. Chris paused and then said, "You don't need me there, do you?" I was utterly dumbfounded, and disgusted, by his reaction.

"Umm, no, I guess not," I said, snapping the phone closed and dropping it into the stroller pocket without saying goodbye, when what I really wanted to do was scream into the phone: "Your son may have broken his foot! Your son is going to the emergency room! How can you not care?" Of course, I'd also wanted company in this terrifying rite of passage. I'd thought Chris would want to be there, too, even though Chris had been trying to tell me for months he didn't want this life.

Marnie and Paul could feel my panic at doing this alone, and so they trooped into the ER with me. But after we'd spent twelve long, slow minutes in the packed waiting room, not a single person had approached me and my still screaming child. Marnie and Paul conferred with each other, and then took charge. Paul told me I was going to go to a different hospital in Manhattan, told me which one, and called a car service. Then Paul took Luke home and Marnie came with Zack and me. I was so grateful not to have to do this alone. In the car, Zack nestled on my lap, sleepy after his panic, my arms wrapped around him. My cell phone rang; it was Chris. I couldn't talk to him, I was so undone and confused and angry. Marnie answered instead, and told him where we were going. After she hung up, she handed the phone back to me and told me he was coming to the hospital. The two of us started to cry together, holding hands, both of us feeling the terror of being young mothers.

When we got to the second hospital, Zack and I were admitted right away. We settled into the sterile waiting room, bathed in fluorescent lights, Zack sitting on my lap and playing with my earrings. Chris showed up about forty minutes later, bringing a dark mood with him, lost as he was in his own emotional stew. Marnie and I exchanged glances and she scooted out the door, back home to her own baby. Chris sat down and asked me all the right questions about how Zack was doing, but he was unable to look at me. When we were shown into an examining room, he stared at the floor during the entire exam and didn't address the doctor once. I was flustered by his stony presence and he didn't even interrupt to point out that I had asked the doctor to examine the *wrong foot* until after the doctor had left the room. When he told me, I had to get up and chase the doctor down the hall to explain my mistake.

Hours later, after the X-rays showed a fractured bone in Zack's foot and the doctor applied a teeny white cast, Chris and I shared a cab back to Brooklyn. We were exhausted from the ordeal, and from the pressure of being miserable together. And so while I held on to our sleeping son and cradled the little cast on his foot as the taxi hurtled down the highway along the black river, Chris unleashed all his frustration and rage on me—for the night in the hospital, yes, and apparently for every wrong moment in our marriage. He lavishly described how horrible I was, how selfish, how everything in life was always about me, and that's why he had to get away from me. His diatribe went on for minutes; I just stared at the dark and shining river, my heart thumping, and tried to breathe through his rant.

When he finished, I turned to him and gathered my wits, setting aside the temptation to blast him. Instead I drew on the quiet spot I'd discovered in my head since Chris had moved out, that place of calm that was bottomless like the river, and I said to him, my voice shaking through tears, "I am sorry that is how you see me and how you experience me. And I know that you do. But I know in my heart that I am a generous and loving person." It was the turning point, the moment I realized that I didn't have to meet anger with anger, that I didn't have to marinate in all the terrible things he wanted me to feel. That I could choose to let go of the idea of scoring a point (when, for so many years I'd thought my favorite thing in the world was to be right, to win!) and instead focus on protecting myself. I also could see clearly that Chris was lashing out at me partly because leaving me hadn't cleared him of his responsibilities to me and Zack, but I knew that whatever anger he was feeling about that was for Chris to deal with on his own.

In that moment of vulnerability, of being open to his anger, I sensed a strength in myself that I knew I could trust.

After I got home and laid my sleeping son gently in his crib and crawled into bed, I cried and cried. I felt so lost, as a mother, as a wife. How could it be that Chris had come to hate me so much? But at the same time, I felt I had found a little pearl in all the pain I'd been through, and I could feel it glowing in my chest. For the first time since Chris had left, I had an inkling of who I might be without him.

✷   ✷   ✷

I was learning that divorce is not a fight, it is a funeral. It is the death of a shared dream, a fatal fall after a beautiful leap of faith. It is tempting to believe we can learn something from other people's divorces, but we can't, because we do not live those marriages. We can't protect ourselves with other people's pain, because what we think we learn through them won't help us when it's time to meet our own. I thought of what my mother had told me about her marriage to my father. I thought of all there must be that I still didn't know about what had happened between Chris and me, even now, a full year after he'd told me he wanted to go. I didn't want people to help me slam the door shut, I wanted people to help me close the door gently.

I was at the Old Town Bar with my guy friends at some point after Chris was gone, drinking beers and talking about the particulars of the divorce—the division of the house and the money and the stuff. Chris and I weren't suing each other and so we didn't have to follow the state's rules for division of shared assets; we'd decided to try to come to an agreement. In fact, a few weeks before he moved out, Chris had said one night as we each smoked a cigarette in the frozen backyard, "You negotiate for a living. I don't want to fight you. You tell me what you think makes sense." I mentioned to my friends that maybe I was going to be able to give Chris more than we'd originally agreed in those backyard chats. Paul, a charming caricature of old-school, forties-era masculinity, told me he thought this was a stupid idea. "Be strong," he said. "Stay pissed. Don't get soft about him. Give him nothing." It was a classic expression of Paul's humor (and his romantic idea of strength), but I knew I couldn't stick to the advice, even though Paul kept repeating it the whole cab ride home. The truth was that nothing would be able to keep me from feeling the brutal loss that had nothing to do with the house or the money or the stuff. If I managed to tuck that loss away and hide it behind self-righteousness or a made-up story about Chris's worthlessness, it would come back at me, turning me into that woman with the rose-colored diamond, my loss all anyone could feel in me when they met me.

I could see in my friends' and my parents' eyes how hard it was for them not to be angry at Chris, especially when I stood before them sobbing about all I'd lost. How do you comfort someone in that kind of pain? It's normal to want to feel something, *anything*, else, rather than be that close to raw grief. I could see how hard it was for friends not to try to move me to a place that hurt less, where they thought they could help me be sure, confident, where I might feel strong for a minute, even if it was false strength.

Zack's second birthday party in August was where I watched my friends and family wage this struggle together, all at once. I had decided to invite Chris—of course! He was Zack's father!—but the rest of the invitation list was made up of my family and the people whom Chris had considered *my* friends. When Chris came into the party, I saw my father's pale blue eyes flash with anger, even though I'd warned him that Chris would be there. I loved Dad for walking toward Chris just a minute or two later after he'd regained his equilibrium and offering his hand; I know what that cost him. My mother already knew what having Chris's presence accepted by my family meant to me, so she approached Chris and the two of them launched into one of their typical lengthy rants against politicians (or dumb people or bad television or whatever had teed them off).

All the others approached Chris in their own time. My brother Scott said to me, "It's kind of strange, you know, having him here."

"I know," I said. "It's kind of strange for me, too, but it helps me." And he nodded. That was enough for him. And it was everything I needed.

I knew that my anger would surface from time to time, but that I didn't have to embrace it. If Chris and I were able to link arms even as we were letting go of marriage, we could both agree that everything we had done wrong in the past would matter less in shaping our lives apart than how we were going to do the right things as we moved forward. I didn't care all that much about the furniture or the money (though Chris was right, I did have very definite opinions about how to divide everything up), but I did want to protect the emotional currency I'd earned in my marriage; I wanted to keep everything I'd learned. And I wanted to be able to pull up some of those memories and share them with Chris from time to time, to know that it wasn't all gone forever and ever. I wanted a connected breakup. That, I thought, was the right way to honor thirteen years of my life and all that those years had brought me.

I knew that not clinging to anger was going to give me my best shot at seeing myself clearly, maybe for the first time in my life. To be me: just me, wholly me, life-size me, okay with me. I was sure that was the prize I wanted.

6

You Are Not Alone, and, Yes, You Are Totally Alone

In my darkest moments of grief, my body sought low ground. The crying often started in my bedroom, after twenty endless minutes of my staring up at the ceiling, waiting for answers to how I was supposed to cope with a falling-down house and a falling-apart life. Tears slipped out of the corners of my eyes, dripping into my ears. Then a sob would break from my chest, and I would get up and head downstairs so as not to wake my son in the next room. Sitting on the couch, I wept, my elbows on my knees; then my body would list until I was lying down in the red sofa's embrace. But the grief was heavier still, and I would roll onto the floor, arms around a pillow, holding on to it as if it were a life raft and I adrift at sea.

On the worst nights I always ended up in the kitchen, the farthest point in the house from my son's bedroom, except for the unusable basement. I'd start out sitting on the floor leaning against the cabinets, but I always ended up lying on the floor in front of the stove, trying to keep the sound of my racking sobs from drifting upstairs and waking Zack. Despite my best efforts, I woke him more than once. I'd quickly pack up the accordion of despair that had opened inside me to run upstairs and hold him, tell him that we were safe, we were fine, everything was fine.

The kitchen floor became my touchstone, the place my body took me when I didn't know where else to go to try to get away from the pain. The nights I ended up lying there, I'd sometimes find myself staring at the crumbs under the stove as I cried, wondering how they got there and how I should go about getting them out. Part of my brain was hurting a hurt so deep I felt like I might be swallowed up whole into the ink spot—and yet, another part of my brain was doing light housekeeping. Dust was gathering, time was passing, my life was still being lived, and some kind of healing was happening, even though I felt I was barely surviving it all when I wasn't at work, where I could embrace the comfort of routines, of being the one in charge.

At those moments in the kitchen, I was in full submission, a circumstance I had spent my whole life furiously fighting to avoid. Action was my anodyne, whether I was trying to keep the volatile energies generated in my childhood home from igniting into a flashover or I was getting a magazine off the ground with less time, people, or money than generally assumed to be necessary. I could suppress all reasonable needs for months at a time, driving myself into the ground so that I could drive myself toward the goal.

But in the past few years, with the help of a wise and good therapist, I was learning that needs and vulnerabilities weren't the same things as weaknesses; I was unwinding ironclad coping devices, so that I could let in the truth that the safe place I'd always imagined I would get to in life didn't really exist. Intellectually, I completely understood this, but emotionally I knew that I still clung to the idea that being strong makes you strong.

And now here I was, facedown on the kitchen floor for perhaps the third, fourth, fifth time since Chris had moved out. I was feeling my fragility in my bones and I could not deny it. I let myself feel how truly afraid I was. I was ready to ask for help; I was ready to beg for it. *I get it now! I am human and weak and vulnerable and I can't control what's coming my way. I submit. I see my smallness. I am not in charge. I need help. I need help.*

Please help me, someone.

But no army of friends, I realized, was going to be able to meet me here in my alone.

How could I not have known this would be so hard? Why was it that the only thoughts I'd ever had about divorce until I went through it myself had involved fighting and affairs and money and parents trying (and failing) to get along for the benefit of their kids? I was poleaxed by how difficult this all was, to have to rebuild my entire sense of self from this point right here: me lying on a kitchen floor, trying to forgive myself for not being able to breathe because I am so afraid.

My friends could love me but they couldn't fix me. All the support and sympathy in the world doesn't help in the painstaking work of starting over. And unfortunately my friends also couldn't untangle my strained finances, straighten out my legal issues, or find me a plumber who would solve the flooding problem. Yes, they could give me company and comfort, but the times I was the most alone and most afraid, they were cozy in bed with their own partners.

Now that I had decided I was weak enough to take whatever help I could get, I tried to think of what my friends *could* do for me. At the very least, I thought they would help me rebuild my decimated social life, but even that wasn't wholly possible. After Chris and I broke up, suddenly many of my old friends no longer fit—or, to be more truthful, I no longer fit them. What's a Saturday night couple date with a single mom? Turns out, it's nothing.

All the couples who'd had had children at the same time Chris and I did were each doing the I'm-dancing-as-fast-as-I-can tango, trying to keep their own marriages connected and afloat in the pressure-cooker environment of life after baby. The truth was that I hadn't been seeing them very much since our babies were born. We had managed one or two get-togethers, and we had the photos of all the babies lined up on different sofas as proof, but as the babies went from darling lumps to high-octane toddlers, the get-togethers had all but ended. Also, a few of my friendships had been anchored with the men in the couples—with Charlie, whom I'd known since I moved to New York; with Paul, for whom I'd been a groomsman in his wedding—and apparently my having had a baby proved that I was not really one of the guys, and changed the nature of our friendships.

My single friends had been busy living their own lives during the time I was married and procreating and getting all domestic in Brooklyn, thank you very much, so they didn't have ready-made places in their lives for me to step into. Alix, she of the old Melrose Place dinners, works in the all-consuming, globe-trotting fashion world, and Eric, my former college roommate, is gay; I didn't have the proper credentials to join either community. My midweek dinners out with them and other single friends remained a mainstay in my life, a time when I could unload about what I was going through, while also feeling a little bit like my old self. But I was still trapped in those seemingly endless weekends.

Adding to my sense of dislocation was the geography of New York City. Chris and I had loved our house when we bought it, and hadn't thought much about the fact that it was in a developing neighborhood, far from our friends, because—of course, we were going to live here *together*. And in my married life, I was always having people over for dinner and a movie, or for parties. But now, on my own, I was tied to the house, financially and otherwise, and the house was neighborhoods away from where my mommy friends lived, so there were no impromptu playdates.

Feeling tethered to the house echoed how I felt weighed down by every decision I'd made, as if the thing I'd wanted were now dead-weight anchors pulling me underwater. I kept reaching back into the past, trying to select the first decision that led me to where I was. Was I being punished for having wanted a house? Was it moving to San Francisco because I just had to launch that design magazine that put our marriage on the path to failure? Wait, was marrying Chris actually the mistake? No, all of those decisions still seemed right, but my mind couldn't stop rooting around for the left turn that had taken me off my road to happiness. I was single, but not quite single; a mother, but no longer a wife; a homeowner who wanted desperately to escape her home. It was obvious to me that I had to set about finding new friends, but that only felt like another impossibly large task to add to my already formidable to-do list. And fixing the house remained Job One, because nothing else would move forward—not the separation, not the divorce, not finding a new place for me and Zack to live—until that was done.

I talked to seven or eight lawyers, and each scenario they painted sounded more awful than the last: since disclosure laws are vague, it would cost at least $60,000 to bring the case to trial, with no certainty that I'd win; it would be six months of paying the lawyers before the case would ever even make it to trial; and, worst of all, the only way to make a successful case was to declare the house uninhabitable and move out immediately. There was no way I could add any of this additional stress and uncertainty into my already stressful and uncertain situation, so I kept making phone calls, convinced I'd find another answer. I finally found a lawyer who handicapped the situation for me in straight cash terms: if I could fix the damage in the house for less than $100,000, I was more than likely going to recoup my expenses in the sale, since house prices were still climbing steeply in my neighborhood.

Done. Or at least doable. But I had no idea what it was going to cost to fix the house. I'd had a string of plumbers in to review the situation, a heating crew who replaced the ruined boiler and water heater, drainage-system crews, and hard-sell old guys with hair-sprayed side parts who were absolutely, positively certain that my waterlogged home was a haven for evil black mold. (I wanted to kick them for trying to take advantage of me, especially because they kept asking if I'd need to make this decision with "the man of the house.") Each expert could solve only one piece of the problem. Finally I got a referral for a contractor, an early-model De Niro type who scared me a little but knew the neighborhood and was able to explain how he would get the job done. He would tear up the ruined linoleum tile floor and the cement subfloor; bash out the walls from shoulder height down; install an impermeable membrane to protect the house from groundwater; install a new drainage system, new pumps, and a check valve to protect the house from the storm sewer's backflow; and install a stone floor, cement-board walls, and cast-iron heaters in the basement so that if water got in somewhere, the room's finish would not be damaged. He would not be able to get a check valve behind the drain in the stairwell that led up from the basement to the sidewalk because getting in front of that drain meant excavating the city street, and that would definitely blow my budget.

My contractor helpfully pointed out that I lived in the lower part of a neighborhood called Park Slope and so of course water was coming into the house, since I lived so far down the hill. In fact that's what the basements had originally been designed for a hundred years ago when my house was built, to take in water. *Gee, thanks for the historical perspective.* All I knew was I had been sold a three-story house with a finished basement, and I was going to sell a three-story house with a finished basement, come hell or . . . high water.

And so after months of consulting with lawyers and contractors and just a week after Chris moved out of the house, the basement floor was jack-hammered up and removed in gigantic concrete chunks. At least it was winter: the rain had turned to snow, so I had one less problem to worry about while all the demolition went on, laying a fine, ever-present dust over everything on the first floor. Chris promised to help with the renovation as much as possible, so I wouldn't be left with the whole of the burden, but he wasn't going to be the one managing the project, living in the dirt and turmoil, writing endless checks to the contractor, or figuring out where to find the money to pay for it all.

The work on the house was slow, and this added to my sense that nothing was moving ahead in my life. The basement had a complicated series of problems that overlaid each other, and each step unearthed new problems, like discovering after the floor was removed that the main waste outlet for the house was an ancient clay pipe that was cracked and leaking into the ground under the house. Getting used to being in charge of the house alone was slow work, too. Simple life tasks, like shoveling snow or moving the car in the morning on street-cleaning days to avoid a ticket, became laden with emotional weight. I'd have to leave the baby in the house alone for a few panicked minutes at a time. I could keep an eye on him through the living room window when I was shoveling, but eventually I gave up on the parking and just paid the weekly tickets, figuring I was buying myself some peace of mind.

The first time I went away on a business trip after Chris moved out, he came to stay with Zack in the house. My flight got delayed on the runway. The pilot powered down the engines and told us that we would be in an indefinite ground hold, so we were permitted to use our electronic devices. Everyone around me called their spouses, partners, boyfriends. I sat there looking at the phone in my hand and wondering who cared that I was stuck on a plane on a runway, a stack of manuscripts on my lap.

That stack of paper was with me wherever I went. If I got stuck in traffic in a cab, or was kept waiting at an appointment, or my lunch date was late, I always made good use of the time, getting down to business with my blue pen. It was a lot of work, but it kept me focused on the good fortune of having a great job and a great team in a field of work that is inherently social. I was essentially kept from drowning in solitude by my work at *Redbook*, the days filled with meetings and talking about photo shoots and writing cover lines, all interrupted by lots of laughter and truth-telling and digging around for the next great story to publish, a story that would reveal the complexities and joys and challenges of trying to build a life you love.

I discovered that the best way to handle all the pressure and the too many to-dos was to let my days take on a very consistent and definite rhythm. I settled into a routine for the first time in my life as a way of taking care of myself. My 10:00 p.m. bedtime became my new religion out of necessity, since Zack was still getting up at 5:45 a.m. and hitting the snooze button was no longer an option for me. I needed to sleep to keep my wits about me, and fortunately fate had sent me a child who slept through the night.

Another night, another round of crying, crumbling under the pressure. I got up off the sofa after the last ragged sobs had stopped and headed into the kitchen to get a paper towel. After I wiped the tears off my face, I turned the faucet on, running the paper towel under the cool water, wringing it out, and pressing it against my swollen eyes as I thought about how many manuscripts I had left to read that night. I thought ahead to how many more months it would be before the house was fixed. I thought about how many more months it would be before Chris and I had a separation agreement, let alone a divorce. I thought about my job, and how much I loved it, but that maybe it was too big, maybe I couldn't handle it all anymore. Maybe getting a different job would be the way to relieve some of the pressure on my life, but that was almost impossible to consider. There was nowhere to go with this line of thinking but back into tears. I slid slowly down the kitchen cabinets until I was sitting on the floor and I cried for all the things I did not know how to do and all the ways I did not know how to fix my life. And in a few minutes, here I was, again, in full surrender on the kitchen floor, with no one to see me waving the white flag.

Breathe in, breathe out. Breathe in, breathe out. I filled my lungs with air a few times. I listened to my breath. I had stopped crying. I was thinking about the people who sold me the house. I was thinking about the repairs the house needed. I thought about a life raising Zack on my own. I was afraid. I didn't feel up to the enormity of it all. I wanted to walk out the front door and never come back. Then a piece of the Rilke quote from the notebook I had given to Chris floated into my head:

> Don't search for the answers, for they could not be given you now . . . And the point is to live everything . . .

Live everything. Live this fear. I let myself fall into the fear, a fear so deep I knew that even my dearest friends wouldn't be able to find me when I was in it. The fear that I wouldn't be able to survive the terrible unraveling in my life and in my brain. The fear that I was falling apart into a million little pieces. The fear that I would cease to function, literally cease to exist. And I followed that fear, pulling aside the curtain in my mind, stepping into the void where my brain didn't even send me words, where it was just pain and agony.

Stepping into that fear led me to . . .

Right here. On my kitchen floor. Safe in my house. In one piece.

The fear that feels like it will swallow you whole can't actually swallow you whole.

Breathe in. Breathe out. Think that thought again, louder this time.

The fear that feels like it will swallow you whole can't actually swallow you whole.

All these months I'd been trying to keep from falling apart, from giving in to my fears, because I was afraid I would cease to exist, sink into a dark place in my head and never come back. But instead, what I found when I hit bottom was solid ground beneath me. And I was still in one piece. I thought about how I had been looking in the rearview mirror for the place Chris and I had taken a wrong turn, a turn I couldn't quite see. And I realized that here on the kitchen floor I had reached another turning point, and I hadn't seen this one coming, either.

✻   ✻   ✻

As winter gave way to spring, and the snow that had sat around in hulking piles on the sidewalks and rooflines started to melt, the house sprang new leaks: in the second-floor hallway, in the first-floor bathroom, pooling into the kitchen light fixture. I was now in the habit of walking the house in the wee hours of the morning, going from room to room, and floor to floor, listening for the evil little plink-plink-plinks that crawled up the back of my spine. I actually shook my fists at the heavens on more than one occasion, begging them to stop sending me rain. (It seemed like the right thing to do.) I called in the roofers again, and they found a few more breaches in the roof that I had been told was new when we bought the house. (It had never occurred to me to ask if the new roof was a good roof.) They patched the roof but many of the drips kept dripping. I started to look for new roofers.

But the basement was slowly shaping up, with all its new underpinnings and mechanics, and the walls rebuilt and painted. The slate tile floor, which was both practical and beautiful, had been laid, and the metal plates to cover the sump pumps in the corners of the room had been ordered. I was desperate to get the house on the market, but realistically we couldn't close the deal until January of the next year so that Chris and I wouldn't have to play a flip tax for selling less than two years after we'd bought it. I'd had to borrow tens of thousands of dollars from my parents (and was so lucky that they even had it to spare) and needed to be sure that I could pay them back when the deal was closed, and still be able to make a down payment on a home for Zack and me. I fantasized every day about living somewhere else. I prowled through the online real estate listings obsessively, trying to handicap how much apartment I would be able to afford—assuming that the house was fixed enough to hold its value and that Chris and I would get all of our money back out of it.

The night the first big spring rainstorm hit, I couldn't make myself stay in bed to wait for the sound of water somewhere in the house. Instead, I got up and went barefoot down into the almost-finished basement and stood sentry, facing down the drain outside the basement door that led to the staircase up to the sidewalk level in front of the house. I heard the sump pumps firing, drawing ground-water away from the house, and nothing was coming in from the two drains in the floor. Five minutes went by. Six, seven, eight, and the rain was still pounding on the house. Then a gray trickle slipped in under the door, very quickly turning into a gush. There was no point in panicking. I just grabbed the push broom and started push-ing the water toward the pumps, across the beautiful slate floor that wasn't going to be ruined by the water. I wanted to fill the entire staircase with cement and brick up the door with my bare hands to stop the water from coming in, but instead I stood there for more than an hour, pushing the broom, sweat dripping from my nose and my brow, escaping to a quiet part in my mind where the house was already sold and this wasn't my life anymore.

The next morning I called the good plumber and told him the basement had flooded again. He was disappointed. Neil Weiss was the owner of his business, and when I'd told him my story, he'd taken the time to come over to my house to look at the basement himself. That morning he came over again, and I told him about my fantasy of bricking up the door and filling the staircase with cement, but I said that I had a different idea, too. What if we just capped over the drain? It was there ostensibly to drain away any water that pooled in the stairwell from a rainstorm, but I pointed out that water pooling in the stairwell would be the least of my problems. Neil stood there with his hand on his chin, thinking. Finally he said, "Well, we could cap off the sewer inlet and then install a small sump pump there to take the water up to the street side. We wouldn't be able to hide the pipes, but it would work."

I almost clapped my hands. I still had a leaky roof, but that seemed like small potatoes when compared to having to face down gallons of water. So in the next weeks, the pump was installed, the drain was capped, and the mason came in and covered everything with a thick layer of cement, sloping the stairwell toward the sump pump. After twelve months of watching the weather reports fanatically and dreading rain. I couldn't wait for the next storm, to see if we had succeeded. Finally, another spring rainfall hit. I stood in the basement holding my breath. Then I heard the little sump outside the door start wheezing, and I could hear it coughing out water onto the sidewalk above from the little white plastic pipe that poked out between the slats of the house's white picket fence. (Yes, the house had a white picket fence.) I danced a victory dance in the basement, and then I got down on my knees and clasped my hands together, thanking the universe for having sent me Neil, thanking God that I had had the strength to make it this far.

And so I dared to consider a vacation. In the past twelve months I had lost my husband, started a big new job, fired two nannies, taken my son to the emergency room, poured $55,000 into house renovations, and survived endless nights of crying on the kitchen floor or mopping the basement dry. There was a little money left in my savings account and I was ready for some time off. I knew that going out of town anywhere with Zack would be hard to handle on my own, so I looked for a house to rent near the beach and near friends in Amagansett for the month of August. Paul and Marnie (with their son, Luke) were renting a house there for the month of August as well, and my friends Rose and Scott (with their daughter, Rachel) owned a house in the Dunes. I found a tiny, cute house in the Dunes, just a four-block walk from the beach. It was a splurge, to be sure. I planned to take a few long weekends that month and one whole week off, to really enjoy being with my son for so many days in a row and feeling out the new shape of our family. I packed up beach towels and bathing suits and sunscreen and all manner of plastic buckets and set out for the beach.

But instead of having an idyllic break, I slammed headfirst into the hard realities of my life and slid directly into depression. Being alone with Zack, a demanding toddler, exhausted me and only served to underline how much I was on my own. On the beach, he wasn't interested at all in playing in the sand. He just ran and ran and ran toward the ocean, into the ocean. Once when we were standing in waist-high water, Zack in my arms, he tried to wriggle out of my grasp just as a big wave came in. We got knocked underwater, and I felt Zack starting to get pulled out of my arms by the waves as I struggled to get my feet under me in the surf and stand up. We lurched up out of the water, both crying and coughing. (Thank God Zack was crying and coughing!) I got us to the beach and pounded on his back and then held him until he stopped crying, but I was still shaking. Two minutes later, he was up and running into the water again. I fell apart. Not knowing what else to do, I dragged him home, him screaming and crying and so disappointed, me with my head down so that I wouldn't have to meet other parents' eyes.

And I'd had unrealistic expectations about how much time Zack and I would spend with our friends. I was starved for adult company in a way that my friends weren't. We met for breakfast, we met at the beach, but they had their own plans, their own nap schedules, and babysitters so they could go out to dinner alone, as couples. Even after all this time, I hadn't learned how to say I needed help, and I needed company. I called Kim at work and burst into tears. I tried to make the invitation I was offering for her and her family (daughter Julia and husband Stephen) to come and stay out here for a weekend sound inviting, not panicked. Alison from work. Eric and Dave and their dogs. I made a list of everyone I thought would come and visit and I called them, to fill the house and buffer myself from that awful feeling of lonely panic, and to surround myself with some helping hands.

The last night of Labor Day weekend, our last night in the house, with Eric and Dave and their dog, Angus, asleep in the guest bedroom, I awakened to the sounds of breaking glass. Thinking the wind must have blown a vase over, I jumped out of bed and ran up the three steps to the living room. As I was turning the corner, I heard a second explosion—Was someone breaking in?—and when

I finished the turn I was met by a wall of flames ten feet away, engulfing the back wall of the sunroom. I stopped dead and screamed "OhmyGodOhmyGodOhmyGod!" over and over, remembering the citronella candles we'd carefully extinguished and checked twice. I knew an ember must have escaped into the dry bushes, and I felt the full weight of the responsibility for disaster in the pit of my stomach. I willed my brain to snap into gear and scream something more useful: "Fire!" Eric and Dave were up and barking out orders: "Call 911!" "I've got Zack!" I was pushing the buttons on the phone, but the call wasn't going through. I jumped back down into the bedroom, grabbed a pair of shorts and my cell phone, and ran out of the house behind Eric, who was carrying Zack, and Dave, who was carrying Angus. We stood in the gravel driveway and screamed to the neighbors' houses for help because my cell phone wasn't getting service. In the meantime, the dry brush around the house was going up in flames.

We stood in the chill summer night, watching the house burn. Lights went on in houses nearby. Neighbors called 911, and they came outside in their robes to start hosing down their bushes so that the fire wouldn't jump. Then fire engines came screaming up the dirt road and firefighters got to work putting out the flames. Police cars pulled in, and police officers started questioning me. The sirens and the spinning lights and the sheer horror of having been awakened in the middle of the night to full-fledged panic was starting to get to Zack, and he began to shake uncontrollably. I wrapped my arms around him, looking for someone I could ask for a sweater. I had to get him out of there, but where? Rose appeared at my shoulder at just that moment—she'd awakened to the smell of smoke and had had a sixth-sense sensation that it was us—and I burst into tears and fell into her arms. She talked to the police officer. She gave them her phone numbers. She found the fire chief and told him where I'd be. All of us got into Rose's car and drove the eight blocks to her house, where she put Zack to bed and found a place for Eric and Dave to sleep. Reeking of wood smoke, I sat on her white sailcloth sofa waiting for the police. I was numb. Totally numb.

At 4 a.m. or so I fell into a fitful sleep, the smell of the smoke in my hair finding me even in my dreams. The next morning, the sun sparkled in the true-blue sky and it was a glorious day, but I was engulfed in a black cloud, a knot in my throat so big I could barely swallow around it. While Zack played with Rachel under Rose's watchful eye, I kept making laps to the house, waiting for the owner to come in from Manhattan. The back end of the house was scorched and black, and that heavy, wet, smoky smell that had been with me in my dreams emanated from the open wound where the sunroom had been. The fire-resistant building materials had done what they were supposed to do and the damage was remarkably contained, but somehow that didn't feel right. In my head the house had burned to the ground, and my sense of resilience and optimism along with it.

That afternoon, Zack and I got in my car and made the long drive home from Amagansett. When we arrived with our bags of clothes that smelled of the fire, we went right to bed. And that night, the fire alarm in our house went off, screaming in the middle of the night when its battery died. I ran down the hall and pulled at the alarm until it dropped to the floor and the plastic case shattered, as Zack cried in his crib. After consoling Zack and getting him back to sleep, I sat in the middle of the living room with all the lights blazing, trying to get the part of my brain that was loose and panicked and flapping around inside my skull to calm down. I could feel my grip on the notion that life would be okay again someday loosening, that hopeful notion starting to slip through my fingers like the fine sand that lined the roads at the Dunes. I had once thought I deserved a nice and happy life, and I had believed that I would have it. Now I did not know what I believed anymore.

I went back to work the next morning, and I could barely look my team in the eye. I felt so small and scared. When I did look at them, the sadness and concern I saw in their faces made me even more frightened, as if they could see that I was floating away from them on a dark sea. I don't know how I could feel so alone with that many people who cared about me all around me, but I felt unreachable, as if I were standing at the bottom of a long, narrow well, faces peering at me from the light, many miles away.

But my friends did find ways to reach me. Like the way Kim had cooked up an escape into a day of fun for me and Zack when Chris moved out. Like Marnie clutching my hand in the back of the car and crying with me as we raced Zack to the second ER. And Rose the day after the fire, standing by my side, stiff and on guard like a Doberman, while the owner of the beach house talked with me about insurance and liabilities. Or Kim and Alison and Melanie at the office, letting me try to talk out everything I was learning and feeling every day, our conversations about love and marriage and divorce and heartbreak seamlessly moving from the magazine articles to our own lives and back.

And there was the comfort that came to me one night, a few days after the fire when my friend Nancy called from Atlanta. I answered, just barely, since I'd been crying, and she listened to me wail and said only "I'm sorry"—said it again and again for twenty minutes and didn't try to offer any advice.

My sister-in-law Melissa, who sent me cards that said "When life gives you lemons, make lemonade" and other simple messages, the inside filled with her love and exclamation points.

My parents, who carefully refrained from asking me questions or telling me how to feel, but lent me money again and again, and then drove up to New York for weekends of patching and painting, and then patching and painting again all the spots where the roof had been leaking. (Engineer fathers may not excel at surprise babysitting duties, but give them a falling-down house and just wind them up and watch them go!)

My brother Scott and his wife, Kelly, who drove up with my parents, and helped to strip and powerwash the deck (which had been shellacked for a temporary sheen, but was now peeling off in long, ugly strips). And then stayed to enjoy my son with me, then listened for hours as I talked at them, trying to explain how I was beginning to make sense of things.

My friends Tracy and Eric, who gave up a gorgeous spring Saturday to help me with yardwork. It took us hours to beat back the grapevines, which were now growing out of control; we filled six garbage bags with their monstrous tendrils.

The surprise birthday luncheon that Alison, Melanie, Kim, and Tracy planned, taking me out for a fancy French meal and giving me a gift certificate for an unreasonably gorgeous (and unreasonably expensive) bisque candlestick I'd loved and coveted for years, to bless the new apartment Zack and I were getting ready to move into, at last.

In being gentle and loving with me, my friends were teaching me how to be gentle and loving with myself, coaxing me to find some self-compassion. It was hard for me to let go of punishing myself for having failed at something important in life, but in my friends' eyes I would occasionally catch a glimpse of myself, the person I used to think I was—loving and loyal, generous and outspoken, not the selfish and self-centered person Chris had had to escape—the person I might still be.

Through my friends, I was starting to see that my life history hadn't been entrusted solely to Chris. I had shared a lot of myself with many, many people. Maybe that meant I didn't suck. Maybe I deserved the love these people wanted to give me. Maybe I actually did know how to have a relationship, to be connected to someone. In the stability I'd had with some of these friends for decades, I started to let go of the idea that I couldn't keep love.

My best friend in New York was my best friend from college. I'd known Eric and trusted him like nobody else for "more than half my life," as we always said to each other.

All my best girlfriends from college were still my best girlfriends, even though sometimes months pass between our phone calls.

I'd made friends with Mary Rose and Alix when we were all assistants together at *Mirabella* eons ago; Alix was Zack's godmother, and Mary Rose was a reliable sounding board about work, motherhood, family, life.

I'd been seeing my shrink for ten years, and I'd stayed with her through lots of hard emotional work, instead of shedding her and finding a new therapist and an idea of me I could like more easily.

My best friend from high school and I were still deeply connected, even though he and his wife lived in South Carolina. I remember when he wore Garanimals; he knew me when I had braces. Our children had been born just three months apart.

The same stylist, Thea, had been cutting my hair for twelve years. The same colorist, Bryan, had been coloring my hair for ten; I'd been his first client in New York when he moved here from Australia. I'd followed both Thea and Bryan to seven different salons between them, I liked and trusted them (and their haircuts and -color, too, yes) that much.

I had a friend I had met nearly twenty years before, when she and I were both summer interns for magazines in college. She'd written for every magazine I'd ever worked for, and our sons both had the same name.

I was still in touch with almost all of my former assistants, all of whom had gone on to have rewarding careers of their own. And many of my coworkers from past jobs (like Melanie, like Kim, like Holly and Daisy and Mary Rose and more) had agreed to—had *wanted* to—work with me again and again.

And other past coworkers said they wished they could work with me again. And I knew that was because I have a reputation for wanting people to love their jobs, and love themselves.

I was a keeper. I both wanted to keep people and wanted to be kept. I was loyal. I could be trusted. I could be loved. I was lovable. I was steadier than it seemed on the surface. I would survive. I was surviving. I was, I was. And my friends are the ones who helped me see that I didn't have to start totally from scratch. Each one of them had a little piece of me, a fragment that he or she was able to help put into place, as if together they were arranging the fractured bits of a broken doll. In their eyes, I was still in one piece, even though I'd been shattered.

And being able to open myself up to them at my most raw—my friends who I knew would do anything if they could, if only there were something they could do—helped me know that I would get through it all. And the days I felt like I didn't deserve love, they gave it to me anyway.

7

Your Child Knows More About Life Than You Do (Think Small)

After the fire, I became hypervigilant. It was an actual physical sensation between my shoulder blades, as if my body were trying to sprout eyeballs there so I could be more aware and perceptive, and see into the mysteries of the universe. I've always been someone who lifts her feet when she drives over train tracks or avoids walking under ladders as a kind of karmic insurance, in case the superstitions turn out to be true, but I'm not one for magical thinking. So I was surprised to keep catching myself ruminating about the symbolism of water and fire and what their powerful presence meant in my life. I was a little spooked by the feeling that there were forces larger than me at play.

Now that summer was officially over and the basement almost fixed, I moved into fast-forward to finally get The Evil House (that's how I always referred to it, in conversation or in my own head: The Evil House) on the market. It wasn't in perfect condition yet (the roof still leaked in one or two places during windy storms), but the backyard was in its full summertime glory, the thriving grapevines on the pergola weaving their magic. I'd propped out the rest of the house with inexpensive Ikea pieces, hiding the gaps in the furnishings created when Chris had moved out, to make it look like the perfect Brooklyn family home. There was the reading nook on the third floor where I'd never read a book, the guest room that had never had a guest of mine in it, the basement playroom Zack had never played in. It felt like my life had stalled as soon as we moved in.

Except that life hadn't stalled for Zack.

When we moved into the house, my son had been only six months old, a baby boy with a haze of white fluff where his hair would eventually appear. I had painted the walls of entire first floor while he supervised from his spot in the blue bouncy seat, kicking his feet to make the toys that hung on the chair dance, and giggling when I sang songs to him from my perch on the ladder. In the ensuing months, as my life started to disassemble itself (lost job, lost husband, lost hope), Zack bloomed and then zoomed, learning to crawl, then pull himself up, then walk. For the first week or two, he walked with his arms held straight up overhead for balance, weaving to and fro until he got the hang of things. He had transitioned to solid foods, and then learned to feed himself bits of strawberries and Cheerios with his chubby hands, and then later, with a spoon. He eventually would amble, stiff-legged, over to the tomato plants I'd mothered in the backyard garden, and he would pluck the baby cherry tomatoes off the vine and stuff his mouth full. He'd figured out that my digital camera captured pictures of him, so I'd had to learn how to take photos on the sly to keep every shot from being of his pink pudgy palm as he reached for the camera to turn it around and look at himself. And he'd started to speak. His favorite expression was "all right," and he relished it like a hard candy when he said it, rolling it around in his mouth: "Awwwwriiiiight!" His sunny personality unfolded as his hair grew in, his sprouting nimbus of white-blond curls an extension of his irrepressible spirit. He was my little lion, my little Leo, and it was blessedly impossible not to be caught up in his joyful wonder at the world.

When Chris had first said the marriage was over, I was heartbroken for Zack, beside myself with grief that he would lose his family at such an early age and that I hadn't been able to stop it.

I was also upset because it meant I was going to be tied to Chris for the rest of my life.

I actually had moments where I envied my friends who were divorced with no children; their exes simply disappeared, sometimes into other cities and new marriages, only months after the divorce was final. I knew how much my friends had been hurt by their exes' instant immersion in shiny, new-and-improved lives without them, but I longed for such a simple ending. Instead, Chris and I were going to have to learn how to spend a lifetime sharing something precious, even after we had failed at sharing our lives.

But in the six months since Chris had moved out of the house, I was slowly coming to realize that in some ways the timing of our split had been a tremendous blessing. Zack had been too young when Chris moved out for us to need to explain anything to him, too young for us to have even considered a traditional custody arrangement, with Zack changing households every few days. It seemed clear to both Chris and me that Zack should have one home, one bedroom, one crib, and a reliable, everyday routine to help him get on with the business of being a toddler. We knew he needed to absorb and learn the world around him without the interruptions and anxieties of constant change. Instead, Chris and I would be the ones to bear the brunt of the discomforts and petty annoyances of accomodating each other in my home, even after Zack and I moved to our new apartment.

This arrangement suited what Chris and I were each struggling with most in our separation. Chris had a roster of anxieties about being able to take care of Zack the "right" way (the way I'd made up on the fly, which he'd been so furious at me for being able to do). So having Zack live in one place meant Chris wouldn't have to learn my mysterious recipes for Zack's nutritional mush, wouldn't have to duplicate the set of bottles, set up a crib in his small apartment, keep up on what size diaper Zack was wearing, manage the nanny's hours and pay. All of this annoyed me, and I complained about it for a week or two with friends before I realized that it meant I would get what I wanted most. Of course I wanted Chris to be a constant presence in Zack's life, but I wanted Zack to be with me as much as possible, since like every other working mom I suffer the gentle heartache of being apart from him during the day. I knew I would put up with any amount of personal discomfort to avoid having to spend an entire weekend without my son.

So not much changed in Zack's routine when Chris packed up and moved away. Zack's father was still there for him three evenings a week, playing with him on the living room floor, reading him bedtime stories, putting him to bed. Zack's being so young had bought Chris and me time to figure out what the shape of our new life would be. It also allowed me to gain perspective before I had to tell Zack a story about his father and me. I could help him put all the pieces into place in his head long after they had arranged themselves in mine.

A few weeks after Chris had moved out, I was upstairs with Zack, taking him through the paces of his bedtime ritual: a story, followed by snuggling in the rocking chair, and then into his crib for a good night's sleep. As I laid him down this night, Zack looked up at me and asked, "Daddy?" I felt my heart catch in my throat. It's rare to be so aware of one of Life's Big Moments presenting itself to you, but here it was, right in front of me. I reminded myself that even married parents are not both at home all day and night every day. Then I said the simplest things that I knew were true: "Daddy's not here right now, sweetie. You'll see him tomorrow. But he loves you very much."

I resisted the urge to say more while I leaned over the crib and rubbed Zack's back, because there wasn't more to say. Not anything that would have made sense to my nineteen-month-old son. As I stood there in my own silence, I felt that I was suspended in a perfect, still moment of ambiguity.

And then I had a brainstorm. "You know who else loves you? Grandma and Grandpa love you, and Grandma Barb loves you, even though they're not here right now." I went on, "Uncle Scott and Aunt Kelly love you, and Kim loves you, and Stephen and Julia, too. . . ." I named everyone in Zack's universe who cared about him. Who cared about us, and me. I was consoled by the thought that lots and lots of people love your child along with you, no matter how lonely it can feel to be a single parent.

I was finding my footing as a parent, and learning to improvise around the hole in my life in a way that felt good and true. That night I went to bed wrapped in a gentle haze of pride.

Zack took to this new little nighttime ritual instantly. Each evening as I laid him down on the changing table to put on his pajamas, he'd look up at me and say, "Annnnnd . . . ," coaxing me to start the roll call of all the people in this big wide world who loved him. As he grew older and spoke more, he started filling in the blanks himself; I'd start with one name, and he'd call out the rest of the names that made up the group, whether husband, wife, partner, children, dogs, or the single friend alone. Every night as we did this I was reminded that families come in all shapes and sizes, and that this was the world that Zack was growing up in. It was time for me to stop mourning the loss of the mommy-daddy-baby family unit and realize that what made the three of us a family was up to us—and that Chris and I were in the midst of creating that, together, even though we were apart.

This, to me, was a challenging notion. We were no longer a family and yet we were still going to be a family. These truths did not cancel each other out in the way it seemed they must. I knew that keeping both ideas in my head at the same time, finding that tensile point where they were both true, was my pathway to eventually being able to let go of my grief.

*   *   *

Zack had other lessons to bring to me. A child's constant engagement and delight with life as it's happening This Very Second is a
boon for any parent, but it was a magical respite for me. Zack taught
me not to will away time—not to close my eyes and hunker down
and wait out the months until the house was fixed, the months until
the divorce was final, the months until we had a new home. Instead
he reminded me every day that I could choose to join him in enjoying life's simple delights. The hour and a half I got to spend with
him in the evening when I got home from work was always my
Happy Hour.

Zack literally pulled me out of living life just in my head, and
brought me down to Earth. He had me crawling around on my
hands and knees with him, grooving on the patterns in the rug,
playing peek-a-boo from behind the sofa, making toys rustle and
toot and click. For Zack the world was a wonder, and when I was
with him I found the world wonderful, too. His utter joy in the
simplest of things—the beep as a cell phone's numbers are pressed,
water pouring from the tap into the sink—led to giggles bubbling
up out of his chest, his gigantic blue-green eyes (just like his father's) turning toward me, sparkling with mischief and delight, inviting me to be with him in his happiness.

The only time that Zack knew was Right Now, and in those evenings on the living room floor with him I learned that the comfort
of Right Now was always there, no matter what else was happening
around me. He taught me that I could set aside my grief, set aside
my worries from work and choose to be where I was that second: on
the living room floor with a little creature I loved beyond all reason.
No matter how big the events were that were unfolding in my life,
they didn't have the power to erase the pleasure of a million small
joys and discoveries that were brought to me by my little boy every
day. Those precious moments, though small, weren't fleeting; they
were like down—small puffs of delight and joy that when collected

together created a featherbed, a buffer between the hard stuff of life and me.

As Zack got older and more expressive, I was able to live more fully in all the small moments we shared, and soon it became impossible not to notice the small moments in my own life. Picking up a perfectly ripe pear at the deli. Running into a friend I hadn't seen in a while on the sidewalk. Catching the subway train waiting and with the doors open when I ran into the station, running late. I started sending a thank-you into the universe every time I caught a lucky break or enjoyed a simple pleasure; it was a humble and yet very powerful way to keep me from falling into the self-fulfilling fantasy that everything in my life—the house, the fire, the divorce—was wrong.

When Chris had first moved out I would keep reminding myself that I had it good: I had a great job, a good career. I could support my life financially without Chris. But those things didn't comfort me. They represented stability; peace was something entirely different. Taking Zack's lead and getting small turned out to be where the comfort I'd been looking for lay. I started to experience that even the very worst of days were peppered with small gratitudes. I started making a list at night as I lay in bed: *Today I finished a memo for work that had been weighing on my mind, really loved my outfit* (never underestimate the power of looking good and feeling good), *ate a delicious sandwich, read an article written for the magazine that just nailed the point I wanted us to make, found the perfect lipstick, made it home on the subway in thirty-eight minutes flat.* Anytime I caught myself thinking *I am cursed* when another piece of bad luck found its way into my life, I would immediately practice some gratitude, to shoo away the sense that bad luck was all I deserved. To this day, I send a little thank-you to the heavens every time I fumble a glass when I'm unloading the dishwasher and it doesn't shatter.

As Zack thrived, I had to accept the simple truth that I was succeeding as a parent and that I had protected him from the worst of my grief. It was clear that Zack had made it through my hard year believing that the world was filled with people eager for the pleasure of loving him, even if he hadn't yet met them. Sitting on my lap on the subway, he would unself-consciously reach his arms up to the stranger standing in front of us, asking to be picked up and spreading smiles among the other passengers. At the playground, he would walk up to children who were crying or upset, and he'd gently lean into them, as if to comfort them. In restaurants, he'd look around until he found a table nearby with people who would flirt with him. It was like being out with the mayor of Park Slope, except that the mayor was in diapers. But Zack's big personality and endless interest in people reminded me that the point was to connect. His irrepressible spirit started to pull me from my shell. He reminded me that I could be living life's rewards every day, if only I were brave enough to do it.

That summer, Chris's mom, Barb, had come to stay with me. When Chris and I broke up, I had emphatically professed to Barb that I couldn't, and wouldn't, give her up, and not just because of what she meant to my son. Barb is practically a professional grandma, with six grandchildren who'd come before Zack, so having her around for a week was going to be a treat for both Z *and* me. I was always happier when there were people around to help me enjoy Zack. Plus, I might even be able to sneak out to the gym one or two mornings when she was there, leaving the two of them to enjoy breakfast together.

Of course, Barb was here to spend time with her son, too, and so I carefully created a schedule of who would be with Barb on which evenings and which weekend days so that I wouldn't have to be with Chris too much. I was planning for the four of us to have two dinners together and one big outing to the Prospect Park Zoo. What I didn't expect was that Chris would be in the house seemingly nonstop, sitting on our old sofa, helping himself from the fridge, and just generally enjoying the comfort of his old home. I found myself retreating, by running errands, or disappearing into another room when he was around, and feeling pushed out of my own life. Why was it so easy for him to step back into the way things used to be? If he still found it possible to spend this much time with me, why had he chosen to destroy our lives?

Because leaving hadn't destroyed his life. I had to keep reminding myself that the end of our relationship wasn't going to affect us both the same. That he had left because he felt he had to, because he *wanted* to leave. That he'd felt he couldn't be who he was around me. So why shouldn't he be comfortable and happy now?

It was hard to see that being free of me had allowed something in his spirit to rebound. People often asked me if Chris was dating again, but I didn't obsess about that so much. Chris + Some Other Person = Happy isn't where my anxiety lived; Chris - Me = Happy was much more difficult to accept.

I had to remind myself that I would just be living different pain if he had up and disappeared, and walked out of my life for good. So I did my best to just wince and then let it go, and instead focus on all that his presence—and the three of us together—was bringing to my son. I tried to find the place where I could get comfortable in this strange new normal, and just live our connected breakup.

Later that week, the four of us—me, Zack, Grandma, and Chris—drove off to the Prospect Park Zoo on a sunny summer day. I found a parking spot right outside the zoo (*thank you, universe*), Zack was completely entranced with the sea lions and the baboons, and I took photos of everything we did, all afternoon long.

When I loaded the photos into the computer a week or so later, I was struck by what I had captured: a photo of Chris, six foot two, holding hands with his tiny son as they headed into the baboon enclosure, faced away from the camera. At first I wanted to cry; the photo was so sweet, and I felt again the loss of the family I thought I would get to have, sharply, just under my breastbone. But then I caught myself: I had *been there* to share in that moment. It belonged to me as much as it would have if Chris and I were still married. What more did I want?

As I sat at the computer, I scrolled back through photos of the three of us when we had all been living together. I was looking for the photos that captured how Chris was there, but not there, with us but not with us, when we were all together. In one shot, Zack is crawling at Chris's feet in a wide-open field in Prospect Park, green grass stretching out in every direction. But Chris, his back to the camera and his hands stuffed into the pockets of his jeans, is staring up and off to the right, away from Zack, and not turning to me even though I'd been calling his name. In another, Zack is walking in Gregg and Melissa's backyard in a tiny track jacket, the white-blond fluff of his hair blowing in the wind; Chris is off in the distance, looking up into the trees at nothing in particular, wanting to be somewhere else. And now I had to get used to the opposite: Chris was here and present with Zack in a way he'd truly never been when we were still together.

And what mother wouldn't choose that for her child? I decided right then and there that if Chris had the ability to be deeply connected to only one of us—Zack or me—then he had picked the right one.

The conventional wisdom on creating a so-called amicable divorce is that you "do it for the kids." I was constantly reminded of this by the people who, after hearing that my ex's mom was staying at my house, or that my ex moved in when I went away on a business trip, instantly chalked up our arrangements thusly: "Well, of course you guys are trying to get along, for your son." Every time I heard that, I felt my blood heat up and rush to my face. I started responding sharply (probably too sharply, but I was reaching the point where I had stopped caring what others thought about my divorce):"No, I'm doing it this way for *me*."

It *was* for me: to heal me, to help me. I was tired of the fact that people didn't know that this was the real work of divorce, the hidden work that no one talks about because people are much more interested in knowing whether your spouse had an affair. I'd met plenty of people who thought they played nice with their ex-spouses, but you could still smell the bitterness on their breath, catch the hostility in the occasional snide comment. And children are like Geiger counters; they can sense the presence of feelings long before the feelings are expressed. Pretending that all was good with Chris and me wasn't going to be enough. I believed Zack deserved to decide for himself what he thought about his father, without my casting my own emotional cloud over their relationship, and I knew that the way to allow that to happen was for me to put my quest for peace first, in the same way that you're supposed to put on your own oxygen mask first in an airplane emergency, and then turn to those who depend on you to help them with theirs. This was a small certainty that was taking root in my life, after I'd had to give up on all my old ones. And so I held on tight.

Armed with this bit of wisdom, I resolved to get good at something I hadn't been very good at in our marriage: accepting the ways in which Chris and I were different. We thought differently and so we would parent differently. I had to accept that the world did not hinge on whether Zack's fruit got cut exactly the way I would cut it, let go of the fact that Chris didn't take Zack to the playground as often as I would like, accept that he had ushered our son into the world of superheroes a year or two too soon for my taste. (I discovered this when Zack, standing in the hallway of our new apartment, said, "Meanwhile, back at the Hall of Justice . . ." and then whooshed down the hall to his bedroom, flapping an imaginary cape behind him.)

I didn't like to have to admit it to myself, but I knew in my heart that if Chris and I were still married, I'd be picking fights about why he should do things my way. Now that we weren't married anymore, it was easier for me to see that Chris didn't have to be me, didn't have to follow my plans. I was humbled to realize I'd learned to be separate from, and therefore more generous toward, my husband only after he'd left me. It took the prospect of divorce to change my idea of what a marriage should look like.

I started to accept that Chris's definition of success and mine were unrelated, and that neither one was wrong; realized that the fact that I like to play within the rules of corporate structures and he doesn't, doesn't mean I'm right; got over the fact that his idea of a fun Friday night, beers with friends at an East Village bar, was not mine. I found dozens of places in our relationship where I had apparently been waiting for Chris to be more like me, although, at the time, the story I told myself was that I was waiting for Chris to grow up. One by one, I let all those expectations go, and started to see Chris as who he really is. And then I forgave myself for getting it wrong. I saw that I had been consumed with writing the story in my head of what my life should look like, and had been racing like hell to get to that safe place I always imagined was waiting for me. I'd just neglected to tell Chris that I'd signed him up for this race, too. And when he didn't take the baton I handed off to him, I didn't wait for him. I raced ahead. I'd been staying connected to the idea of "our marriage," instead of doing the more complicated and ambiguous work of staying connected to him, especially because it was hard to be connected to someone who'd x-ed off large "no access" zones in relation to his own work and his unfolding sense of self. I couldn't know what those years had felt like for Chris, but I could piece together that what he had been asking for was solitude, and solitude was not at all what I wanted from marriage. I was starting to see where we'd begun to lose each other, and starting to see why our marriage had worked until, quite suddenly, it didn't.

I'd spent the last five years waiting for Chris to "catch up" to me. Maybe he had been waiting for me to slow down, or maybe he had been realizing that he was happier with me ahead of him, leaving him to himself. Maybe when I slowed down after Zack was born and wanted more of Chris's life was when Chris became sure that he couldn't live with me.

It was hard to have to keep living these reasons and answers—or, more accurately, living the questions—but it was better than having no answers at all.

*   *   *

One sunny Sunday afternoon in September, after weeks of people trooping in and out of our home, we finally got a bid on the house that we could accept, from a couple who would wait until January to close (relieving us of the need to pay the flip tax). The price was lower than what we'd listed for, but it would pay for all the repairs, repay my parents, preserve the money that Chris and I had put into the house in the first place, and give us a very small profit. It meant that Chris and I could begin moving forward with the divorce in earnest, now that we had pulled ourselves back from the brink of losing everything we had saved together.

And—joyous delight!—I could finally start looking for a new home for Zack and me.

Now that I was a single mom, I was finished with fringe neighborhoods, and I started looking in an established area of Park Slope in Brooklyn that had restaurants, fish markets, and dry cleaners. I fell in love with one specific block, with its double-wide street, wide sidewalks, and row of grand limestone apartment buildings on either side. It was just one block from the public elementary school, and two blocks from the park in one direction and two blocks from the playground in the other.

And so I stalked all the open houses for this block, making sure I was the first to arrive each time. I wanted an apartment on either the first or the second floor, and one that needed absolutely no work done to it. I was finished with home renovations.

Then, one Sunday, I walked into the apartment I could call home. All the apartments in these limestone buildings were laid out more or less the same, so it took only seconds for me to check room arrangement and confirm that this apartment was in amazing shape, having clearly been lovingly renovated by the young couple who were selling it now. I approached the real estate agent and told her that I was as ripe a buyer as she was ever going to get—with a house in contract, a preapproved mortgage, and a strong personal motive to find my new home as soon as possible—and that I was going to bid that way. I bid almost ten percent over the asking price, happy to pay more to make sure that I got the apartment.

After I had placed the bid, I went home and found Chris and Zack playing in the green backyard. I told Zack all about our new house and said I couldn't wait to show him the long hallways he would be able to run up and down. Chris was happy for me, happy that we were moving forward and were going to be able to be rid of the house, too. I had gotten used to the way Chris was rooting for me and it didn't feel strange anymore. I sat under the pergola, feeling good, looking up at the evening stars. "What day is today?" I asked, so I could do the math on how many weeks it would be before Zack and I could move. Chris looked at me strangely for a second. Then he said, "Today is October first." I sat forward with a start. *Ah. Our wedding anniversary.*

I had forgotten! Earlier in the week, I had been dreading the approaching date, but it had snuck up on me over the weekend. It seemed impossible that only a year ago Chris and I had been away together, attempting to save our marriage. I winced at the memory of the awkwardness of that weekend, which Chris misinterpreted as my being hurt about remembering what today was, flashing me a lips-turned-down smile. But I didn't bother to correct him. I was too delighted that Zack and I were going to move out and into our very own place, just the two of us. My new life was about to begin.

8

Grief Is Not a Mountain,
It Is a River

I had assumed I would survive my divorce by lacing up my hiking boots and conquering it, as if it were a mountain to be summited. When Chris first made clear that he was really leaving, I had comforted myself with the mantra "left foot, right foot, left foot, right foot," to remind me that I had only to take one step at a time. I assumed that I would climb up to the peak with determination and will the way I'd attacked everything in my life, make my way to the apex of the hard stuff, and then start my slow victory walk down the other side, feeling better and stronger with every step and every passing day as the grief loosened its frightening hold on me. I thought I would heal on a predictable arc, one that heads gently down, down, down, a little less pain every day.

I believed that I was now cresting the summit, since I'd found both a buyer for the house and a new apartment for Z and me. Any moment, my life would start to come together as Chris and I finished with the details of coming apart—finalizing the separation agreement, filing for divorce, checking items off the list of legal undoing—as if real estate had been the only thing binding us together. I started to feel confident and strong. I started to believe that, a year later, I had almost made it.

I was back in the swirl of planning the annual Redbook Heroes event—the same one I'd had to prepare for in Maine the year before, at my friend Tina's wedding. But now I had fifteen months' of running the magazine under my belt and I was working with a fantastic team, many of whom had been at the magazine when I got there. The changes we'd made to the magazine—adding style, complexity, honesty, more powerful photographs, and more and more stories from real women—were being very well received by readers and advertisers alike. I was ready to take the stage at Heroes and I felt I'd earned my spot at the top of the masthead, because now I knew the magazine, its readers, and our business inside and out.

As I shopped for an outfit to wear at the event, I noticed I'd lost about fifteen pounds without really trying, as if I were shedding an old skin. After a year of frozen dinners (at least they were organic) and two glasses of wine (Hey, it's got heart-healthy polyphenols!) at the kitchen table while I read manuscripts every night, I had started figuring out how to take care of myself in my life alone. Although I had cooked dinners for Chris and me almost every night, as soon as he moved out I found I couldn't conjure the energy or enthusiasm for it. Even just making an arugula salad—something I could eat seven days a week—seemed like too much effort and time when there was so much on my daily to-do lists. I started running on the treadmill again, and I quickly came to rely on that physical energy outlay as the best kind of stress reliever—yes, even better than pinot noir—even if I managed to fit it into my schedule only once or twice a week.

All those small steps toward taking care of yourself are like the first soft, green undergrowth that shows up on a mountain after a forest fire. I marveled at how good it felt to feel good, like a rush of pure oxygen, as if I hadn't taken a deep breath to the bottom of my lungs in a year. And it's possible that I hadn't in all those days of being clenched up, willing days to unfold, waiting for time to pass.

And then out of the blue, the Internet age ushered in the perfect first postbreakup boyfriend: an e-mail appeared in my in-box from a former not-quite-lover from college. He had contacted me on a whim after fifteen years—on his fortieth birthday—no less, and I was instantly seduced by his potent recollections of my both my freewheeling, younger self and our brushes with sexual adventure. He was in recovery from alcoholism, and we bonded instantly over doing the hard work of rediscovering who you are at life's midpoint.

We went from long e-mails to late-night phone calls and then all-day-long text-message volleys. I carried my phone with me everywhere, like a teenager, surreptitiously peeking at it during meetings, feeling a surge of delight every time there was a message from him. I took photographs of myself to e-mail to him, wearing a green T-shirt and a big fat grin, and in the pictures I could see that being excited about him—and the way he made me excited about me—had put a sparkle, a sense of lightness, back in my eyes.

We had marathon phone conversations at night—after Zack was in bed and the day's allotment of manuscripts had been read—talking for hours about life and love and chance and changes, and we tumbled easily into a fantasy of being together even though we lived thousands of miles apart. Talking with him felt as if I were being reintroduced to the younger me, which was both heady and poignant: I couldn't believe how far I had drifted from my sense of myself as an interesting, engaging, and attractive woman. And not just in the aftermath of Chris's leaving me; I'd lost touch with her years before. Sometimes when I got off the phone I would cry for having managed to lose my best idea of myself.

I felt a lurking desire to taunt Chris with my new relationship. I would let him catch me whispering into the phone as I walked in the door at night, or I'd rush to the kitchen table to pick up my phone and read a new text message with a big grin on my face. I wanted to hurt him to see just one second of regret in his eyes. But I never got a payoff for my efforts, even when I intimated that I might need "a weekend to myself" because an "old friend from college" might come to visit. Chris was happy for me, and happy for himself; I could see him shrugging off more and more guilt. I wanted to pinch him sharply, to let him know he wasn't living by the rules: *I* was supposed to be scoring points here! But he kept lobbing back my volleys with genuine goodwill.

It took me a few days to realize there weren't any points to be scored, unless I was trying to live the story of divorce that everyone had been offering to me all these many months. But I reminded myself that that wasn't what I wanted.

Halloween was coming up, and Zack was old enough to trick-or-treat for the first time. Our neighborhood does Halloween to the nines: houses are decorated, neighbors sit on their stoops cradling bowls of candy, and a Halloween baby parade of hundreds marches down the main drag, with thousands more people lining the street. I couldn't wait. I am sure I was more excited than Zack. But in the previous weeks, as I'd been making Zack's costume—he was going to be Bamm-Bamm from *The Flintstones*—I'd been feeling sad about doing Halloween with Zack alone. From my experiences in the past year, I knew that trying to hook up with paired-off parents for events such as these was futile. It was already enough to coordinate for two parents coming from two jobs and hooking up with one or two children and their babysitter while the neighborhood was exploding in hysterical Halloween celebration without also trying to connect with me and Z. and I was tired of feeling like the desperate divorcée. Which is how Chris and I ended up spending Halloween together with Zack.

The three of us went trick-or-treating as we made our way to the parade, Zack getting out of his stroller and hesitantly taking candy from our neighbors. He looked back at Chris and me for permission the first six or seven times, not fully comprehending why these people he'd never met were handing him chocolate. (He got the hang of it.) Then we headed to the starting point of the parade, joining a cacophonous crowd that surged around homemade floats—a sailboat bedecked with fairies and mermaids, an aquarium filled with little toddler crustaceans—and costumed children being pulled in wagons by costumed adults. I knew Zack would want to walk in the parade and be surrounded by people. But as I walked into the fray with him in my arms and Chris pushing the stroller behind me, I felt dread trickle into the back of my throat, realizing that I was putting Chris into a crowd situation, which he hates, hates, hates. I tensed up, but then I reminded myself that he'd chosen to join us, and so I could will myself to relax. And then actually relax. I zeroed in on Zack's wide-eyed awe. All these people! When Zack heard the drum corps at the front of the line start up, with its heavy, happy beat, he shimmied down out of my arms so that he could stand there and shake his groove thang, feeling the music and the thrum of the crowd.

The parade began its lumbering pace, and Zack went into performance mode, scooting up through the paradegoers to get closer to the beat of the drums, doing his funky dance for a stretch of the twenty-block, jam-packed, shimmy-walk processional. Halfway through the parade, we walked by Marnie and Paul on the sidelines, with Luke all dressed up as a little lion. A few eyebrows were raised at Chris, Zack, and me all being there together (Marnie and Paul both exchanged meaningful glances with me on the sly), but I just shrugged, and the three of them joined us for the last leg. After a few more blocks, Zack hit his limit, so Chris and I traded off carrying him and pushing the empty stroller before turning around to head back home and put our tired little caveman to bed.

Halloween had been a kind of victory. It wasn't quite planting my flag on the top of my mountain, but it was close. But right on the other side of Halloween, the big holidays loomed large, and I found myself starting to backslide. Just thinking about Thanksgiving and Christmas served up a fresh platter of grief. I didn't want a lifetime of having only half of those holidays with my son! I didn't want to have to pack him up and send him off with his father to create his childhood memories of the holidays without me! And even worse was the thought of my having to be alone. Going to my parents' house to celebrate with them and my brothers and their wives was going to feel like I was fresh out of college and just beginning the work of creating my life, instead of being an almost-thirty-seven-year-old, a mother, a successful career woman. And, yes, a divorcée, a loser. I felt all the growth and acceptance that I'd laid as groundwork for myself in the past few months start to tremble and shake; my mind flashed back to images of my house's foundation being jackhammered up, revealing all the dark earth hidden beneath.

I told myself to be a grown-up and just get on with the impossible task of choosing which holiday with Zack I would give up to Chris. For the past thirteen years, we had been spending alternating holidays at our respective parents' houses, so in theory this year meant Thanksgiving in Illinois, since we'd been there last year for Christmas, when we'd had to tell Chris's mom that we were breaking up.

The truth was that *I* wanted to go to Illinois to stay with Chris's mom for Thanksgiving. There was a lot about the life that Chris and I had shared that I didn't want to have to say goodbye to, and his family was the biggest part of that. Chris's two sisters, Kelly and Jennifer, had three children each. The oldest of Zack's cousins, Colin, had been born just weeks after Chris and I had started dating; the second oldest, Danny, was born a few weeks before Chris and I married. Of course I thought of all them as family; they *are* family. Three of the cousins lived near Barb, and the other three cousins often showed up around one holiday or the other, making the long drive up from North Carolina with their parents in their minivan. I wanted that rumbly-tumbly seven-kids-in-a-house holiday chaos for Zack, and I wanted it for me.

But giving up Christmas this year with my two-and-a-half-year-old was unimaginable. My father, a lifelong train enthusiast and hobbyist, was all revved up to give Zack a gigantic play table for his wooden train set so that he would have a place to make amazing track layouts for Thomas the Tank Engine and all his friends. My mother was just about to finish knitting the "Zack" stocking that would match the one she made for me thirty-odd years ago, with Santa peeking up out of a chimney, his angora beard all fuzzy and white. And I wanted to be with them; they had helped me with so much in the last year. I couldn't bear it that I had to live without one of these; it was fueling new anger toward Chris and reigniting all the old hurts.

One weeknight I got home and Zack was asleep; Chris was packing up his work piles and getting ready to head to his apartment. I worked up enough nerve to start the conversation, asking him which holiday he was planning to fly home to Illinois for this year.

"I hadn't thought about it yet," he said.

Of course not, I thought, ungenerously. I had always been the one who bought the tickets and made all the necessary arrangements.

"I don't really feel like going out there at all," he said. "I can't stand traveling that time of year. It makes me crazy."

That's an understatement, I thought. I felt all the places where Chris and I rubbed each other the wrong way rising to the surface. This you hate, I reminded myself, this you don't miss, his inability to just deal.

I willed myself to calm my prickles, and instead took my window of opportunity, suggesting that maybe I could go out there with Zack. And then I just went for it all.

"Except, Chris, I don't think I can not be with Zack for Christmas this year. I know we should share, I know we have to share, but I don't think I can right now. By next year, I'll be ready." I tried not to get teary because I didn't want to be manipulative. I tried to just say it straight, but I felt all my sadness pushing up into my eyes.

Chris didn't even look at me. He said, "Okay. That's fine."

I should have been happy. I *was* happy. But there was still an aching hollowness, both for whom I'd wanted Chris to be when we were married, and for what was gone. When would what was gone stop being what I wanted?

I had to face facts. In the year since Chris had said he was done I had not really taken any steps to rebuild my life. I had rebuilt my house, I had rebuilt the magazine, but doing so in conjunction with caring for Zack had kept me from the labor of starting over. I knew I needed to find other single moms and dads, to create a new social life around who I was now, but I felt too tired and closed off to do the work (and take the risk) of connecting. That's why my text-only boyfriend was right for this moment in my life. He lived so far away I didn't have to actually *be* in a relationship with him.

I remembered watching my friend and coworker Melanie go through the end of her own marriage when we were working at *Marie Claire*. I remembered how raw she was, her tears lurking just below the surface and how much she struggled with her sense of not fitting into her tight-knit suburban neighborhood anymore, with all her friends married and starting their families. I recalled offering her what I hoped was useful advice. I'd advised her to be gentle with herself, and to be forgiving about her grief, and said that it would get better, slowly. I'd reminded her that her friends would find ways to keep her in their lives, and she didn't have to start from scratch. I'd believed every word I said to her, fervently.

Now swimming in the rapids of my own divorce, I recalled my well-intentioned advice, and I longed for it to feel as true and as certain as it had when I was doling it out.

On the last day of work before Thanksgiving break, I couldn't keep my sadness at bay, even though Zack and I were getting on a plane tomorrow to go to Illinois. I was worried that I had been fantasizing about continuing to live in a past that was gone, that I was setting myself up for disappointment. While all this was running through my head, Melanie came out to the elevator bank, loaded down with bags to take home for the long weekend.

After a minute or two of chitchat, I looked at her and said, "It's so hard, Thanksgiving."

"Yes. Yes it is," she replied, instantly understanding exactly what I was talking about.

"I know I believed everything I ever told you when you and your husband were breaking up," I said. She nodded. Then I said, trying not to cry, "But it just doesn't help, does it?" Melanie shook her head, her eyes filling.

I brightened my voice, as if it would brighten my mood, and said, "It feels better now, right? You're better now?" And she nodded and said, with as much conviction as she could muster, "Yes, it's better now. It's still hard, but it's better."

Two years later and it was still hard for her. I went into the subway hearing the word "alone" playing in my head over and over: *Alonealonealonealonealonealonealonealonealone.* It was all I could think about, me, who had never wanted to marry. I didn't understand how I could have given all my self-reliance away in my years with Chris. I tried not to hate myself for feeling so weak; I tried to hear the advice I'd given Melanie and to believe that my life was moving forward even though I still, one year later, felt like I was drowning.

I decided that all this was Chris's fault. Not the divorce, but the way that I still felt so terrible. It had to be because he was still too much in my life. Maybe my friend Paul had been right that night at the Old Town Bar: I needed to get tough, be mean, just seal off the place where Chris and I had been connected, and snap the emotional ties in the way everyone else in the world seemed to think was normal, as if thirteen years of connection could be rejected overnight. Maybe I wasn't an optimist, doing my best in a hard time;

maybe I was actually a masochist, and keeping Chris in my life like this was a way of hurting myself. I vowed to get better at separating myself from him. I was selling the house we'd lived in together, and Zack and I would start our new life soon—without Chris.

I had to go before my apartment's co-op board to be approved as a buyer. Such a meeting usually entails a simple review of the buyer's financials to make sure he or she can afford the apartment. But I felt exposed and not a hundred percent sure that I would be approved. I could definitely afford the monthly mortgage payment and the monthly maintenance, but I would be putting every single penny I had into the down payment for the apartment, leaving me with no cash reserves. Meaning that if I happened to lose my job, I would pretty quickly be unable to pay my mortgage. As I'd prepared for the meeting—sending in the sheaves of financial documents that detailed the financial tornado I'd been living in for the past two years, managing the house and all its repairs—I'd caught myself wishing I were a chemical engineer or a teacher or something that seemed *stable*. But then I reminded myself that the last time I'd been fired, I had managed to line up a well-paying freelance job in just days. I would be fine. If the worst happened, I would find work quickly. Hadn't this past year taught me I could survive anything?

When I headed to the interview in the apartment building in Brooklyn, it was pouring rain, curtains of water sweeping across the streets, chased by a bitter wind. Of course it's raining, I said to myself as I negotiated the storm with a giant umbrella, hailing a taxi near the office. The weather is wailing back at me because I'm going to a meeting tonight to put the stake in the heart of my house. I tried to shoo these magical thoughts from my mind and set aside the notion that the weather was proof that my house didn't want to let me go. As I rode over the Brooklyn Bridge, I rested my head against the cool glass of the window and stared out at the black river, water meeting water in the storm.

I was ushered into the apartment just above the one I hoped to buy, and led to a small chair surrounded by a semicircle of people who lived in the building's other seven apartments. I welcomed the sensation of facing my future. And it felt good to know that when I needed to park my car or unload groceries there would be people above and around me. For years I had wanted the independence of living in a house, and now I could hardly wait to give that up and be surrounded by others again.

The interview was straightforward, but I still felt vulnerable. One of the board members kept circling back to what my outstanding liabilities were, because I hadn't shown any on my net-worth statement. I hadn't remembered to list my credit cards and show their zero-balance statements; I hadn't remembered to show that I owned my car outright with no loan to pay off. So I haltingly told the whole story of the house and its repairs and the divorce and the way I'd had to borrow money from my parents and that I'd spent the last two years living up against the threat of losing everything, and that the last thing I had any interest in was taking on any more debt. That the apartment was debt enough, an investment in my son's and my future and in our stability. I told them how I'd chosen this very block and waited months for the right apartment to become available. I told them how all I wanted was to move in and move forward, and put all that had happened in the past two years behind me, and live somewhere that didn't leak, somewhere that felt safe. After all my talking, there were a few seconds of silence, during which I could hear the rain still raging against the windows. And then the interview was over. I got an e-mail from the sellers the next morning letting me know that I'd been approved, and that I'd been declared "lovely." I stood up and danced a little jig at my desk, sending my thank-you into the universe.

In preparation for packing up the house, I started going through all our belongings, a task that quickly became overwhelming, stifling.

Where had all this stuff come from? So many things I'd really cared about had been destroyed by this house—like my precious "shoe archive," a duffel bag in which I'd stowed shoes I no longer wore but couldn't part with, like my black Justin cowboy boots (1990–96), my thigh-high flat suede boots (1992–94), my six-inch-wedge platforms (1992), and my ivory suede sample-sale Manolo Blahniks (so very 1995), which had been destroyed by mold after the basement got wet. We'd had to toss out a dozen garbage bags' worth of toys and clothes and tools that had been ruined before the basement renovation, so I couldn't understand how there could be this much left. There were pots and pans of every kind and serving platters and wine coolers and cheese knives and ice buckets and at least a dozen vases and a seashell-themed cheese plate and an asparagus steamer and a fondue pot with its color-coded skewers and other equipment for entertaining. Everything that was left seemed to mock the security I had thought these items represented, the grown-up life in which I would be safe and happy. Many of these items were wedding presents, which made my heart ache. I felt I should return all the gifts with a note of apology; the givers had offered me and Chris all their love and faith (and a piece of cookware) and we had squandered it.

Why hadn't we registered for video games and a big television set and video cameras, items Chris would have loved? All this gleaming stuff of dinner parties felt like a reproach, archeological evidence that I had expected Chris to step into *my* dream of what our life would be.

I became a whirling dervish, shedding belongings as if they were tainted with anthrax. I dropped off fifteen bags of clothes and tablecloths and shoes and random household items like board games, two ice chests and all sorts of other things at the Salvation Army store. I kept searching for things Chris would *want*. In the end, I gave him our collection of everyday plates and cups and glasses—which had been given to us a wedding gift by my dearest friend, Eric—because I wanted Chris to have *something* from our life together. I deflated the AeroBed that, propped on cardboard boxes, had made the third-floor guest room look real; I gave away the cheap furniture I'd bought to dress up the house. I set almost-new stockpots and omelette pans out on the sidewalk in front of the house with a hand-drawn sign that read PLEASE TAKE. I needed to get lighter, have less, want less, need less.

But the past kept making its presence known. Chris got news about one of his best friends who'd disappeared from our lives some years before: Matt, Chris's best friend from college, and my boyfriend just before I had started dating Chris, had committed suicide in California.

We hadn't even known that Matt had been living in California. Dynamic, hilarious, gregarious, good-looking, Matt had been at the center of what was happening in a room. He loved music and being cool, and he was really good at being cool. But he had been struggling with depression and drugs and alcoholism and threatening suicide for years; he was furious at the world for not handing him the life he wanted to live. Chris and Matt's other friends had done everything they could to help, but Matt was too in love with being dark.

Matt had been the best man at our wedding, and he had been Chris's best friend for a long, long time. Matt was the first person Chris had met at NYU; an oft-told story about the two of them on the rooftop of the city dorms and something about a sandwich one of them was eating always made them laugh. A big group of us ran around in a pack in the East Village for years, spending Wednesday, Thursday, Friday, Saturday, Sunday nights out together, going to see bands, drinking too much cheap beer. At our wedding, Matt had made the only toast, a twenty-minute saga that kept everyone in the room enraptured, earned long and lusty applause, and silenced anyone who would have spoken after him. His toast was the benediction for our marriage.

I was standing in the dark purple living room of our house when Chris got the call on his cell phone; he'd been on his way out the door after spending an evening with Zack. Before he had even hung up, I knew what the news must be. I sat down, suddenly heavy, and my legs shook. When he put the phone back on its cradle, Chris turned to me and said, "Matt," nodding his head slowly.

I stood up and went to him and we held each other, wrapped up in the memories of everything we had shared with Matt—the youth that was gone, the dreams that we'd all had of what our lives would be—and the strange confusion of being so close and being apart at the same time. I pulled back and looked up at Chris and his sad eyes and said, "It feels like the end of something, doesn't it?" He just nodded, and we held on to each other some more.

We planned for both of us to go to the memorial service, but at the last minute I cancelled the babysitter. Matt had belonged to Chris; Matt still belonged to Chris. I didn't want the memorial service to turn into a eulogy for the end of our marriage, too. I hadn't seen any of Chris's friends since we broke up, and I couldn't bear the thought of marking two deaths on one day.

Out of the blue a few weeks later, after Zack and I had come back from Thanksgiving in Illinois, Chris decided to take Zack home to see his mother over New Year's, a surprise move that would have him traveling with Zack alone for the very first time right smack in the middle of the holiday crush. I chalked it up to his feeling alone after having spent Thanksgiving by himself in his apartment with a bottle of bourbon. So I said sure and seized the opportunity, planning a weekend ski trip over the New Year's weekend with two friends. I was thrilled Zack was going to be with Grandma and all the cousins; I knew that he would have a great time. Chris and Zack left town and I hopped in my friend Patrick's car and made the five-hour trek with him to Vermont; Alix would meet us there the next day.

But the winter cold with which Chris had boarded the plane turned into a full-blown sinus infection when he was in Illinois.

He started to slide into a crisis, and the two- and three-times-daily phone calls from him—theoretically about giving me updates on Zack's doings, actually about how Chris was so miserably sick and so unhappy during the visit—started to drain me. He complained about the flight, the hell of travel, and the horror of having inane, stupid humanity all around him; he complained about his mother, his sister, the way his mother and his sister talked over the television, and how his sister's husband just kept turning up the volume until Chris couldn't tolerate the din; he complained about his sinus infection, his boss, his company's Web site, and all the work he was being asked to do remotely. All the while his anger, his anger, his anger was pressing into my cell phone and pounding into my skull. This time, though, he wasn't mad at me; his anger wasn't my fault. But I still felt that he was asking me to help him carry it.

These repetitive conversations with Chris made me feel that I was living my own version of *Groundhog Day*. They were conversations we had had—or, more honestly, monologues I'd been captive to—when we were married. As his wife (still his wife), I could read all the signs that he was starting to nosedive: The amped-up energy, his cyclical arguments to himself, his pressing need to talk to me at great length. I guessed that the initial elation of being freed from our marriage had started to wane but not much else had changed in his life. He was overwhelmed by hating his job, a job I had assumed he would quit when he left me, the same job he'd been suffering miserably for eight or nine years now. He was still trapped in the cycle of needing enough money to live but then not having enough time to work on his movies, his company, his dreams. And now he'd sacrificed one of his release valves for this stress because everything that he hated in his life couldn't be my fault anymore.

I knew Chris was trying to puzzle his way out of feeling trapped in his life, but I didn't want to help him with that, dammit, because he'd puzzled his way out of our marriage! I understood that Chris was missing me, since this was the first time he was visiting his family since we'd broken up. I had missed him when I was at my parents' house, too; I'd felt his absence when I needed someone to commiserate with after the holiday dishes had been washed and put away and it was time to take stock of the ways the people you love most make you crazy. It was good to have a partner to remind you who you were as an adult when you found yourself facing your teenage self.

But I felt like I deserved a break. To be caught in these very same circular, solve-nothing conversations with him while I was skiing with friends and flirting with my cell phone boyfriend was more than I could take. I did my best to be polite, but I could feel anger come flooding back. I didn't want to comfort him or console him or commiserate with him. I wanted to punish him, though I couldn't bring myself to do it. I retreated into monosyllables, but Chris didn't even notice; here he was, needing me and erasing me at the same time.

Every time I hung up with him I was angry, and hurt, and trying to hide both feelings from my friends. I was ashamed that I didn't know how not to make room for him in my new life. My friends were confused, as everyone always was, by the way Chris and I still seemed connected. "Cut him loose!" one of them said in a joking way, trying to make light of my mood as we drank our wine over a fireside dinner. I was going to try. There was my New Year's resolution.

When we returned from our respective vacations, I decided to act as if Chris didn't exist, and the blur of preparing for the move out of the house and into the new apartment made that possible. I felt like I was holding my breath for three weeks straight, waiting to get the house packed up so Z and I could start over again in our new home. I took Zack over to see the apartment a few times, to prepare him for the idea that he would be living somewhere new. He took to the place instantly, pumping his little two-year-old legs furiously as he ran up and down (and up and down) the long hallway that stretched from the foyer to the still-empty bedrooms in the back of the apartment, his footsteps and laughter echoing off the high ceilings. I felt the tingle of anticipation, of moving into a place that had never been a home to the three of us, of claiming something as just mine.

It was so important to me to get this transition right. I had typed up a long list of every single renovation and repair I'd had done on the house, with the name and phone number of the workmen who'd completed it, to hand over to the buyers. I was disclosing everything, even tasks and work I didn't need to, because I was afraid that after I'd moved out, I'd find myself lying in bed awake on rainy nights, waiting for the phone to ring.

Just around this time, as luck would have it. I ended up at a business meeting with a feng shui healer and lifestyle guru, Ellen Whitehurst, and we talked through a range of ideas for possible partnerships with *Redbook*. At the end of the meeting, I couldn't keep myself from asking Ellen for advice, since she is an expert in the ancient Chinese practice that believes your home and your luck are intertwined: "I think I'm cursed by my house, and I'm getting ready to sell it. What can I do to make sure the house lets go of me? I'm afraid I won't be free of it."

Ellen asked me a question or two to understand just what I was talking about, and my whole story came tumbling out in a torrent of words, as it always does. Ellen just calmly looked at me across the table and said, "We can take care of this. We can fix this." I almost swooned with relief.

She sent me an e-mail a few days later with two different "cures" to help break my ties with the house. I read the e-mail and loved her suggestions, their poetic nature and elegance. One was a visualization, which I practiced every night for two weeks: me imagining the house whirling away from me, like Dorothy's house in the tornado before she lands in Oz. But I particularly loved the way Ellen recommended that I bless my new home: On the first night in the apartment, fill a basket with a box of coarse salt, a loaf of bread, a bottle of red wine. Then, pour some salt in a dish and put it in the basket. Pour a glass of wine. Tear off a piece of bread, dip the bread in the salt, eat it, and drink the wine, all while walking from room to room with the basket on my arm, carefully and potently envisioning the new life I wanted to see unfold in each room, down to the most minute detail.

It sounded lovely, and just reading the e-mail and telling all my friends about how the idea conjured a sense of calm in my head was comfort enough. I intended to do it, but then the labors of packing up my entire life with a two-year-old underfoot got in the way.

Moving day arrived on a brutal, bitter-cold day in January, the temperature well below freezing for the second week in a row. My family—Mom and Dad, both brothers, and Scott's wife, Kelly—all trooped up to Brooklyn to help me get unpacked. After three weeks spent packing up the house while trying to take care of Zack and do my job, I finally just gave in and paid the movers to pack the rest—easily the best $500 I have ever spent. And despite everything I'd given away in my panic to shed my past life, I still had nine or ten extra-large boxes of glassware and kitchen stuff. It was a nice reminder that no matter what had happened to me in the past year, I was now and forever the daughter of a Southern woman who really knows how to throw a party. Scott and Kelly started tackling the kitchen and my father took on the most important job of all, which was to get Zack's crib set up in his bedroom so he could come back home to me that night. After Dad was finished, he called me into Zack's bedroom, which I'd painted a beautiful, bright spring green, a color I believed would help my son keep growing into his naturally sunny personality. I was startled when I walked into the bedroom to see that the crib took up most of the space in the little room. I knew the room was just a little over eight feet by six feet, but suddenly it seemed too small.

I felt panic light up in my chest. *Oh, God, this will never work.*

As my head spun, my father drew my attention to the heat riser in the corner of the room, saying that the crib couldn't be too close to it because it was blazing hot and Zack might burn himself. But if the crib wasn't going to be close to the riser, then it would have to be in the middle of the room, and that meant the dresser and the rocking chair wouldn't fit. I couldn't not have the rocking chair that I'd rocked Zack to sleep in every night since he was born. We needed to keep our rituals in place! He needed to feel safe here. *I* needed to feel safe here.

I started to cry; I couldn't help it.

My mother had come into the bedroom as this was happening. My father steered me to the windowsill to sit down and my mother came over and laid her hand on my shoulder and said, "There, there. Everything will be fine after a time. You just need to get adjusted is all. This is a beautiful apartment and you and Zack will be very happy here. The room is plenty big enough and we'll figure out how to make it all fit."

I gulped a few times, and just drank in the feeling of my parents standing there wishing for things to be better for me. I'd believed myself to be the "strong one," in the family, the one they counted on to get things done and do the right things. But it felt so, so good to be small and sad and be allowed to be just that.

Again, I was surprised to feel the bad in the good. This was supposed to be my day of beginnings, but the truth is there would be no Here and There, no Before and After. I needed to continue to find the way to make peace with the challenges of the way every day contained a little sad and a little good, the way the grief was a constant undercurrent to my moving-forward life.

Much later in the afternoon, Chris came by to drop off Zack. Zack tumbled in the front door, thrilled to see my family and delighted with all the commotion, all the boxes and paper. Just seeing his beaming face was enough to take my blood pressure down a notch. I dropped to my knees to catch his running hug, which nearly bowled me over.

As my family and I continued our furious unpacking, Zack went to look out of the three big windows in the living room. He spotted my friend Kim approaching the building and called out her name: "Kimmmmm! Kimmmmm!" She'd come to see the new place and congratulate us, and she was carrying a bunch of tulips, a basket, and a shopping bag filled with a bottle of red wine, a box of coarse salt, and a loaf of bread. Here she was again, helping me keep my life moving forward, just as she had rescued me and Zack on Chris's moving day. I was touched beyond words, a lump in my throat.

Hours later, when my family had packed themselves back up into their cars and driven home to Philadelphia, and my sweet, happy son was asleep in his crib in his brand-new room with its bright, happy paint—and the rocking chair and dresser in place, after my father and brother did some finagling—I went into the kitchen and started my ritual of blessing. Because Kelly and Scott had unpacked my kitchen, I was able to find a wine glass and a little bowl for the salt. I walked down the hall with the basket on my arm and started in Zack's playroom, imagining him making ever-more-complex arrangements of track on the big train table in the ocean blue room, with his dad's help; and then I imagined turning the room into a place for him to do his homework and play video games as he got older, with a built-in desk and bookshelves. I went into my bedroom and envisioned it all furnished and finished, with a cozy warm-gray color on the walls, and an aqua ceiling that I could gaze at every night as I lay in bed. I looked at the bed and dared to think about sharing it with someone again someday; this made my heart race not from titillation but from anxiety, but I just held the image in my mind. I went through every room this way, pausing to conjure all the good moments I hoped to create there with my son, letting myself conjure my best-case scenario for what my life as a single mother could look like.

After I finished the long, slow walk through all the rooms, and I was back in the kitchen, I set down the basket and just stood there and smiled to myself. It had been such a simple thing to do, but I could feel its power, I could feel the pull and promise of the life that comes next.

After that lovely declaration of independence, I thought long and hard about trying to find a way to change the coparenting arrangements. I wanted to tell Chris that he would have to spend his time with Zack at his own apartment, or suggest that we move toward the more conventional custody arrangement, where there wouldn't be so much contact between Chris and me, but I just couldn't do it. I still couldn't fathom putting myself in a situation where I would go more than a day without seeing Zack, and I didn't want to move him to a new home and then suddenly give him two homes; it would be too much for both of us.

So instead I withdrew from Chris. In all our interactions, I spoke to him as little as I could, my eyes cast down, while he talked at me, barely even registering that I was trying to make myself invisible. I felt as if his talking would grind me into the wood floors—going on and on about his conflicts with his bosses at work, his attempts to have more time to work on his screenplay, his struggles not to be so angry all the time—but I remained polite, if distant, even though I felt I was being crushed by the weight of his burdens. When I went away on a business trip a few weeks after moving into the apartment, I told Chris I didn't want him to sleep in my bed anymore. That bed had been our bed, of course, but I felt as if it had gone through some kind of cleansing process in the twelve-block move that brought it to the new apartment. Chris ignored me, of course (the big red sofa now lived in his apartment, and my new aqua velvet sofa was too small for a six-foot-two man to sleep on), but just having told him what I wanted made me feel better.

When I came home from the airport after the business trip, Zack was asleep in bed and Chris was a fountain unstoppered. I heard every last detail of what had been playing out at his office, the same intramural struggles, the same communication issues, the same pecking order, and yet Chris was still in the same place with it all as he had been for the last several years. I unzipped my suitcase in the front hall and proceded to sort its contents, giving Chris as many "mm-hms" as seemed necessary and trying not to get pulled back into this conversation I'd had with him so many times. My take has always been: Accept the truths of how an organization is organized. If you don't have the authority to change those rules and structures, then you have only the authority to decide whether you can take it (and stay) or you can't take it (and then go). Why hadn't he left? Why hadn't he marched off in a whole new direction when we split up? I felt he was wasting the divorce that he'd wanted, and worse, that he'd gotten to walk away from what he didn't like about me, but hadn't had to give up one single convenience of our married life—me always taking care of things, making the plans, keeping the household going—except that I didn't cook him dinner anymore.

I kept unpacking my suitcase, getting angrier, and using my anger to create a wall between his troubles and me. I walked down the hall to deposit some dirty clothes in the laundry basket, Chris following me, still talking. I walked into the bathroom to start putting away some toiletries, shielding myself from his chatter by opening the medicine cabinet, putting the door between us. I walked back down the hall and got down on my knees in front of the suitcase to pull out more clothes and Chris finally snapped at me, "Could you show me some compassion here?"

"*Compassion?*" I shrieked as I looked up at him, totally incredulous. "Compassion? You don't get to have that anymore! You left me, remember?"

He slammed out of the house that night, and I felt for a moment that I'd won some small victory. But what had I proved? That I could be a bitch? That I could choose to reject him, too? Big whoop. The poison of the anger seeped into my stomach, making me nauseous. I was a world away from the calm I'd created walking through my home with my basket and my visions.

Nonetheless, I spent the next two weeks holding my anger like a small, hot flame in my chest, shutting him out. Chris figured out what I was up to. "Oh, you're not talking to me now? Okay, Fine. I get it." I started packing my Sundays full with errands and gym time and dinner with friends to avoid being around my apartment when Chris and Zack were in it, and our evening transitions shrank down to six- or seven-word exchanges, Chris picking up his bag and whooshing out the door; me flouncing down the hall.

But after a few weeks of this, I realized that my anger was leaving me exhausted and empty, and disconnected—and not only from Chris. I was losing more than I'd bargained for: I was losing myself. When I thought ahead to who I wanted to be when I got to the other side of the divorce—and I was fervently praying these days that I would actually discover that there was "the other side," as I'd been reassured by so many people—it wasn't this woman. The anger that had helped me throw up a fireproof screen when Chris and I were coming apart was putting distance between me and myself when I really needed to be listening to my instincts, so I could be learning not only who I was separate from Chris, but who I was for *me*.

And worse, I was denying myself moments I really treasured: the Sunday afternoons and evenings of my sitting at the dining room table reading manuscripts, or cooking, or doing laundry, while Chris and Zack played together in the living room, ate dinner, did the evening bath routine. Even though it caused poignant pain sometimes, I loved watching my son spend time with his father, hearing them make each other laugh, and witnessing as Chris grew more confident in his role as a parent. I loved to watch Zack just be instead of attending to his needs. The actions I was taking to try to protect myself were hurting me. And I was so tired of hurting.

It was in this frame of mind one afternoon—feeling stuck, and hopeless that I would ever get back to feeling "normal"—that I went to see my shrink, Dr. G. When I got into her office that day, she kicked off the session with her usual question: "And so how are you?" That triggered sobs. I lay on her sofa, chest heaving.

After a few minutes, I managed to croak out a few words. "I'm so tired. I'm so weak. I give up. Everything hurts so much, and I feel like I will never be free of it. It's like I'm in a river, almost drowning, being swept along by the current."

"And what does that feel like, being swept along?" she asked.

As I lay there on the sofa, I could feel only the whooshing sensation of being carried by water. I realized that it felt quiet, even though it hurt. "I'm just going with the flow, I'm just floating along. It's all I can do. I don't have any fight left."

"Maybe you shouldn't be fighting," she said. And that statement landed like a big, soft pillow right in the spot in my chest that ached so much I could hardly breathe. I knew she was right, but I was afraid not to fight, not to push for whatever I thought should be next; it was the only way I had ever known to live and to be.

Dr. G. sat there with me as I cried. We darted in and out of the conversation, but I was unable to stop the tears as the session ticked away. The expression on her face was tender and questioning; I could see how broken I felt reflected in her eyes. Finally I sobbed the last sob, stood up and gathered my bags, and headed toward the door; she stood up, too, and stepped toward me, putting out her arms and gathering me into her embrace. I fell apart again as she held me, sobbing into her shoulder, humbled by her reaching across the professional divide because I so obviously needed the comfort.

In my head, though, I was a little alarmed. To have your shrink take you in her arms? This person who gets paid to be professionally detached? Now I knew without a doubt that I was in a really bad place.

But in a few days I realized it wasn't a bad place; it was an open place. I was just yielding, and it was a totally unfamiliar sensation for me. I had done a lot of crying in the past year, but I hadn't yet given in to the miserable pain, even after that scary night on the kitchen floor when I pulled aside the curtain in my mind. I could now see I had tried to give myself some sense of control by holding fast to my idea of a tidy time line. I kept promising myself that I was getting better, even when I knew deep down that I wasn't. I was going to have to come to terms with the fact that the pain and grief would ebb and flow in unpredictable patterns, for months, even years, after I thought the healing was complete.

I thought back to the contractor who had told me that my basement had been built for the express purpose of taking in water, because I lived at the bottom of a slope. And I realized now that my soul had been carved deep to take in life's water. The grief of my divorce would stay with me and leave its mark. But I reminded myself that in a way this was exactly what I had wanted. I had wanted my marriage to leave its mark on me, and so I would simply have to learn to take the undercurrent of grief along with it.

I was starting to feel that letting go and giving in to the pain was somehow giving me comfort, like that quiet space in my mind I discovered at the kitchen table after Chris was gone. In fact, I was being buoyed up *because* I had lost my fight, because I wasn't thrashing wildly against circumstance. Grief isn't the mountain I'd first imagined, a visible terrain to be conquered one step at a time. Grief is a river, with hidden depths and coasting shallows; sometimes you're swimming for your life and sometimes you're being carried along by the same entity that threatens to drown you.

I realized that it was a relief to just give over and feel what I was feeling, instead of instantaneously reacting against it and creating a battle plan. I was learning that being gentle with myself when life hurt was a compassionate thing to do, a way of making room for the inevitable ups and downs of the journey, and it had simply never occurred to me before my divorce to do that. It brought a grain of truth to Chris's accusations that I was "never happy." It's not that I wasn't happy, it's that I wasn't *still*, because I had always been pushing, pushing, pushing myself to get to the next goal, unable to relax enough to be in the moment. I started to understand a little bit better who exactly it was he had been living with all that time, which was more gentle than blaming myself. And in that moment of clarity, I started to forgive myself for the simple, human failing of trying to solve life, instead of just living it.

I stopped willing myself to feel strong and started to let in the truth that feeling vulnerable is a condition of living. I would not be able to win my divorce, and I would not be able to win life, either. It suddenly became clear to me that no one had been keeping score, except me.

Everything I was learning was a Zen puzzle of sorts. Being carried by grief was better than always fighting to get away from it. Bringing Chris closer was making it easier to let him go. My infant son knew more about life than I did after all my years on the planet. I had friends and family to help me, but in this process of falling apart and putting myself back together again, I was truly, deeply, untouchably alone. As I talked all these thoughts through with my friends (and yes, with strangers, massage therapists and shop clerks and subway companions), shaping them and turning them into river stones I could store in my pockets, I started jokingly calling myself a Zen warrior goddess, but the comfort I was getting from these seemingly contradictory thoughts was serious indeed.

I e-mailed a friend from college who had always lived more on the woo-woo side of life than I did, running a yoga retreat in Africa and doing the hard, good work of bringing the best of East and West together, and gave her an update on how I was feeling and what I was doing. I wrote, "I'm either going to become a Buddhist or a talk-show host," explaining that as all these simple and obvious truths took root in my head, I found myself unable to keep from sharing them with others, that I kept finding myself with a ring of women around me at the playground or cocktail parties, all wanting to hear the story.

Her e-mail back to me was perfect in its simplicity: "Why not be both?"

I laughed. Why not? But I also could laugh because I was starting to discover the lightness in knowing that I had absolutely no idea what was coming next in my life.

9

When You Accept That You Can't Be Safe, You Can Be Safe

Every night when I got into bed in the new apartment, I lay on my side and gazed out my bedroom window at the big, tall tree that grew in the back of the building, its skinny, mostly bare branches reaching up into the sky, and the expanse of dark night all around. I loved the tree for how it pulled me out of myself, out the window, and into the wider world that existed beyond my own heartbreak and worries.

The tree came to represent my appreciation of being able to live life, even when it hurt—especially because it was a "weed tree," the humble alianthus, found all over Brooklyn. It became the first item I named on my nightly list of gratitudes, the mental tally of all I'd been thankful for that day: I was happy I had the tree, I was grateful for the friendly neighbors in our building, I had drunk in my son's loving nature in our bedtime ritual, I was still thrilled by the orange boiled-wool slippers my parents had given me for Christmas, I was humbled and happy to be living in a home I wasn't afraid of, a place where I felt safe.

I settled into our new home and our new routines, and I set aside my plan to freeze Chris out of this life. I also had to set aside my text-message boyfriend, the electronic connection being both too much and not enough: I became desperate for him to bring me answers about me and my worth, and life and love, and I had to be gently reminded, by both him and my shrink, that those answers, in the end, had to come from me. So I let my text-message account go dark and let him recede into memory, but I held on to what he had relit in me and dared to imagine a day when I might actually try to share that spark with someone in the flesh.

And then I was finally able to shut the door on the house Chris and I used to share. He and I both attended the closing—Chris being sure to take careful note of numbers on the big checks I would walk away with and deposit, so we could divide and divorce at last. There had been some complicated legal tussles in the final days and hours before the closing, which didn't surprise me at all; I had known there was no way this house would let go easily. When we arrived at the lawyer's office late on a Friday afternoon, the buyers' lawyer still wasn't there, refusing to show up until my lawyer and I made some last concessions regarding permit violations that had stood on the house, unchallenged and uncollected, since long before I'd lived there. I paid, of course (and argued about it with my lawyer later, since he should have caught those violations two years before, when we were the ones buying the house). I had to be rid of the house today. I would pay any price to close this chapter of my life; to close the door, turn the lock, and hand over the key.

When all was resolved and all the signatures were in place and the checks duly recorded, I stood up, handed over the keys to the new owners, a young couple, and said, "I hope you enjoy the house more than we did." Then I turned to Chris and said, "Okay, now let's get divorced." And I went home to my apartment, sending a huge thank-you to the universe as I walked in the door, Zack careening toward me, all smiles.

✻   ✻   ✻

Zack was now two and a half. He was absorbing the world and his new environment with abandon, and was in love with this brand-new concept of "neighbors." Having been freed from the vertical restrictions of a house with four stories, he'd run from end to end of the apartment, from playroom to living room and back, squealing the whole way. I winced for Marc and Pat, our downstairs neighbors and apologized to Pat when I saw her in the hallway. She demurred and said, "Well, he goes to bed pretty early; it's not like he's keeping us up at night." Pat and her generous spirit made my gratitude list that night, and many other nights, especially as Zack gained in speed and size and energy.

One Sunday evening as I was giving Zack his bath, there was a knock on the front door. Zack loved the surprise visitors who happened by in the apartment building, and as I made my way down the hallway to the front door he screamed after me, "Who is it? Who is it, Mommy?" It was Pat. She'd come upstairs to let me know that my bathtub seemed to be leaking into her bathroom.

Oh, God. Water leaking?

I focused on pretending I was calm and upbeat, even though I wanted to lay myself down on train tracks. It's not a big deal, I said to myself. This isn't the house coming to haunt you. This is easily fixed.

I offered to call my plumber—the one I trusted, who had fixed the basement, and have him take a look. I dreaded that he might have to open up the floor or a wall in my nice, new, recently renovated bathroom to look at the pipes.

When I called the plumber and made the appointment, I also placed an order to have a pricey bit of prevention installed elsewhere in the apartment: an automatic sensor and shut-off valve for the clothes washer. When I'd had the apartment inspected before I bought it, the house inspector had mentioned that the washer, like those in almost every New York City apartment, didn't have an industrial drain—make that any kind of drain—under it, so that if it or the pipes malfuctioned, gallons and gallons of water would pour into my downstairs neighbors' apartment. "Everyone thinks, 'Yeah, well, I have insurance to cover that,'" said the inspector. "But they forget that it's just a big mess and a pain to have to deal with the damage and the repairs. It's not a small problem." Well, I was familiar with the spectacle of gallons and gallons of water and the damage that went along with it.

The plumber came and detected a pinhole leak in my bathtub drainpipe, which he was able to fix from Pat's ceiling. And Pat was delighted to hear about the extra steps I was taking with the washing machine sensor. At the very least I figured I'd just bought myself a few more months of Zack running amok in our apartment, but I know deep down what I was really trying to buy was a little peace of mind.

Three weeks later, I had drifted off to sleep after my moment of gratitude for the tree when I was jolted into full consciousness by the sound of water somewhere in my apartment. I was up and on my feet in an instant, adrenaline rippling up and down my spine. How could I possibly be under siege by water? I stepped into the hallway and heard it pouring down between the walls. I padded onto the cold tile floor of the bathroom and saw it dripping from a spot over the sink and another breach in the ceiling right over the doorway. But it was the sound that made me sick, the sound of water coursing unseen above and around me.

I bolted down the hallway, out the door, and up the flight of stairs to my upstairs neighbor and started pounding on the door. Lori, startled, let me in; she'd been visiting with a friend in her living room, far away from the bathroom, and hadn't heard a thing. But as we headed down her hallway we spotted water pooling outside the bathroom door, and inside, the toilet was overflowing like a fountain, two inches of water covering the entire floor. The toilet was instantly fixed with a jerk of the handle, but as I headed downstairs to find Pat in the hallway, knocking on my door because the water had found its way into her apartment, too, I couldn't calm my heartbeat. It was just a leaky toilet, I kept reassuring myself, but I wasn't able to get back to sleep for a long, long time that night.

"Wow. What is it with you and water?" my friends commented when I told them the tale of the latest leak. I just shrugged. When people said it was creepy, I had to agree, but I said that instead I'd decided to call it "poetic," another of these weirdly literal and dramatic expressions of all I was struggling with: beating back floods, treading water, rebuilding foundations, trial by fire.

The unsettling memories of the fire at the beach house were all stirred up again one spring evening a few months later. Zack and I were sitting on the floor in the dining room, pushing a ball back and forth between us, our legs open in Vs to catch it, when he pointed at the bulky carbon monoxide sensor plugged into a nearby outlet and said, "It beeped." After a few more pushes back and forth, I learned from Zack that the battery had died, making the alarm go off and "beep," and that Sezi, our nanny, had unplugged the alarm and replaced the batteries.

Then Zack said, "Fire."

I felt prickles up and down my arms, but I calmly pushed the ball back to him and repeated, "fire."

"Fire," he said more firmly, as if making a point. "Big orange. Beeping." Now I was afraid, feeling the terror of that night, remembering the wall of flames, the sound of the sirens. I stopped the ball and looked straight at him.

And then he said, "Scared," in his little baby voice, pronouncing it "Skeeoud."

"Are you remembering the fire at the beach house?" I asked. He nodded. I tried to figure out what I was supposed to do with his memory of that terrible night. I said, "Yes, that was a very scary thing, but we were always safe, the fire was never going to hurt us."

I pushed the ball back to him, and back to him, and we drifted off the subject of the fire.

But as I was tucking him into bed that night, Zack said, "I see fire, big orange, Mommy." And then he said, "Eric," naming one of the two friends who had been in the house with us that night. Trying to prove to myself he wasn't recalling the fire with such intense clarity, I asked, "And was Kim there, too?" Zack shook his head no. And then he named Dave, Eric's partner, and Angus, their dog, all the people and creatures who'd been in the house that night.

I gathered Zack up in my arms and said, "Oh, Zack. I know, honey. That was a scary time. Mommy and Eric and Dave were scared, too. But you and I are safe. And they are safe, too. It's Mommy's job to keep you safe and we are safe here where we are. This is a big, strong building and no fires can burn it. Don't you worry." Our apartment was in a limestone building, so this wasn't a total lie. I stayed in his bedroom with him for a long time, rubbing his back until he was asleep, but my mind stayed restless. What was it I was promising him? What was it I was trying to promise myself?

I decided not to go to Amagansett that next summer, after four years of summer weekends out there. It wasn't quite that I felt it had been ruined for me by the fire, but it wasn't quite *not* that, either. Renting the house for the month had also been a lot of responsibility and work and a lot of planning. It was also a lot of stressful driving in heavy summer traffic, which was hard on Zack and hard on me. More than once I'd had to career off the highway onto the shoulder in a panic because Zack was getting carsick or just crying because he'd had enough of the traffic and being in the car. The mantras that I invoked whenever I was making a decision for myself and my life became "Choose simple" and "Choose the path of least resistance." I envisioned myself as a delicate egg, and imagined carrying myself around in my two cupped hands, as a way of acknowledging that I still felt hurt and fragile all these months after Chris had moved out.

And so instead of planning a big vacation for the summer, I accepted an invitation from my friend Tina to stay at her weekend home on the Cape for a week. Her husband and one-year-old daughter, Julia, would join us for the weekends on either side. I had spoken with Tina and she knew I was feeling very vulnerable and very needy. She said the magic words that I could not resist: "Let us take care of you."

Another college friend, Nancy, was going to join us for the first weekend with her infant son and husband, and Eric and Dave were going to join us for the second weekend, a perfect complement of personalities and people I trust—and a relief from the challenging and exhausting one-to-one adult-to-child ratio that I lived every day. It had been a year since I had taken a week off from work, and I allowed myself to dwell in vacation fantasies: the outdoor runs I'd be able to sneak in while Zack napped and the other adults were in the house, or the thought that I might actually get to read a book or a magazine on the beach while Zack was entertained by Julia and the sand.

But things did not go as planned. (Of course they did not go as planned. When would I stop expecting things to go as planned? When would I stop *having* plans?) First, I injured my hip while running right before the vacation, and wouldn't be running anywhere on the Cape. (And of course I'd hurt myself because I was running through the pain, instead of giving in to it. Another lesson.) Then when we got to Tina and Matt's house, Zack, used to having me all to himself, had no interest in sharing me with my friends. In the late afternoon of the first day, as Tina and Matt; Nancy and her husband, Kevin; and Matt's mom, Elsa, and her husband sat around the grill in the backyard, sipping wine and beer and dandling babies on their laps, Zack kept devising different tactics to pull me away from the adult conversation I craved. He would either drag me by the hand or arm up out of my chair and across the lawn, or would simply take off running, toward the street, toward the wooded trails, into the garage. I went into the house and came back outside with different toys to engage him, but he leveled a steady, flat gaze at me when I told him Mommy wanted to sit down and spend some time with friends, and could he play by himself for a few minutes. His answer, unspoken but clear, was no.

I felt foolish, being held hostage by my toddler. "Stace, come and sit and talk for a while," Nancy would say. "I'm trying," I would answer, keeping my voice as light as I could. I felt as if I were standing behind a glass wall, and though I kept playing scripts over and over in my head, I couldn't open my mouth to speak the words to ask my friends to help. They were busy with their own children and divvying up the duties of getting dinner ready. I was hideously jealous of their ease, the unspoken sharing of the tasks, the way their partners seemed to be managing the challenges of parenthood without feeling like they were being robbed of something else, the way Chris had.

Eventually all the babies, including Zack, were put to bed, and I got ready to nestle into the conversation I'd been hoping to enjoy around the fire pit with a nice glass of red wine. But when I rejoined the group, I still felt as if I lived in a different country and didn't speak their language, that language of quiet confidence and contentment and daily doings and lives that are unfolding just as they should be. No matter how mundane the start of the conversation had been, after a few minutes I'd be coughing up the viscera of my life, and that kind of unvarnished truth-telling wasn't going to fit into the relaxed mood here. After listening for about twenty minutes, I realized I was disappearing into myself, so I got up and walked out into the middle of the lawn and lay down, staring up at the dark, dark sky dotted with stars. I listened to the husbands chat about mountain biking and kayaking and muse about doing these things together in some potential someday, Tina and Nancy making encouraging noises. I counted the minutes to see how long it would take the others to notice that I was brooding in the grass, collecting sour apples while their laughter washed over me.

I had thought that I hadn't planned a vacation in a year because I'd been busy, but as I lay on the lawn, feeling the weight of silence and grief pulling again on my mind, I realized it was really because I'd been afraid of this: the way that having a moment to reflect still revealed so much hurt.

Later on, after the fire was extinguished, and the fourth or fifth bottle of wine had been emptied, my two girlfriends and I got some time alone together, sitting on the floor in the living room. I tried to express the loneliness I'd been feeling in my life, and even here with them. I fell apart, crying for all the months of crying alone, and for the relief of being with two people I knew loved me deep and wide. Nancy had to leave early the next morning, but she just held me tight, and Tina held my hands in hers and said, "We're your family, Stacy. You can count on us."

But there's an unbreachable divide between what people *want* to do for you and what they *can* do. Though Matt and Tina were generous in their hospitality, planning the meals, arranging activities, we could not get our children's schedules to mesh. Julia's two-naps-a-day schedule and Zack's one-afternoon-nap routine meant that we were always in the house at different times, and, like most couples, Matt and Tina had their own schedule-sharing, with one or the other of them disappearing for an errand, a run, or a bike ride when Julia was asleep. I found myself knocking around with Zack alone a lot, the very situation I'd been hoping to avoid.

After a difficult morning getting Zack to slowly eat breakfast, slowly get dressed, and then slowly getting ourselves together and out the door, I started pedaling my bike, with Zack in the carrier, the few miles to the beach to meet Tina and Matt, who had left an hour or so earlier. As I turned the corner to the final stretch, Tina and Matt drove by me, on their way back to the house. I stopped, confused, and turned around and pedaled all the way home, walking the bike up the big hill that led to their house, exhausted and disappointed. I tried not to feel I was on the outside of their life looking in, but it was hard, and I was miserable about being a bad guest.

Zack and I began to take long walks together each morning, down the hill, across the road, and down a long, winding path that led to some abandoned train tracks that crossed over a marsh. I felt safest when it was just the two of us, which was both comforting and ironic. But I simply breathed in and enjoyed the hours we were alone together, Zack looking for ways to charm me, me looking for ways to make him laugh, the two of us holding hands and taking in the beautiful scenery, his blond curls whipping around in the wind.

When all of us were together in the house, I felt very self-conscious about Zack's classic toddler behavior, which didn't bother me in quite the same way at home. Here I felt as if it was unsettling the household's calm order in a way that wasn't welcome. We kept bumping into rules that I didn't have at home and that Zack wasn't prepared for. On Wednesday, he put surface scratches in a much-loved coffee table when we were playing in the living room with Julia, despite the fact that Tina had put a towel on the table to try to protect it; he took all the toys out of the toy basket at once, spreading them around the playroom, while Tina quietly picked up behind him because Julia played with only one toy at a time; he grabbed toys away from Julia in a way I knew was just a normal part of toddler life, but that made Julia cry and thus put Tina and Matt on edge. I found myself saying no to him over and over and over. Zack was confused by his new role as a bad boy, and he reacted against it, throwing tantrums and expressing his frustration in a way he didn't at home. He could feel the tension in the house and he was reflecting it back at me, the way children will. I was desperate for him to settle down. I was desperate, period.

I kept thinking, *I hate being a parent alone.* If I just had another person here, this wouldn't be so hard. I needed someone to help entertain Zack. Someone to help discipline him. Someone to distract him. I wondered when I would stop missing my lost partner. I felt weak and worthless that this was where my brain went, and I cursed myself that free time only created the space for me to feel all my fears, all my loss, still. And I felt even more foolish that I had dared to believe that I could let down my guard, relax, be safe.

I spent the next day racing after Zack, trying to keep him quiet, trying to make him play more like a one-year-old girl than like an almost-three-year-old boy, an experiment that failed. Matt and Tina bought Zack a brand-new truck, to distract him and thrill him—which it did—but it didn't change the dynamic of the situation. By dinner that night, we adults were all strained and polite, tiptoeing around each other. After dinner, Tina and Matt disappeared into their bedroom without saying good night, and I heard snatches of an argument.

The next afternoon I stood in the living room, tears streaming down my face, begging Tina just to call the week a failed experiment and let me go home. She prevailed on me to stay, but in the morning I caught Tina and Matt in another row after Zack had made Julia cry by grabbing a toy from her again. This time I hurriedly packed up my car, hugged Matt and Tina goodbye, and left, two days early, on Zack's birthday.

We drove the seven long hours home—seven hours during which I replayed every incident in a hopeless spiral—and parked in front of the house. To decompress from the trip, Zack and I played out front of our building for a few minutes before unpacking the car, blowing bubbles, both of us relieved to be back in our regular orbit. As a neighbor's babysitter let herself into the building, Zack stopped to give her a big welcome, but then he stumbled and fell down the stoop, his face slamming into the cement. He sat up, screaming, blood pouring out of his mouth. I ran to pick him up and take a closer look, and through the copious blood, I could see he'd put his teeth all the way through his lower lip, making a big, ragged tear. I carried him inside to try to clean off the wound. I got a good look at the tear and saw it was even worse than I thought, so I grabbed hold of him, ran out of the apartment, and ran the three blocks to the hospital, amazed by how little attention we garnered along the way, a mother and her screaming son, blood all over both of us.

In the ER, we attracted almost no attention, either, and after ten or so minutes in the waiting room, which was lined with people who looked like they'd been waiting for hours, I once again took a car service to that hospital in Manhattan. We were admitted instantly, and seen by a nurse in ten minutes; she gave me a friendly, sad look after she asked for Zack's birth date. She leaned over and gave him extra stickers, while he, exhausted and bloody, leaned his head into my shoulder. I called Chris to let him know what was happening; he offered to come but I declined, not wanting to add him to the mix after our last ER visit. Zack perked up again when the doctors tried to examine him; he screamed and kicked and would not let the doctors get near his face, no matter how I tried to reassure him. The doctors left and a nurse came into the room and gave me the tools to clean the blood away from the wound, and then she left the two of us alone. I did my best to soothe Zack, explaining what was happening in soft, slow tones as I sponged off the blood from around his mouth and nose, and reminded him that I would never do anything to hurt him, and so he should let me clean his face so that the doctors could see his boo-boo. The fear in his eyes was so big, and when he tried to talk to me—"Mommy, let's go. Mommy, I want to go home"—it was hard to make out the words with his lip swollen to more than twice its usual size.

In the end, the doctors had to sedate Zack in order to give him the necessary six stitches (two inside, four out), but even in twilight sleep, he cried out, "Mommy, no!" as they put the needle in his lip. I was holding his hand, turned away from him so I wouldn't ever remember what it looked like to have my son's face sewn back together, but his cry made me weak in the knees. Spots spun in front of my eyes and I came right up to the edge of passing out. A technician made me leave our little curtained area and got me a glass of orange juice while the doctors finished the procedure.

When Zack came to in my arms twenty minutes later, he looked at me and said, "Mommy, you left me." There was no explaining that he'd been the one who left me, disappearing into the anesthesia, but I felt guilty for having had to leave during the procedure anyway. I just kept smoothing his hair and trying to wipe the dried blood from his hairline, telling him that we were fine, telling *me* that we were fine, though all I could feel was the sense that my life was closing in on me.

A taxi dropped us off at our home at two in the morning; our car was parked out front, still packed with our vacation luggage. My son had turned three today; he was growing up, growing older, and I was growing more and more certain that there was nothing in this life that was for certain.

If the safe place wasn't an actual destination in life, then where would I find it?

In the following weeks, Tina and I exchanged cautious letters, the confusion too heavy for e-mail, the thought of a phone call unbearable. We apologized to each other for . . . nothing, really, except for how it had all turned out. Because sometimes that's how life goes. Because sometimes life is hard and hard is what you get.

I headed right from this emotional maelstrom into another busy fall season at work, another year gone by, another Redbook Heroes luncheon to produce. We had been able to build on the success and buzz we'd created for the magazine and had attracted a fantastic celebrity lineup including an appearance by Harry Connick Jr. He was the first man we were honoring at this event, chosen in acknowledgment of all the incredible work he'd done in his hometown of New Orleans in the months after the floods caused by Hurricane Katrina.

But before hosting that luncheon I had a wedding to go to in Santa Fe, New Mexico. Holly, my assistant at *Marie Claire*, and now a writer and editor at *Redbook*, was marrying her longtime boyfriend, Gabe, and I wanted to be there. The week immediately following the wedding, I was scheduled for back-to-back black-tie events for work, the same week that our nanny would be on her annual two-week vacation home to Turkey. And it was the same week Chris had decided to claim as his own, for a week off from his job and his parenting duties, a week to write and work on his stuff.

When I realized that Chris's vacation and Sezi's vacation were going to overlap, I called Chris and asked him if he could change his plans, since he was staying home. The answer was a very brusque no, seething with disdain. Clearly I had pissed him off by asking this, as if I had insinuated that his vacation was unimportant. Once again, I was the selfish, bossy wife, who thought her complicated schedule mattered more; I felt all the terrible things Chris can think about me in the back of my throat like a bad taste. I cursed myself for having even called him to ask. I cursed myself for having any needs at all. *If I could just stop needing help, if I could just stop having wants, then I could be safe, and not be vulnerable to the way other people disappoint me and let me down.* I felt myself think this thought, and then chastised myself for having it. This was not the way to healing; this was the path to being hard. I desperately longed to go for a run, a half hour on the treadmill usually being enough to clear the voices of fear and self-loathing from my head, but because of my hip injury, I couldn't even do that.

So instead I invited myself to a half-hour self-pity party, where I listed all the decisions I'd made that had brought hard things into my life: I had married Chris, I had launched a demanding career, I had refused to give up the career to save my marriage, I had refused to give up the career when my marriage was over, I had bought an apartment that was too small for a live-in au pair even though a live-in would have made my life slightly more manageable, I hadn't spent enough time finding backup babysitters, I hadn't just gone for a shared custody arrangement, I hadn't learned to stop being afraid of Chris, I hadn't learned to expect that bad would almost always go to worse. And so, after having taken the blame for the shape of my life while at the same time realizing that if I hadn't made those decisions it probably would have changed nothing, I took a deep breath, let it out, and started to make other arrangements.

I picked up the phone and called Gregg and Melissa and asked, straight-out and simply, if they would be able to take Zack for that week. Nothing would be more fun for Zack than to spend a fall week on my brother's farm; running around with his cousin Anna and getting to see Gregg's cool tractor; by now Zack had graduated from Thomas the Tank Engine and was fully in thrall to John Deere. Taking Zack there meant I would be adding a two-hour drive down and back to two different days of an already-packed week, but it seemed like the best solution. I almost cried when Melissa said yes.

I hung up and reminded myself that it wasn't that hard to ask for help. That it didn't take a piece out of my heart to ask for help. That it didn't mean I was weak to ask for help.

Before Zack and I left town for Santa Fe, I had to squeeze in another visit to the emergency room with Zack, to get the ER doctors to take a look at his lip and figure out why two of the dissolvable stitches hadn't dissolved. They stuck out like the pin bones on a piece of salmon, and when I gave one a tug to try to pull it loose, Zack's lip would tug with it, making my stomach turn over and making him cry. Surely the stitches would eventually disappear, I had been thinking for weeks, swatting away the thoughts that their failure to do so was a sign of universal ill will against me. Finally, I called the ER, hoping to get the name of an ointment that would do the trick. Instead I was asked to bring him back in.

After examining Zack and the stitches, the doctors were visibly befuddled—which was not reassuring. They kept referring to his chart to check the day the stitches had been put in and made scary sounds about how long it had been, confirming for each other that, yes, the stitches most definitely should have dissolved by now. The doctors reached over and pulled on them the way I had. When that failed, they decided to try to pluck the recalcitrant stitches out with tweezers: two doctors and a nurse holding Zack down and clenching his head, Zack screaming in horror because of being restrained, but still managing to thrash his head around. I got up on the table on my knees and stared into Zack's eyes, telling him that the doctors were trying to help him, but after five minutes of his screaming and flailing the doctors gave up. I left the ER, the stitches that should have disappeared weeks ago still in my son's lip, and with no further advice from the doctors except that "they really should dissolve eventually." They were reassuring themselves more than me; in any case, my anxiety was not assuaged.

So, his stitches firmly in place, Zack and I made the long trip to Santa Fe for the wedding. He was a great traveling companion, charmed by the Dallas airport and the cobalt blue monorail cars we got to ride in when we had to change flights there. And in our two-hour drive from the airport, he was amazed by the scrabbly red Southwestern landscape, so different from the green and trees we had at home in Brooklyn; he asked me the name of every piece of brush he could see. He was slowly making that crossover from baby to boy, even though he was still in Pull-Ups. At the rehearsal dinner that night, Zack quickly located the only other child near him in age, exclaiming to this boy he'd never met, "There you are! I've been looking for you everywhere!" His confident, outgoing spirit helped make the event an even lovelier occasion, as he pulled me through and to things and people, always with his incredible sense of happiness and joy, my constant reminder that life was good, life was *meant* to be good.

The next day was the wedding, the first I'd attended since Chris and I had broken up. I worried that being a witness as Holly and Gabe made their beautiful commitment to each other was going to be too much to bear, that I was going to be selfish, and cry for my own loss. Instead I found myself holding my breath, hanging on every word, tears slipping down my cheeks as I craned to see and hear and take in all of it. The poignancy and power of watching these two people stand before a gathering of family and friends to make their vows rang even more clearly to me—the nakedness, the daring, the sheer beauty of it. It was all over both their faces, each of them overcome with emotion at different moments, all of us in the audience in those moments along with them.

The most beautiful weddings aren't the best-made parties; I smiled to myself as I remembered trying to impart this knowledge to the readers of *Modern Bride*, drunk as they were with choosing flowers and colors and party favors. The best weddings are those where the bride and groom dare to reveal and affirm to each other the soft places where they meet, and the audience is then able to become a part of the covenant. I remembered so clearly the way that Chris and I had met in those tender places, and had connected there for a long time. I remembered the love that had brought Chris and me together, and the bravery it took for us to stand up and share it so publicly, so joyfully, with a roomful of our family and friends. It had been real, what we shared. And it was still real for me, the memory of it, the history of it, all the ways it had changed me and fed me still visible in who I was today. Sitting there, a weeping guest at Holly and Gabe's wedding, I felt proud that I had dared to marry, and proud that I was surviving my divorce with a sense of optimism intact. I felt certain, in a way that I hadn't even when I married Chris, that I truly believed in marriage, and believed especially in the beauty and ritual of publicly declaring your gamble, of daring to hope for the best and chase after it with an open heart, bringing all the guests along for the ride.

After less than forty-eight hours in Santa Fe, Zack and I packed up and started the ten-hour journey back home: it would be one car ride, two planes, an hour stuck in the hell of getting out of a New York City airport, and then, after an hour-long cab ride, home at last. I was supposed to be up-and-at-'em the next morning, driving two hours to Philadelphia and back, so that I could be at my desk by noon or so, if the traffic gods were smiling.

But as we landed at JFK and I turned on my phone, I picked up a voice mail from Gregg: "Stacy, listen, I know this is pretty awful timing, but . . ." One of the dogs he and Melissa had recently adopted was having emergency pulmonary surgery that night. It wasn't clear how things were going to go, and there was just no way they could take care of Zack for the week. As Zack sat in his stroller, tired and hungry from the long trip, I replayed Gregg's message twice again to be sure I'd heard him correctly, waiting for the part where he would offer up an alternative plan. Then I put down the phone and just sobbed, grateful for the never-ending hustle in JFK so that I could hide in plain sight as I completely fell to pieces in the baggage claim area. Zack called out, "Mommy? Mommy?" but all I could do was take his hand. I finally calmed down and, wiping my eyes, looked at him and said, "Mommy's fine. She's just crying because something didn't go right, but we're fine." I would tell him later about his not getting to go see Anna, Melissa, Gregg, the farm and the tractor, but not now. He looked at me, believing me and not believing me at the same time. I felt my heart break even more. I wanted to protect him from all this. I wanted him to believe we—he—could be safe; it was my sole purpose as a mother to make him safe. But as the two of us sat there in the airport, waiting for our bags and waiting for my answers, I saw clearly that this divorce was going to touch him in ways I couldn't control.

I didn't know what to do or what to think or who to call or what to think or what to do or anything anything anything. I couldn't, absolutely flat-out wouldn't, call Chris. And I couldn't call my parents, because although they would probably offer to take Zack, I might not be capable of managing the emotional fallout I would feel if they didn't.

And so I called Kim, leaving a barely coherent phone message that ended with me in hysterics, apologizing for being such a mess. In the meantime I focused on the words "path of least resistance" and wondered what that was. Kim called me back just as my bag was showing up on the conveyer belt, and we agreed it was this: me, not calling Chris; me, not calling my parents; me, going to work; Zack, going to emergency day care; me, canceling my work-related events. That was the path.

Monday, I managed. I got up, dressed me, dressed Zack, fed him breakfast, fed me breakfast, packed his lunch, put him in a stroller, got on the subway, rode in a jam-packed subway car with the commuters all around me being annoyed by my stroller, got off the subway, and dropped him off in the emergency day care center after getting lost in the confusing hallways of the subway station/shopping center/maze that lies under Rockefeller Center. I had somehow come up from the subway platform on the wrong staircase and couldn't find the hallway that connected to where the day care center was tucked away, so I ended up carrying Zack in his stroller up two flights of stairs out of the subway, breaking a heavy sweat in the warm fall weather (always a nice experience in work clothes and high heels), and then pushing him two blocks to the center's street-level entrance. I was wiped out, mentally and physically, when I got to work.

I sat at my desk and tried to dive into the day, but as soon as Kim came into my office, I started crying again.

"How is this possible?" I asked. "How can these things keep happening to me?"

"I know, I know," she said. "It's a lot of hard all at once. You really aren't getting a break."

Not a single one. My running injury had taken away the one coping device that made life more manageable, and had added a raft of doctor's appointments—X-rays, MRIs, physical therapy—to my packed schedule. Zack's stitches from his birthday injury had not yet dissolved, and I still had to find someone who could figure out how to get them out. My divorce lawyer kept disappearing, and no matter how many times I called or e-mailed her, no updates were forthcoming about the state of the separation agreement that Chris and I weren't even disagreeing about. I had called on my family to help me, and then they couldn't help me. I was still afraid of my not-quite-ex-husband and the way he seemed to hate me. And I still had to start over on starting over, because here I was almost two years later, still stuck, still falling apart, still floundering, still drowning, goddammit. Still under water.

I managed to make an appointment with a pediatric plastic surgeon on Wednesday morning, to look at Zack's stitches. The doctor's office was a short walk from our apartment, but when we woke up on Wednesday, it was pouring: miserable hurricane-rain weather that put me on edge, a vague sense of dread creeping up on me until I caught it and reminded myself I didn't live in that house anymore and to let the feeling go. So I buckled Zack into his car seat and drove the seven blocks to the doctor's office and we scooted inside. When we got in to see the doctor, he sat Zack on the examining table, took one quick look at his lip, and said, "Hold still." He put his hand on Zack's forehead and gently but quickly guided him down onto the examining table. Before I even saw him reach for the tweezers—One! Two!—the stitches were out and the doctor was pressing a cotton pad against Zack's lip. Neither Zack nor I had had even a second to see what was coming, and now it was done. I was so relieved—and so angry. Zack had been through hell in the ER a second time, for no reason. This doctor didn't fuss about *why* the stitches hadn't dissolved; he had simply dealt with the fact that the stitches were still there.

It was such an obvious lesson. Try to solve the problem that's here in front of you. Try to focus on why your life is hard this second and fix that; don't keep getting all caught up in the reasons that your life became difficult in the first place. Everything isn't about the divorce and your bad luck. Sometimes rain is just rain.

But as I stepped out of the doctor's office into the downpour, carrying Zack and a huge umbrella to try to shield us, I couldn't help but think how everything in my life felt like an allegory. Or a poem. Or some kind of message handed down from the heavens.

When we made it back to our block, there were no parking spots. I drove slowly around the block in every direction once, twice; twenty minutes went by and not a single spot opened up. I double-parked outside our building and sat there trying to figure out what to do. I wasn't dressed for work, but I could just drive into the city with Zack to take him to emergency day care and wear jeans in the office. But then I would have to find a place to park in Manhattan, and wheel Zack through the streets, carrying his diaper bag and lunch and an umbrella, to drop him off at day care. And I hadn't made his lunch yet, or packed his diaper bag for the day care center. So maybe I could stay double-parked here, and bring Zack inside and put on a video for him to watch while I got ready for work and made his lunch and got his diaper bag. Or, I could keep driving and looking for a spot, and then have to carry him back home in the rain, because I hadn't brought the stroller to the doctor's office. Or, I could go inside and get the stroller, come back to the car, and then find parking. . . .

None of these options was good. I was going to get to work really late and really wet no matter which one I chose. *Decide! Decide! Choose the path of least resistance!* I couldn't decide. Every path created problems. I started to feel an anxiety attack setting in, the breath-lessness, the pounding heart, the dizziness. I tried to talk myself down, under my breath: "Calm down, stay calm, be calm. Breathe in, breathe out."

"Mommy?" Zack said plaintively.

I started to cry, for the eighteen-millionth time since Chris left me. Except that this didn't have anything to do with Chris or the divorce. It was that my sense that life was good—or even just good enough—was slipping away. I was going to fall apart right now, sit-ting here in my car in this torrential, unforgiving rain, right outside my apartment building, because I could not decide what to do next. I took in one long, ragged breath, reached for the key in the ignition, and turned off the car. I got out in the pouring rain and untangled Zack from his car seat and ran inside with him in my arms, leaving the car parked in the middle of the street, having managed to decide, at least, that, yes, a ticket was the least of my worries.

We were soaked to the skin when we got into the building. As soon as I unlocked the apartment door and opened it, I sank to my knees and cried raggedly, unable to hold myself back from giving over to the feelings. I took off Zack's jacket and his boots, while he stared at me wide-eyed. Sobbing, I offered him all I had: "I'm sorry, Zack, I'm sorry I'm crying. I just don't know what else to do. Mommy's just sad, honey. But we're safe, we're fine. I love you."

Then I lay down on the hallway floor, and I gave up. For the first time in my life, I felt what it was to actually wish I were not alive. I didn't want to kill myself, I just wanted not to be Not Here Anymore. I wanted to will myself into nonexistence, to disappear in a puff of smoke. This was actually the path of least resistance, as far as I could see. Zack just walked around me, saying, "Mommy? Mommy? Mommy cry?" But I was too far away for him to reach me. And that was the scariest feeling of all.

I did get up off the floor. And take then Zack to day care and go to the office. Yes, I'd hoped that by now I'd be finished with this crushing grief, this continually reappearing astonishment that life could hurt so much and that I could be so unprotected. But in that state of utter resignation, lying on the floor of my front hallway, I'd heard the truth I needed to know: I didn't want to be dead. I wanted to be here. I wanted to live this, even when *this* didn't feel so good.

More than once since Chris had ended our marriage, I'd been brought to my knees—or, more literally, been brought to a prone, please-God-take-me-away-from-all-this position—and I still believed that this life was worth living. Or, more to the point, *I* was worth living. I was worth it. I possessed worth. I played with these words over and over in my head in the days following my breakdown the way you slide tiles around on a Scrabble rack. I used the words to console myself for having let Zack see so much pain, to forgive myself for having failed to be a parent in that moment, to remind myself that wisdom comes only when and where it comes, and you have to be open and ready and willing to accept it whenever it lands on your doorstep.

In the same way I'd had to accept the divorce that landed on my doorstep.

I realized that if I have no idea what's coming next in life . . . then, well, I really have no idea what's coming next! That if I'm not in charge, then I'm not necessarily to blame when my life gets hard. And that what's coming for me could be good and surprising and wonderful as easily as it could be stitches that don't dissolve or vacations that don't work out as planned.

After months of endlessly asking myself the question "Why me?" I was reaching the point where I realized "me" wasn't even in the equation. The events that came into my life—the floods, the fire, the stitches, the blood, the rain, the water, the endless water—had come into my life . . . just because. In trying to comfort me through this last round of unfortunate events, friends would reflexively say, "You are due for a break." And I would reply, "Nope. Not necessarily." Not because I was being negative, but because I was being realistic. I was learning that these situations that tested me to my limits didn't come into my life because I deserved them, because of my karma, because I was cursed, because they were life's way of proving to me that I would never be happy. They came Just Because. Because each one was what came next.

The concept of Just Because used to be totally terrifying to me. If it all came down to chance, then what could I do to be sure I was safe? Nothing. You can count your blessings or practice gratitude. And then you have to let go and fall into all we cannot know and live your life. My myriad attempts to master life would be foiled again and again, or, more accurately, more confusingly, my attempts would be foiled sometimes and rewarded sometimes, leaving me to wonder whether I'd been "good" or "bad" or hadn't invested enough in the karma tip jar at my local Starbucks, or whether those mean, petty thoughts I'd had about the guy in the car next to me on the highway had rebounded through the universe, ricocheting back to me. Yes, it mattered to be a good person, to be compassionate, to care about others. But it mattered because of what it made me feel about *me* and about life, not because that quarter in the tip jar was buying me a golden future. Because, no, I don't get to know what's next, just as my mom told me when I said I was in love with Chris but so afraid. I didn't get to know then, and I don't get to know now, or ever.

Yes, this is a scary thought. But getting away from causal thinking—from "if this, then that" thinking, from thinking that I have any ability to program my life—was helping to lighten my load. Because if I'm not actually in charge of what happens to me, then all I have left to focus on is: How close am I living to my truth? And that is a Buddhist TV-talk-show-host way of asking, Am I who I want to be—inside? Not my accomplishments: a woman who made her girlhood dreams come true, a wife for ten years, the editor in chief of *Redbook*, a would-be poet and a dreamer, the owner of a really outrageous collection of four-inch heels (of which I am extremely proud). I hadn't wanted to be divorced partly because I feared what it said about me. But I came to see that it says nothing at all—except whatever meaning I give it, and whatever credence I give to the opinions of others, who know nothing about the inside of my marriage, much less the inside of me.

And so I realized that what my divorce was teaching me was that I am an optimist—something I'd always wished or hoped was true about myself. It had been part of my public persona since I was a precocious, know-it-all girl. "I'm a relentless optimist," I'd say, feeling proud of myself for having such a deep and thoughtful statement to make about myself. I said it then as a way of pronouncing that I was strong, but today I hear those words and know I say them because I dare to admit that I'm soft. That I believe in the power of love. That I believe that life is worth living. That I believe it is just as likely that there is something good, something amazing, waiting for me around life's next corner as it is that there is something terrible. I expect some of both, frankly. But I know that my optimism will prevail.

It was only through my divorce that I realized how deeply I liked and loved who I was. And that I would be fine, I would be safe, because I was safe in how I felt about myself, I was safe in knowing that I could trust myself to get through anything. And I was safe because I'd had the opportunity to lift my proverbial hood and take a long look deep within. And I had discovered that I really liked what—and who—I saw in there.

And so I found ways to really begin again. I joined an online group, Park Slope Single Parents, reveling in both the intimacy and the anonymity. My first post after I introduced myself to the group was a lengthy one detailing my confusion about the vacation gone wrong, and how I didn't know how to help my friends understand the grief and aloneness of being a single mom. I printed out the responses that people sent me, and I felt that I'd been understood.

I checked in on the site almost every day, reading long, impassioned posts from moms who were struggling to make ends meet, or wondering aloud how their ex could just not show up for a planned visit, leaving their child wondering why. I was blown away by the stories of single moms by choice and how they grappled with all the difficulties of being a solo parent—how to run errands, buy groceries, park your car in the city, afford day care—without even having the luxury of blaming their worst days on someone else's departure. I was heartbroken to read how many divorces and custody battles were tipping into full-on wars. With topics such as love, money, parenthood, divorce, and honor in the mix, it's not surprising that the occasional fight would break out in the group, with people typing as fast as they could, occasionally SHOUTING IN CAPITAL LETTERS, jumping to refine or challenge a perspective they felt called their own choices and actions into question.

One weekend, after one mother had described a poisonous exchange with her ex, and four or five other mothers had chimed in with tales of egregiously bad behavior from their own exes, one poster asked: "What is it that you are doing that is making them react like this?" I was shocked by the insensitivity of the questioner, and I rushed in to defend the women who'd shared their tales of woe.

> *To your question I say: It is not one's actions that cause the other's actions (i.e., most single mothers do not willfully create monster exes who use the children to spite the woman for her independence or whatever other evils she's visited upon him), but rather the CHEMISTRY between the two adults. To think that one has total power to control how a divorce plays out is naive. Like a relationship, a divorce/separation/breakup/custody agreement is controlled and managed by two people and how they dance together. And sometimes the dance goes awry.*
>
> *As for me, I am very lucky. I have an extremely unusual co-parenting relationship with my soon-to-be-ex-husband. I am lucky because Chris (my ex) was very invested in the idea of redeeming himself for walking away from our ten-year marriage (with no counseling, no effort, no hope) by remaining an active partner in Zack's—and therefore, my—life. But he totally broke open the marriage of his own will, and not with my agreement. I was devastated. And angry. And hurt. But what I found in this horrible, horrible two years since this all unfolded is that (1) I'm bigger than I thought, and (2) Chris is bigger than I thought.*
>
> *Having generous thoughts about Chris isn't always my favorite thing to do, but the paradoxes of what he and I have been through since we broke up are truly awesome. I feel closer to understanding myself than I ever have before in my life because of having to face the pain with wide-open eyes, and to continue to think well of him, even when he did (and continues to do) things I didn't like. And the truth is, I actually wasn't so good at that in our marriage. And being forced to finally learn it because we broke up? Well, that's God's way of laughing, I suppose.*

But I feel as if this whole experience has been like yoga: it's a practice. I practice being big enough every day to will myself to forgive him his many failures. And not because I'm a saint. And not for my son. For me. For my sense of self. For being able to trust myself to make a choice to have a partner again. For not punishing myself because my marriage fell apart despite how much I wanted it to work.

And having been through all that consciousness-raising, I can say: IT'S NOT FUN! And so I am not surprised when it is a path people can't choose, because there are so many other tantalizing options, like being "right," or being cruel, or being unforgiving, or wanting to demonstrate to the ex that YOU WILL HOLD NO POWER OVER ME!! Fear and fear of not having control are powerful forces, and it's no wonder the brain offers up a hundred more savory options.

The human spirit is flawed, and it wants its rewards fast. This is how people can end up in such a terrible place. And I truly am awed by all of you going through what you do, because it was freakin' hard enough for me, and I had it easy. To you I say, brava! And you didn't do anything to bring this on yourself. But the question remains—and it's a life's work, this question—how can you make it easier on yourself? Are you practicing that?

Stacy

Mom of Zack, 3

Finding this community meant I could explore what was happening to me out loud instead of blurting it out to a colleague at a black-tie dinner—which I did more than once. It was a place where I started to understand the me who I was becoming, the me I'd probably always been. I realized many things by sharing myself in this community, beginning with the fact that I was not actually a single mom, but a mom who was no longer married to her child's father. I had too much support and presence from Chris to pretend I was on my own in parenting, and so I let that go and felt grateful for what remained between Chris and me. I discovered that I had a bottomless resource of compassion for and interest in these people I didn't know who were sharing their struggles and successes on the message board, which inspired me to shine a little of that compassion toward myself. I finally came to accept that I wasn't a loser or a failure or a freak or flawed or any of the dozen other negative labels I had tried to apply to myself, because there was a lot of very interesting and worthwhile company to be found in this land of broken dreams. Even though I was totally alone in the slow, hard work of putting myself and my life back together, there was an entire world of people who knew expressly what that quicksand struggle felt like.

Best of all, not one of these people needed my story to be anything except my story. They didn't automatically start to use my life to serve whatever it was they already thought about divorce and love and failure, because they weren't people who already had answers; they were people with questions. And I was now someone who was trying to live life's questions, too.

One Saturday afternoon in November, Nicholas, a single father of two boys, and a prominent voice of reason and compassion on the site, hosted a potluck. Zack and I showed up at his house with a big bowl of homemade tabbouleh and spent the afternoon among a roomful of families that looked kind of, sort of, but also not quite, like ours. It was the happiest kind of chaos, with all the adults trying to align our first names with our online names, and put faces to the voices we'd all been reading online, and the children wreaking havoc all around us, leaping and screaming and brandishing plastic swords and yelling and laughing, so pleased to find themselves in a full-size army of playmates.

On the surface, I didn't have a lot in common with many of the people in the room. We had all had wildly different life experiences, different educations, different backgrounds. A handful of the women had come to the United States from other countries: Sweden, Slovenia, the Dominican Republic. A couple of the women were lesbians who had adopted their children or given birth to their children on their own. Some of the parents were parents of teenagers. One parent had lost a spouse to drug abuse. Some of the women had had two children with different fathers, single moms twice over. Everyone had a unique story of how he or she had come to be a single parent, and the complexity and diversity of our stories was comforting. But for all the ways we were different, what we shared was what counted: for the first time in months and months, I didn't feel I had anything to explain about my life.

I waited until Zack was two tantrums past time to go, because I wanted never to leave that room, with its table of homemade dishes cooked from scratch by all these people who, I knew, had the least amount of time to themselves. And yet they had taken the time.

Soon Thanksgiving was upon us again. Chris was going to take Zack to Illinois, and this year, I was ready. I made four days of plans, packing the time as much as I could to try to protect myself from hitting a wall of grief. (All the while shaking my head at myself a little bit, because I knew I wouldn't be able to protect myself if the grief was going to come.) Eric and Dave and I made reservations for Thanksgiving dinner at one of our favorite restaurants. I invited my family to my apartment on Sunday to join me for the very first proper Thanksgiving feast that I would prepare myself, ever. I intended to spend the rest of the weekend on an ambitious DIY project I'd been planning for months: painting a huge gold-and-silver floral stencil on the wall behind the bed in my bedroom (with its gray-beige walls and aqua ceiling), something I'd never be able to do with Zack underfoot. It was a perfect way to pass the days without him, and I'd have something to show for it all when he came back.

But things didn't go as planned. Zack threw up all over himself on his way to the airport, and Chris, with a big, fat mess on his hands, freaked out and decided not to try to fly with Zack, unsure whether he was carsick or he'd caught a virus. Chris called me three times in his panic, trying to figure out what to do, but I stayed calm and didn't feel burdened by his indecision. I suggested that he go to the airport and get Zack all cleaned up and see if they could take a later flight that day, but Chris decided to turn around and come back to Brooklyn, to my apartment, so he could figure things out from there.

By the time they got back to my place, Zack was feeling better, though he was covered in "red," as he kept calling it (strawberries having been on the menu for breakfast). I stripped him down and started the laundry, then gave Zack a bath as Chris, extremely upset, and probably feeling like the universe had it in for him (and I knew the feeling), got on the phone with his mother and the airlines. Chris decided he didn't have the energy (or the desire) to try to make it back to the airport over the busy holiday weekend, and that he would postpone the trip for a few weeks. He turned to me and started to talk about how we would share Zack for the weekend. I felt a lick of panic start in my stomach: *Oh, God, there go all my plans. Oh, God, Chris is going to be so mad that I don't want to just take Zack back for the whole weekend, with Chris coming in and out for his shifts. Oh, God, Chris is going to tell me I'm a selfish and awful person again!* But I got a grip, took a deep breath, and said, "Chris, I made a lot of plans for these four days. I would love to have Zack all day Saturday when my family is here for Thanksgiving, and I'll take him overnight Saturday, but I am packed with plans on the other days, and I can't change them—I don't want to change them."

I did it. I stood up for myself with Chris, and I hadn't needed to make him look bad or turn myself into a martyr. I had merely said what was true for me: I had opened myself up to the possibility of no, instead of trying to scheme my way into yes. And Chris had heard me and said, "Okay." Yes, feeling vulnerable is a condition of living, I reminded myself. I still didn't love this notion, but I felt a lot of gratitude for the moment I was living: a successful exchange with Chris, three days for me and my plans, and Zack with me and my family for Thanksgiving dinner on Saturday.

On Thanksgiving day it was pouring down rain, but for once it didn't feel like a curse. Eric, Dave, and I hopped in my car and drove into Manhattan for our night on the town—our night on the empty town. Because of the rain and the holiday, we were able to park right in front of the bar where we went for drinks, and then we parked directly in front of the West Village restaurant where we had made a reservation for Thanksgiving dinner, the cobblestone streets shining with rain and lamplight. The prix fixe menu at the restaurant offered three choices in each course, and so we got one of each, tasting everyone else's meal until we were stuffed full of good food, good wine, and the great feeling of doing just exactly what we wanted to do. Friday, I precooked some of my Thanksgiving dishes—lyonnaise potato gratin, sausage and cornbread stuffing—in between hours of mapping out exactly how the stencil would go on the wall and testing my painting techniques on cardboard. I was happy as a clam to be filling my brain full of things other than work and toddler time. It was like being reintroduced to a very familiar stranger, this side of me that belongs to me alone (an expression I use at work to capture the part of our readers' identities that *Redbook* is serving). And I was really looking forward to making a holiday in my own home, to filling my house with happiness and family.

The next day, my turkey came out perfectly. And I mean perfectly. The tented-foil trick my mother had suggested worked out great, and I had been able to "borrow" an upstairs neighbor's stove so that the seven different dishes were all hot and ready at the same time. I set up a beautiful buffet on my wobbly dining room table, lit tall candles, arranged some harvest flowers, and beamed while my family heaped their plates with my beautiful Thanksgiving meal.

Before we ate, I made a toast, thanking my family for standing by me during so many difficult months, and for having helped me in every way that they could. And I tentatively announced that I believed I was truly through the worst, and said I was so happy to have them here with me today to celebrate family and gratitude. Zack said "Cheers!" when we all raised our glasses, lifting his sippy cup in concert. Of course, if things had gone as planned this Thanksgiving, Zack wouldn't even have been with me today. I just smiled at him, and to myself and the universe.

My January birthday is somehow now irretrievably tangled up with my divorce and the years of instability surrounding it. I broke the news to my family on my birthday, shortly before Chris moved out; the year before, five days after my birthday, we had moved into the house with an six-month-old baby; the following year, two days after my birthday, I moved out with Zack. All those events had overridden whatever desire I might have had to celebrate my birthday in those years. But in 2007, I was beginning to breathe again. I had celebrated Christmas at my parents' house and New Year's Eve with the Park Slope Single Parents (we drank our champagne at 6 p.m. to toast midnight in Paris, since our kids would all be in bed asleep at midnight in New York City). I made plans for a nice dinner out with Patrick and Alix and Eric and Dave for the weekend after my birthday. But on my actual birthday I found myself riding the subway home from work with no real plans in mind other than going home to Zack.

I came up from the subway and started to walk past the French bakery in my neighborhood as I do every night, except today I turned around, walked into the bakery, and bought a little chocolate mousse cake. When I got home, Zack was already in his pajamas, and I asked him if he remembered what today was.

"What, Mama?"

"It's my birthday," I said. "And I have cake."

And so once we had sent Sezi on her way home, we sat down at the dining room table and I snipped open the red-and-white-striped twine around the pastry box. I put the cake on a plate and stuck a candle in it, and once it was lit, I started to sing "Happy Birthday" to me.

"No, no, no, Mommy!" said Zack. "*I'm* going to sing it!"

And sing it he did, keeping his eyes fixed on the chocolate mousse cake the whole time, just in case it should decide to wander away. I was filled with all those oogy mommy feelings you get when your child is being impossibly cute. But more than that, I was feeling something new: *This is my family. We are a family. And I am so, so grateful.* When he finished the song, he let out a big, lusty "Yaaaaaaaay!" and then said, "Okay, blow out the candle, Mommy!"

I closed my eyes and leaned over the cake and made a simple wish that my life would forever be filled with these kind of unexpected moments of love and sweetness. Because I knew I didn't know what was coming next. But I could make my wish—and, actually, call it a pretty safe bet—that at least some of it would be as magical as this.

10

The Answer Is a Riddle

On a late-winter day a few weeks after my birthday, snow still on the ground in big piles, Chris and I met for a long mediation session with our two lawyers, to finish negotiating some of the fine points in our separation agreement. The broad terms of our financial separation had not changed at all in the eighteen months since the hushed nighttime conversations Chris and I had had in the backyard as we stared into the black sky, but my lawyer had been inexplicably slow. Over the past year I'd sent her many cranky or pleading e-mails and left prodding phone messages to urge her along, with little result. I had considered dropping her, but I simply couldn't face adding "find a new lawyer and start all over again" to my to-do list.

So after I'd made it through the upheaval and labor of moving, I insisted that my lawyer schedule this mediation. I wanted to dispose of all the remaining questions in a single face-to-face meeting, rather than lose another two or three months in the back-and-forth paper-pushing that defines the legal process of divorce.

It felt a little awkward and a little stiff to be seated at the big round table with Chris and his lawyer, whom I had found for *us* when we first thought we would try a mediated divorce. That was before some friends reminded me I was the one with money to lose, and so I should definitely have my own legal representation. It was probably bad advice; Chris and I weren't fighting about who gets what, so we definitely could have divorced with a single lawyer to write the separation agreement and handle all the paperwork. But as I'd never been through a divorce before, in the beginning I'd found it hard not to take whatever advice came my way. At the very least, it was comforting to sit at the table now and feel that my faith in my own judgment had come back. But it was strange to have these two people doing all the talking for the two of us, as if they were protecting us from each other—especially since Chris and I talked almost every day on our own, like adults. Like friends.

But in this meeting, Chris appears tense, studiously looking at his hands or the table, avoiding my gaze. His mouth is set in a firm line. There's one issue we've disagreed about in the document, and Chris seems to be focusing all of his energy on it, preparing to do battle. The lawyers start going through the separation agreement and outlining the broad points, rounding up a dollar amount here, eliminating some retirement fund–sharing there, and again confirming that in regard to Zack, Chris and I are adopting the language of "primary residence": Zack will live full-time with me and Chris will have plenty of scheduled time with him. We review the visitation schedule: Chris is to have Tuesday nights, Thursday nights, and either Friday or Saturday night (to be discussed and agreed on in advance) as well as most of the day Sunday, and one morning a week. The morning is the third-rail issue, the one Chris has his prickles up about. It's in there so that Chris could take Zack to school once a week, participate in that routine for himself, and for Zack—and in the process make it possible for me to attend early meetings and schedule early appointments once a week. What has his back up is that I am asking him to come early enough—6:45 a.m.—that I can also use that morning to go to the gym, since on every other morning I am home with Zack until the babysitter gets there.

When my lawyer brings up the morning visitation time, Chris snarks out some comment about how the visitation rights are for taking care of his son, not taking care of me. My lawyer reminds him in her calm, lawyerly tone that sometimes helping take care of the primary residential parent is, in fact, part of taking care of the child, and his lawyer concurs. Chris cedes the point, but thinks it's too early in the morning and I'm asking too much. I am fuming inside: I have agreed to take on the bulk of the parenting responsibilities—all the shopping, the cooking, managing the child care, the schools, buying all Zack's clothes, everything—and Chris won't even help me fit in one workout a week. I acquiesce, feeling sheepish (and selfish) that I was trying to get some time for myself, while at the same time feeling pissed and hateful. I am confused by feeling both things. I am tired of feeling both things. We finish the mediation session, agreeing that the document is now complete with one morning a week at a later hour added—which will allow me to get to work early, but not get to the gym—and I hang back to talk to my lawyer, so I can avoid having to talk to Chris in the elevator on the way out of the building.

It's a Thursday, which means tonight Chris will be the one to go home and relieve the nanny and put Zack to bed. As my cab pulls up in front of the apartment building at 9:30 after my work event, I'm annoyed that I'll have to face him, since I'm still feeling bruised from the day's mediation. I give the front door to the apartment the hard push of my palm it needs to groan free of the doorjamb, and then I step into the foyer. Chris is sitting at the dining room table, as he always is when I get home, at work on his computer on making his dreams come true without me.

"Hey," I say, tossing down my keys on the table and flipping through the mail, moving past him into the kitchen, opening up the fridge, surfing for a snack.

Chris is all energized and bright. I can feel he's happy to see me, that he sees the light at the end of the tunnel in finishing our separation agreement.

"Didn't you think today was good?" he asks.

"Yeah, sure," I say into the refrigerator.

The kitchen is a tiny anteroom that opens onto the dining room. I close the fridge and find myself standing just behind the glass cabinet that hangs between the two rooms. I'm eyeing Chris through the panes, trying to hold on to the sense of superiority that being self-righteous gives me, but he starts talking about how the process today was a relief, how we accomplished so much after months and months of being stalled.

This is true, but I don't want to admit it to him just now. I still don't want to be his partner in this undoing, despite how far we have come. But Chris is clearly feeling relieved and happy and is trying to connect with me. Then he apologizes for being on edge at the mediation session and explains that it came from how much he hates early mornings (which, of course, after being his partner for thirteen years, I already knew). I want to cry. I'm tired. And I'm tired of resisting his niceness.

So instead of cooking up a manipulative response, I just speak.

"You made me feel like I was asking for so much, like I'm insane for wanting one morning a week to myself." I say this standing halfway hidden by the doorway; I have to protect myself with distance and wood and wall. "When you get angry at me like that," I continue, "I feel like I am a shitty person for trying to have something for myself."

Chris looks down at his hands. Then he looks up at me and says, "Angry?"

"Yes. You were angry. I know you think it's not true that I'm scared of you, but I am scared of your anger," I say. "I always have been. I can't function around it. It makes my brain go blank."

As I say this I feel as if I am slowly stepping onto very thin ice, sliding my feet forward in a shuffle, mindful of the steep drop-off into freezing-cold water that my sixth sense tells me must be some-where around here.

Chris pauses, considering what I've said. Then he speaks again. "Angry like how?" he asks, as if he really wants to know. "What did I do? Did I . . . ?" And he goes on to describe, very distinctly, the three different ways he gets angry: (1) the quiet fuming, clenching his jaw, looking up slightly at the ceiling or down at his hands, the angry I got from him when I would surprise him with an unex-pected event on the calendar or a change in plans or a new idea for what to do on vacation; (2) the snide talking down, which he'd em-ployed that morning, disdain and disgust so thickly partnered in his voice it was as if he were trying to erase me, a feeling I remembered from my childhood experience of my parents' anger, and something I have never been able to tolerate; or (3) the blaming anger, the one in his loudest voice, telling me I'm crazy, I'm unhappy, I'm selfish, that everything is always about me, that I create all the drama, or, in other words, that I am too big for this world, too big for him, too big to be loved.

As I feel what is coming, this moment of Chris trying to build some kind of bridge toward me, I take a step back into the kitchen, even though I am the one who took the steps out onto the ice. I start to cry as Chris calmly describes himself at his worst—as he finally admits that he can see, maybe just a little, that it might be possible that I could have been scared of him in our marriage, and could be scared of him now, even me, even strong, dominant, always-in-charge me.

He turns toward me, with those big blue-green eyes I know so well, the eyes that now stare up at me every day from my son's face, and shrugs, apologetic, and nods his head as if to say, Yes, that's me, I know it is.

After that, Chris went on to explain the ways I trigger his an-ger—but he wasn't blaming me. He was explaining himself, suggest-ing ways that we could interact and make all the inevitable calendar adjustments that coparenting requires so that I wouldn't set off his anger: let him know my plans as far in advance as I can, give him a set schedule, don't push my stress onto him as a way of trying to guilt him into helping me when a calendar crisis strikes, which makes him want to tell me no. Just ask. By the time he finished, I was on my knees in the kitchen, clutching a paper towel, trying not to sob, and failing.

I managed to get out: "So you don't think I'm selfish?"

He shook his head, with a gentle, almost loving, expression in his eyes, and said, "No, I don't think you're selfish."

"Really?" I squeaked.

"No," he said. "And I'm sorry if I made you feel that way when we were married."

And with those words he set me free.

I sat on the kitchen floor and bawled like a baby, feeling as if I were taking off a thousand pounds of weight as I let go of the sense that he had been married to somebody who wasn't the me I knew at all. I sat there as if dead naked in front of him, stripped of all my protection, and cried, while Chris looked on, with compassion in his eyes, not anger.

After that night, I felt something shift in my questioning the end of our marriage. Maybe Chris and I didn't make it because our emotional baggage wanted to live on the same luggage rack and so we kept trampling on each other's deepest vulnerabilities (Reason #314). Maybe we didn't make it because his need to turn inward was becoming more pronounced as I was discovering how much it means to me to live my life nakedly open (Reason #315). Or maybe it's simply because we had totally different ideas of what life should look like (#316) x 2.

I am still stumbling across reasons why we broke up, but I don't get lost in the dark eddies of my mind when it unfurls a new thought about how I might have failed him and us and why he decided he had to go. I've started to understand that this searching is just part of the mental furniture divorce leaves behind, a stool that I'll stub my toe against from time to time—a quick, sharp pain and then it's gone.

I will never be a hundred percent sure why Chris and I broke up. But I am finished with those questions, even though strangers and new friends can't help but ask them, even now, because they still need their magic, their prayer, their proof, their certainty that if they can put the end of our marriage in a box, they can keep divorce from coming to them. I'm done with certainty, at least in this one area of my life. It took me more than a year before I could accept all this vagueness as being the most I, and we, would ever get to know about the end of Us. I didn't get the answers I thought I needed—the answers that would keep us together, the answers that would make me look good, the answers that would hide all the messy, unhappy stuff that lives inside even the very best of marriages—but by being unafraid to see the ugliest of things, I have laid my whys to rest. They won't haunt me anymore.

I was able to take all the reasons from the long list that I had been compiling for two years, and let them go, one by one, allowing them to float into the sky and bump up against all the thank-yous that I send into the universe.

And as I've gotten stronger, the urge to answer other people's questions—or accept their hastily offered answers—has faded away. When friends or strangers ask whether Chris and I had married too young/spent too little time together/collapsed under the weight of our disparate incomes, I can now calmly say to them, "That question is for you, it's not for me." And I don't mean it to be rude; I say it to be generous. The best time to ask questions like these is when you are still married, and to ask them of each other, spouse to spouse. But Chris and I did talk about many of these things, just as his mother had said when we told her we were breaking up, and it still didn't save us.

In the end, some couples just don't make it. And it turns out we were one of them.

*   *   *

Now that I was almost divorced, I became a student of divorced people. I asked them all the questions that I was asked, but not because I thought they had answers for me. I asked because I was puzzled by the fact that we don't have a shared story in our culture about how hard it is to break up, no matter the circumstances that may have led to it. I had been a women's magazine editor for years, an "expert" about relationships and love and sex and marriage, yet I was totally unprepared for how quickly everything in my grasp, even my sense of who I am, turned to dust when my marriage ended.

But more than a student, I've become an emotional activist, because I am so saddened by how much people don't know about their own marriage's demise, by the sheer number of partners who walk away from three, five, ten, or twenty years together with a simple "I don't love you anymore" or "I've changed" or, worst of all, "I am in love with someone else." I see now that if we are part of a couple that's disintegrating, we don't know how to truly explore why the relationship is over, even though, as spectators, we cannot squelch our curiosity.

I understand the curiosity, I forgive the curiosity. I wish I were evolved enough as a human being that I didn't crane my neck when I drive by a highway accident, in a mixture of prayer and dread, but crane I do—and what's a divorce but an emotional highway wreck?

But we move too fast to bury other people's marriages, because of all the discomfort their failure awakens in us. So many times I was asked whether Chris had cheated on me—a question that was asked with the assumption that I would say "Yes, he did." It was unsettling to realize that this was the answer people *wanted*, because somehow it would have affirmed that the end of my marriage was about Chris's failing, instead of being about the way the many moving parts that make up a marriage can shift just slightly out of place, bringing the whole thing to a grinding halt. We fall in love or into an affair with someone else long after those forces have been in play.

In our culture, we romanticize marriage and love, despite plenty of evidence in our own homes that marriage is a lot of work. We pick sides in celebrity couples' breakups: Christie Brinkley and Peter Cook, Reese and Ryan, Marla and The Donald—admit it, you have opinions. At weddings where we deem the couple ill-matched, we slyly invoke the (misunderstood) statistic that half of American marriages end in divorce, and we shrug. When our neighbors' marriage is breaking up, we think we are in a position to pass judgment. We are not insensitive; of course we comfort our friends should they be so unfortunate—all while plumbing the depths of what we believe we know about their relationships, essentially digging through their emotional trash cans, weighing pieces of arguments we've witnessed, comparing notes about their conflicts. We can't help it; we want to believe there is a reason why.

Imagining affairs is fun: the raised pulse, the hushed phone calls, the scent of sex creating a tantalizing swirl in our heads. Sex belongs to everybody; solitude belongs to no one. We can dare to ask about the dirty details of an affair—"How did you find out?" "How long had it been going on?" "Did you ever catch them together?"—but it's impossible to imagine asking our friends and neighbors about the ponderous slide that is the decline of a marriage: the intermittent silences, the bungled communications, the pressing of wills against each other. It's way too personal. But that's exactly the point. Breakups are personal. They are deeply, wholly personal.

An affair we can imagine; the much more brutal act of looking at someone you share a life with and saying you want to go is something we struggle to envision. It's too hard, too scary. And so instead of trying to name the vague, complicated reasons a marriage starts to fray—those reasons that don't seem on their own good enough or big enough to throw away three, five, ten, twenty years—we inflate annoying personality habits and small transgressions, we blow ourselves up and make ourselves Right or make ourselves Wronged, and make things as unbearably awful as we can stand to, so we can give ourselves permission to let go.

But I believe there has to be a better, more connected, more compassionate way to help the people around us honor the end of one of life's most beautiful leaps of faith.

The bravest, and best, thing Chris did when he said goodbye is that he didn't wait until we had nothing left. He didn't have the affair that obliterated our relationship, sweeping all the complicated truths of our marriage under the rug. He didn't walk out, saying simply that I'd changed, he'd changed and we were done. He did his best to be my partner in the breakup, to be present as we both tried to make sense of what was happening to us. He accepted that he was the one who had to carry the guilt for ending the marriage. People tend to give me too much credit for the kind of relationship Chris and I have today, because, of course I am the holy one: The One Who Was Left. But in the same way that he set the tone for how we would fight when we were married, he set the tone for how we would connect when we divorced, by not being hateful, by staying open to me. And I am deeply grateful to him for that gift.

Yes, I know, it sounds like I still love him. And believe me, I do. But I don't want to be married to him anymore, either. I got a close enough look at our marriage, and at my hidden fears, and at how we really wanted to live our lives, and at how much we each erased something important, something *vital*, in the other that defined who we are, that I was able to truly let go, too. Apart, we have found a new connection. A far better one.

At some point, almost imperceptibly, my breakup stopped being a secret. I had completely lost track of whom I had and hadn't told. I repeatedly found myself in the circumstance in which I'd run into a friend or colleague, casually refer to the breakup, and watch the person I was speaking with rearrange his or her face quickly, moving from shock to composure in an instant, and then attempt to say something polite: "Oh, I didn't know. I'm so sorry."

I always resisted the urge to grab the person by the lapels and say, "Oh, my God, you mean there is actually someone on the planet that I haven't backed into a corner at a cocktail party and told the whole sordid saga to, with footnotes and references?" Instead I stumbled into something more like this: "Oh, that's okay. Thanks. I mean, it's good. I mean, I didn't want it, my husband left me, but it's fine now. We're getting along great, I mean, it was really hard for a while, and, you know, thanks. Anyway . . . , uh, you were saying?"

It amazes me to this day that I, of all people, still haven't found a smooth way to handle these moments. I'm a professional talker: I make up speeches on the fly, I can do live TV appearances with my eyes closed (though generally TV producers prefer them to be open), I can answer any kind of tough question that is sent my way without flinching, and I have mastered the even tougher skill of not answering any question I don't want to answer. But on the topic of the end of my marriage, I remain as tongue-tied as ever, or, more accurately, un-tongue-tied: I stumble over too many words and too many thoughts, because I cannot pack the whole experience into a simple sentence.

Instead, I have relied on the phrases that I repeated to myself to calm my mind when the panic felt too big—a different phrase for each stage of my profoundly humbling journey. *I will never really know why we didn't make it. I am not alone in all this, but, yes, I am totally alone. When everything is too big, focus on what's small. If I truly come to terms with the fact that I can't be safe in life, I can find my safe place within me.* These small truths are the stones I picked up off the bank of the raging river of circumstance and emotion that threatened to drown me. They arose from the questions I lived during my quest. I didn't find answers. Instead, what I found was me.

My two years under water forced me to let go of all my false strength and come to accept the ways in which I am vulnerable. Accepting these weaknesses has, in turn, made me more flexible, more forgiving. I am better able to see and react to what is happening in life, as opposed to reacting to a story I've made up in my head, a plan I am trying to fulfill, a fear I am trying to ignore. And I feel more connected to the nature of life: it isn't black *or* white, right *or* wrong, good *or* bad. It's everything all at once, many shades of gray, a beautiful, poetic mess.

My apartment—where I live my wholly unexpected and lovely life—is aqua and blue and gray, every single room the color of water and clouds and uncertainty, as if it's reflecting back to me the experience of these two years of falling apart in one piece. This was unplanned. I painted the rooms one at a time, some of them two or three times—the dining room yellow, then chocolate brown, then finally a warm, earthy gray—before it all felt right to me. People always comment on the colors of my apartment, and say they find the place "very soothing." I just smile to myself, remembering my hardest-won lesson: that accepting my vulnerability was the only path toward feeling safe. And I do feel safe in my apartment, and in my life. I do, I do. Even though I don't know what comes next. When I get nervous about all I don't know, I just recite my favorite mantra, the closest thing I ever found to an answer.

Life is good. Life is hard. These two truths are unrelated.

As I like to say at work, "Everybody bleeds." Everyone faces his or her own struggle in life, whether it's the death of a spouse or an intractable case of vanity. There's no weighing one against the other; there are no degrees of "hard." When I used to stumble into a conversation in which a colleague was complaining about a bad meal at a restaurant or a petty fight with a boyfriend, sometimes that person would turn to me, open his or her eyes really wide, and say, "Oh, I'm sorry. I don't mean to complain. I mean, you have so much worse to deal with in your life." And I always responded the same way: "Everyone has pain in their life. It all counts the same."

I didn't want my pain to be that different from someone else's. I didn't want to comfort myself with my agony. I wanted to count myself among the ordinary. I wanted it to all just be a part of life. We all have to take the hard with the good; we don't get to choose.

And how you handle the hard that you get will help you understand who you are and what you believe about this life, and what you believe about yourself.

And what I believe, at last, is this: It is, and I am, Enough.

The first time I felt those words land in my head, I had to laugh at myself. Because, of course, that sentiment is the reason I wanted to be a magazine editor, to reach women and remind them to breathe it all in, to put themselves on their to-do lists, to feed their mind and continue to invest in becoming who they are, all to help them celebrate the love all around them. To "Love Your Life" as *Redbook's* new official motto urges. All those messages I wanted to share with the millions of women I'd never have the chance to meet—I realized those messages were also and always meant for me. It had just taken me thirty-eight years to hear them, to let go enough to let them in.

So I decided I was ready to write in the magazine about the fact that my marriage had ended. In the November 2007 issue, we were running an article called "The Changing Shape of the American Family," which included mini profiles of ten very different kinds of families, from the traditional (husband, wife, and their children) to blended families; married couples who chose to have no children; grandmothers raising their own children's kids. I had been totally moved both by the article and by the voices in a survey we'd commissioned to go with it, and by the myriad ways people create security and love in an uncertain world. And so when I sat down to write my editor's note, it took me no time at all to type up what I wanted to say:

"What Makes a Family?"

At Redbook, *we think about "family" all the time, especially about that amazing transition we make from belonging to our family of origin to creating one of our own. But what it means to start a family has changed dramatically in the last 40 years, as Americans have found different ways to come together and create that special sense of place and peace we call home. This month, we take a look at the changing shape of the American family, to put a face on just what all this change has wrought.*

My own family has changed in ways I wouldn't have imagined or hoped for, as I am now a single mother to my three-year-old son, although I am fortunate that his father and I are still raising him together. Suddenly finding myself outside the mom-dad-child unit has forced me to think really hard about what it is that makes a family, because I have felt so deeply that I simply lost mine. But I comfort myself with company: Only 25 percent of all American households today are made up of mother, father, and their children. In the end, I would rather that I were still in that 25 percent, but for the so many of us who find ourselves caught in different circumstances, isn't it wonderful to know that we can create loving, happy homes of our own, by our own design?

Wherever and however it is you make your home, treasure it. The comfort and solace we get from—and give to—those we love is the greatest reward in life. So this Thanksgiving, be sure to hold your family, however you define it, close.

I finished writing the editor's note and hit "send" to drop the article into the executive editor's in-box. Then I sat back and thought some more about how amazing it is that I don't know what's next and how good it feels not to worry about the next step. What I was feeling was the relief of *not* being the one in charge.

The mediation meeting had accomplished what it was meant to, and so in the beginning of March, Chris and I met again at my lawyer's office to sign our separation agreement so the papers could be filed and we could have our divorce at last. That day was not one of the saddest in my life. In fact, in a weird twist that I have now come to expect in my day-to-day, it was one of the happiest.

Once we had all filed into my lawyer's conference room, Chris, his lawyer, and I sat at the big round table, trading chitchat, while my lawyer zigged in and out in a flurry, bringing in and removing various papers, then sitting down and getting up to retrieve something else she had forgotten. She and Chris's lawyer had one last, polite disagreement about how to word the complaint and about how to file it, and she left the room to make the final adjustments. His lawyer looked at me somewhat apologetically for the delay, and commented that trying to get two lawyers on the same page was like herding cats. I smiled. And then I said, "I'm glad I hired her, because if this had all gone quickly, I wouldn't be able to sit here and be happy that we are almost finished with this." Truly, I would have been devastated and sad, feeling that my life was ending. And so what had felt like a curse for many months now felt like a blessing.

At last, the stacks of paper were approved by both lawyers, and Chris and I began the signature rally that leads irrevocably to the end of the marriage, two years after the marriage had already ended. When Chris and I had finished signing the papers and were each handed our own copy of what thousands of dollars in divorce fees had bought us, we made our way around the table toward each other and we hugged. We had made it to apart, together.

Our lawyers gaped, and one of them mumbled, "Well, we don't see that too often." Chris and I walked out of the building together and shared a cab uptown, since we work in two big buildings just two blocks apart. It was one of those beautiful spring days, a day filled with sun and clear sky and optimism. It was the day after my second exhilarating date with a man who thought I was fascinating and smart and maybe even sexy, a man who was helping me rediscover parts of me that I had thought were gone forever. As the cab headed uptown, sliding through the canyons of the Fashion District, I got an excited phone call from a mentor at work, who was calling to let me know that *Redbook* had just been nominated for a very prestigious industry award.

It all could have been much too much—as an editor, I would have rolled my eyes if I'd been reading the story—except that at this point I had been living my lessons for months, and so I merely recited in my head what I know now to be true for sure: Life is good. Life is hard. These two truths are unrelated. And so today just happens to be a good day.

And I'll take it.

11

The End Is the Beginning

Two months after that sunny spring morning when Chris and I signed the papers, our divorce was finalized by a judge, and a few days later I received my crooked copy of the official notice in the mail. I held the papers in my hand, expecting to feel Something, but the truth is that by then the fact of the divorce's becoming final didn't mean anything to me anymore. Finally reaching the other side was just another day among days, in the best way.

I spent two years living in hell because of my divorce, counting every single day and willing time to pass, waiting to be whole, to be healed. Now life and time are back on their regular tracks, moving quickly, days unfolding one into the other, my life being lived. I marvel at how much more I trust myself and know myself than before all this happened. And I think about how strange and lovely it is that the end of my marriage has been the beginning of so many good things.

I think about how Chris is a much better partner now than he could ever have been if we had stayed married; our relationship as coparents is warm and calm. I know also that it may not always be this way between Chris and me. Life will intervene yet again with some unforeseeable circumstance—or even one of many foreseeable circumstances—and Chris and I will have to adjust. But I have faith that we will continue to find our way, both together and apart, and keep refining the dance we do that supports our son, as longtime friends and forever partners in parenting.

When Chris first told me he wanted to leave, almost five years ago now, all I could feel—all I could imagine—was the terrible, wrenching loss of what was ending, the loss of the love that was being stripped away from me. What I lacked was the imagination to conjure all the love I would find on the other side: from Chris, from Chris's mom and sisters, the great love of my friends, and, of course, that solid love for myself.

Three years after our last Thanksgiving trip to Illinois, Zack and I flew out to Chicago again, to spend the holiday with Barb, Chris's mom, and his sister Kelly and her family. I couldn't wait to see everybody, though I worried it would be awkward. But the visit was heaven: Zack and his youngest cousin, Holly, played together for hours; eight of us gathered around the table for Thanksgiving dinner, the oldest cousins now teenagers, and we remembered Chris's father, Cole, and others who weren't with us, expressing gratitude for the food and family; and I got to lace up my sneakers and set out for long, long runs across the flatlands of Illinois, during which I enumerated the many blessings in my life, including all this, which I'd thought was going to be gone forever.

When all the other relatives had gone home, Barb and I talked for hours on end, about movies and celebrities and family news. I got on the phone and talked with Chris's other sister, Jennifer, for the first time since Chris and I had broken up, the two of us quickly brushing aside the years of not being in touch with apologies and understanding. Barb and I also talked at length about my life, the strangeness of dating again, my job, Zack, and what was new with Chris and how Chris and I have made it all work.

Later in the trip, as the three of us were driving back from a movie, Zack asleep in his carseat, Barb said to me, "You know, when this all first happened you told me you would never marry again. I hope you don't still feel that way."

I had to pause to think back to the night Chris and I told Barb we were breaking up. She had said to me then, "Please give it a year. Don't rush into anything." I said that of course I would give things time, that I hoped we would find our way back together. And then I told her that the only thing I knew for sure was that I would never marry again. I had never meant to marry, and this just proved to me that there was no point.

"That was what I felt then, Barb, that was me then," I said. "Now I think I appreciate marriage even more, all it means. I certainly hope I get the chance to do it again."

"Well, good," she said, satisfied. She turned to me and smiled, and I felt my eyes well up from the gift of her love, of her ability to keep moving forward with me in my life, separate from her son. And I thought of all the love out there in the world that was waiting for me to find it, love I couldn't even imagine.

I used to judge the success of my life by the answer to this question: How close am I living to my dreams? But I realized that somehow I turned my dreams into a list of things to accomplish no matter how I had to get there. Now I judge my life by my answer to the following: How close am I living to my truth? Am I learning more about who I am every day? Am I surrounding myself with people who help me be the me I love the most? And the answer is definitely yes.

I flashed back to the bright September day, just over two months earlier, when Chris and I had taken Zack to his first day of kindergarten. Zack was nervous and excited, jumping up and down like a pogo stick as I tried to pose with him while Chris took some quick photos of us on our stoop. I opened the iron gate that led to the sidewalk, and the three of us fell in with the other clumps of parents and children heading up the street to the public elementary school.

It felt like another neighborhood parade, all the kids wearing their shiny new backpacks and carefully chosen outfits, the parents beaming or grousing with good humor.

The three of us held hands as we crossed the street, and Zack greeted the crossing guard with gusto. I started snapping pictures of Chris and Zack as they merged with the large throng gathered outside the school entrance, waiting for the doors to open. Zack turned around and looked nervously over his shoulder, flashing a toothy fake grin, and I blew a kiss at my baby, suddenly so grown-up and getting ready to walk away from me into his new world. I felt tears smart in my eyes, but I blinked fast to whisk them away.

The three of us wended our way into the school and found Zack's classroom. We found the hook in the closet with his name on it for his backpack and located the table where he would sit every day. Zack yelled with delight each time a friend from his preschool walked in the door, and I greeted the parents I knew from the neighborhood. It was a happy chaos and I could have stayed there all day, but the teacher eventually gently nudged the parents from the classroom. I snapped a final photo of Zack sitting in his spot at the blue table, looking at me with wide eyes, and seeming both so big and so small at the same time.

On the walk back to my apartment to pick up our bags before we both headed off the work, Chris and I recapped the morning, laughing about the kids' amped-up spirits and reassuring each other that Zack seemed to have been settling in fine. It was all so normal and everyday, but Chris and I had been down a long road to get here. I felt exultant, joyful.

I extended my arm up in the air toward Chris for a high five, and as our hands slapped, I said, "Good for us! Good for us for what we've done."

Chris nodded in agreement. We'd done it. We'd broken up without breaking into bits.

After we grabbed our bags and reviewed the details of the evening—the babysitter picking up Zack from school, my night to relieve her, Chris on duty tomorrow night—we headed off in different directions to our respective subways. As I walked the sunlight warmed my back, and I marveled that more than four years had passed since Chris had brought our marriage to an end. I thought about how much our little blond boy had grown and I imagined him trying to sit still in his classroom, barely able to contain his excitement about getting to know all his new friends.

I descended into the cool stairway that led to the subway and passed my card through the turnstile, then folded into the crowd waiting for the train that would take us all to Manhattan. I pulled out my stack of manuscripts and fished around in my purse for one of my blue pens, but I couldn't quite focus on my work yet; I was still thrumming from the morning's events. After I'd settled into my seat on the subway car, I stared out the window and waited for the view to appear as the train climbed the Manhattan Bridge to cross the river: the Brooklyn Bridge stretching grandly over the sparkling water, the Statue of Liberty tucked off in the distance behind it, the skyscrapers of Wall Street reaching for the blue sky. It's a scene I never tire of, that always makes me feel so lucky to have made my way here in New York.

That day I felt even more lucky than usual, with a sense of satisfaction infusing my spirit. I'd made it to the other side in one piece. "Good for you," I thought to myself. "Good for you!" I clutched my fist around my blue pen and made a little victory pump, and then without even thinking I reached up and put the pen in my mouth to remove the cap so I could get to work.

The subway finished crossing the bridge and hurtled back into the tunnel on the other side of the river, but I didn't notice; I was already immersed in the next manuscript on my lap, deep into the groove of another day. It was just another day in the new life that had been waiting for me—a glorious day.

Acknowledgments

I must thank Chris first and foremost, for allowing me to tell this story—my story, which both is and is not his story.

To Janet, Alison, Kim and Melanie at *Redbook*—the curly girls— there aren't enough words to thank you for living all this with me the first time around. And then making it possible for me to write it all down and turn it into this book.

To Cathie Black, Ellen Levine, Deb Shriver and everyone at Hearst: my thanks for your generous support. And my gratitude to Alexandra Carlin and Lindsay Galin for your enthusiasm and PR genius. And to Mary Morgan, *Redbook's* amazing publisher, thanks for being a great partner and friend.

I'd like to give a standing ovation to the entire team at *Redbook* for your passion, dedication, and creativity; getting to work with all of you is a great joy in my life. And to all the *Redbook* readers, thank you for the words of support and love you've sent any time I shared a piece of my life as a single mom. You inspire me every day with your honesty and sense of community, and I'm so glad I get to work for you.

And a huge thanks to all the people I couldn't have done all this without: Jessica DeCostole, Dr. Carol Glassman, Mary Rose Almasi, Eric Hunter, Ellen Whitehurst, Sezin Sengul, Marilyn Machlovitz, Rik Misura, Brian Hajastron, Izzy Gonzales, Michelle Rorke, and Camille Charles. And of course, my family: each of you reached out and helped me in so many ways that this book wasn't big enough to contain.

These acknowledgments wouldn't be complete without a deep bow of gratitude to all the people who helped the book itself come into being, but most especially my agent Karen Gerwin, who first told me I should write a book and then made it happen, and Sydney Miner at Simon & Schuster, who convinced me that I could tell this story—and then, somehow, managed to find a gentle way to edit me, a lifelong editor.

To Derek: You helped me write this book in more ways than I'll ever be able to express. I send a thank you to the universe for you and your lovely, steady spirit every day.

And a final bow of thanks to the curly girls—because, really. Thank you for signing up daily for the ride that is me, and for being as good and smart and talented and challenging and fun as you are. But most importantly, thank you for being my friends.

Made in the USA
Middletown, DE
23 October 2018